Briefly,
ABOUT THE BOOK

> *Deep in my heart*
> *I do believe*
> *We shall live in peace some day –*
> *Black and white together ....*

These words, out of the hymn of the integration movement, could have been written
by Captain Hugh Mulzac – for they express
the principle which has guided his seventy
odd years of life. In *A Star to Steer By,*
he tells his story in the simple manner of
a sea-farer. And yet the heartwarming (and
often heartbreaking) facts come into sharp
focus because of this simplicity in telling.
His has been a courage that refused to be
downed by bigotry and segregation. His has
been a spirit and a will that sent him out
into the world of ships, that carried him
onto the bridge of a U. S. Liberty ship in
World War II – the first Negro to become a
ship's captain in United States history . . .
His story has a deeper meaning than a re-
count of one man's struggle; for it becomes
the story of eighteen million Americans of
his race. His story is also a paean of hope
for a better day to come for his people . . .

INTERNATIONAL PUBLISHERS
381 Park Avenue South NEW YORK, N.Y. 10016

Hugh Mulzac
A STAR TO STEER BY

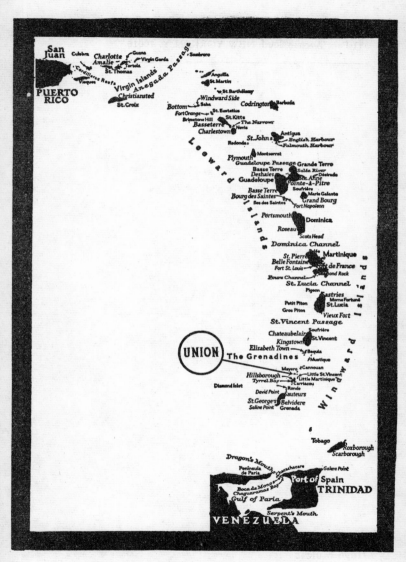

MAP OF THE WEST INDIAN ARCHIPELAGO

A STAR
TO STEER BY

By Hugh Mulzac

As told to
Louis Burnham and Norval Welch

INTERNATIONAL
PUBLISHERS
NEW YORK

First published by International Publishers, New York 1963;
published as a Seven Seas Book 1965.
This edition is published by
International Publishers, New York,
in association with Seven Seas Books, Berlin 1972
ISBN: 0-7178-0352-X

CONTENTS

1. Recollections of an Island Boy   9

2. I Discover Black and White   22

3. The Wide, Wide World   35

4. Sailing Ship Days   45

5. On the Beach   65

6. Marcus Garvey's Dream   78

7. The Dark Years   91

8. Stirrings of Hope   110

9. The World Revisited   124

10. The Commission Will Not Interfere   136

11. On the Bridge   145

12. Action in the North Atlantic   160

13. To All Brave Sailors   185

14. The Routine of War   198

15. The Commander Is Dead   209

16. A Peacetime Sailor   219

17. Painting and Politics   235

18. Blacklist   244

19. To All Young Sailors   254

I

Among the beautiful islands of the Caribbean Sea, at a point where Latitude 12°, 35′ and 55″ north crosses Longitude 61°, 27′ and 25″ west, the sea thrusts two peaks, Tibree and Rafall, toward the sky. From these heights the earth slopes gently into lush tropical lowlands that embrace an area of some twenty square miles before returning to the tides. Few of the islands of the West Indian Archipelago have placed so small a claim on the world's curiosity as this little parcel of land, where, on March 26, 1886, I was born, a howling, mewling addition to the 5,000 inhabitants of Union Island.

All 5,000, save one, were of African origin, the descendants of slaves captured, bound and carried across the ocean in the centuries-long slave trade between the West Coast of Africa, the West Indies, and the eastern shores of the United States. Their forefathers' lives had been a hell on earth, and they, "emancipated," had achieved a kind of purgatory.

One white man, a Scotsman, lived and reigned among them with benevolent but unquestioned authority. In 1863 he had left the *braes* and *lochs* of Scotland to find his fortune in the British West Indies, finally settling in St. Vincent, government center of the British Grenadines. The main island satellites of St. Vincent, then as now, were Bequia, Batwia, Mustique, Carriacou, Cannonan, Mayro and Union, among some hundreds of others.

The year of his arrival in St. Vincent the adventurous Scotsman married a native woman, leased Union Island, forty miles away, and ran it as a large plantation on which the entire population worked on a sharecropping basis. To protect and nurture his investment he built a home on Union, and maintained it the rest of his life. The Scotsman's name was Charles Mulzac. He was my grandfather.

My recollections of grandfather are hazy, for he died in 1893 when I was only seven years old. I remember him as a small man with a long white beard who walked around the island carrying a cane behind his back. Through the mist of years only one incident stands out sharply. Grandfather had a strange custom: He imported a kind of round cheese from Scotland, cut off the top, scooped out the center, and filled the hollow with fine Madeira wine. Then, replacing the top, he let the whole thing stand until the center was rife with maggots! When this delicacy was "ripe" he settled down in a large chair and gobbled it up with a spoon, wriggling worms and all!

I used to watch this culinary adventure with horror. Often the worms would fall into grandfather's fine white beard and hide, and on these occasions I stayed away from the old man for weeks. This was not easy, for I loved to sit on his knee and run my fingers through the silky beard, but the fear that I might dislodge a worm was just too much for my young imagination.

Grandmother lived quite a long time after grandfather's death. Pious and sedate, she looked very much like a dark Queen Victoria. She was extremely pleasant, though proper, in her relations with others, and the people of Union Island seemed to hold her in high regard – whether out of fear or respect I really didn't know. She had borne two boys and two girls for the little man with the maggotty white beard – Richard (my father), Mary, John and Emma.

My mother's parents were of pure African descent. Her father, James Donowa, was born and educated in Antigua in the Leeward Islands, and ordained a minister of the Protestant Episcopal Church in Barbados. A student of

Bishop Bree, Anglican Bishop of the Windward Island group, he was sent to Union to serve as clergyman and school master. Shortly after his arrival he married my grandmother, Jessie, and in the succeeding years she bore him eight children, one of them my mother, Ada Roseline. In 1885 Richard Mulzac and Ada Donowa were married, and a year later I was born, the first of seven children. My father had married earlier, and two older sons, John and Edward, were part of our household. After me there came Irvin, Una, Luvina, Lamie, James and May.

For me, growing up on Union Island was like growing up in Paradise. Even now, two generations and many miles removed from the scenes of my childhood, I can conjure up the taste of the sweet sugar apple, the lovely sabadilla, and the juicy java plums. What boy has ever had the ultimate in desserts who has not taken freshly picked sour sops, mixed them with fresh milk, added nutmeg and spice to produce a delicacy like ice cream but much better? And what pale and artificially flavored jam bought from the supermarket can challenge the tang of marmalades and jellies made from the succulent guava?

Where but on these islands could you walk into a room and be all but overcome by the fragrance of a bowl of mangoes set invitingly in the center of the table? Or walk in any direction with the sweet essence of jasmine pervading your nostrils from a block or more away? Where could a boy grow, gather strength, and test his skill better than on a tropic isle, warm, but spared from enervating heat by constant northeast trade winds wafting from the Horse Latitudes to the equator and carrying with them as they passed the natural perfume of everblooming flowers?

Or what pleasanter way to fill a belly than with the rich variety of dishes prepared from the vegetables yielded by our island earth – yams, eddoes, tanyas and many more. Or the water coconut, and the breadfruit, rising sixty or more feet into the resplendent sky?

Of meats the sea afforded a never-ending supply – jack fish, Spanish mackerel, red snapper, cavali, flying fish, whale, barracuda, and dolphin all made their home in the waters surrounding our little island; and most made their way sooner or later to our table. They were the fruit of the other world to me, the vast, mysterious world of water which bathed the shores of Union and stretched in all directions to lands and peoples who existed only in picture books and stories for an island boy.

But oh, the waters were beautiful – and close by, never more than a few minutes from any spot on the island. I only suspected as a boy, but now I know, that the reef-rimmed shores of Union Island are dotted with the most beautiful sand beaches to be found anywhere in the world. The land slopes ever so imperceptibly from the mountains to the water's edge, surrendering to the gentle tides of the Caribbean on the west and the limitless expanse of the Atlantic to the east. You could walk out into the sea for a mile or more in water no deeper than your waist. And underfoot, through translucent blue water, pure white sand formed a bed for millions of exquisitely shaped white shells, sea eggs and starfish. In my early years I loved to gather shells and make picture frames and other household ornaments from them.

Childhood, then, was happy for me. It was not long, however, before I began to understand that other boys and girls did not have the same opportunity to enjoy the gifts of nature on our island as had I. After all, Union was one big plantation, and every boy was not the son or grandson of the master of the plantation. For those lads who were not, and their parents, life was unending toil with little to show for it. The tenants were required to plant most of their land in cotton, the single cash staple of the island, and their agreement with grandfather, and later father, required them to turn over all their cotton to him. Grandfather then ginned it and shipped seed and cotton to England. In return for their labor the farmers received a pittance, the exact amount of which I was never aware, but which could not have amounted to much. Nor was the sum grandfather received from the sale of the cotton and seed any concern of theirs.

So long as the land was well planted in cotton the people of Union Island could put in whatever vegetables they wanted or the remaining land could bear. For the most part, the little garden patches around their homes provided their main source of food.

After grandfather's death father, as the eldest son, took over the island. He was a man of medium build, about five feet eight, and of quiet nature. He had been called "Sonny" by his own father and Dad by his older sons. Through the years he was known to us as Dad-Sonny. He never smoked and drank very little. For a number of years he ran the island exactly as his father had before him, but with the death of the patriarch dissatisfaction among the people began to spread and gradually found channels of expression.

Finally father went to St. Vincent and arranged with the colonial authorities to divide the land so that each family owned its own little plot. This arrangement worked for several years, though nothing, really, had been changed. Father continued to buy the cotton at his own price and to export it as he had before. Gradually the farmers understood that they were no better off, and that their real problem was that they were compelled to market their cotton through one broker who had a complete monopoly on the trade.

The people demanded further reforms and under this pressure father decided to abandon the cotton business. He opened a shipyard at Frigit Rock, a tiny island a mile offshore, and began to build whaling boats and small schooners to run among the West Indian islands. With four boats: the *Paragon, Priscilla, Pursuer,* and *Providence,* he went into the whaling business.

Father's shift from a landlord's affairs to the sea was,

of course, the major turning point in my life. From that time on the family's fortunes were tied to the sea. Most of my waking hours away from school, church, and chores, were spent at the edge of the water or in boats upon it.

Whaling had a special fascination. The whales came in February, March, and April, driven by the cold from the Grand Banks of Nova Scotia to our more hospitable waters to calve. And as soon as the first schools began to arrive the contests would begin.

Eight strong and daring men – a captain, six oarsmen and a harpoon man – would head out toward the deep, where the water turned a heavy blue and was alive with mackerel, king fish, sharks, and barracuda. With the captain standing in the stern, steering with a long oar, and the harpoon man poised at the bow, the oarsmen would bring the boat quietly among a school of whales, until one of the huge mammals loomed alongside. "Lift your harpoon!" the captain would command. Then, precisely at the right second – not too soon to assure a good strike or too late to hit the alarmed target – the order would come, "*Strike!*"

With a whirring sound the four-foot harpoon, attached to a five-foot rod, whirled from the strong, black arm and lodged in the whale's side. As the head of the harpoon opened inside and the whale picked up speed, the harpooner gave her rope until the slack was gone. Then, with the boat in the mad whale's tow, sometimes careening over the sea at breakneck speed, one of the sailors would give her the gun. The explosion of the shell inside the whale slowed her immediately, and as the whaleboat came alongside the hand lance found its mark under the fin and the whale was dead.

Then the oarsmen, the great dead weight trailing behind, pointed the boat toward shore where an excited boy stood in open-eyed amazement at their gallant exploit.

The whale was hauled up on the beach by "Norwegian steam" – hand power with block and tackle – cut up and its meat given to the islanders for a dish tastier than beef. The fat or blubber would be fried in big iron kettles, and the oil put in barrels to be shipped to St. Vincent in transit to England. The captain, oarsmen, and harpoon man would then return to the sea for another strike.

On Union Island our home stood on the gentle incline of a hill, about 200 yards from the church and school-house. These institutions provided the moorings of my early life. As a boy I ranged in play and exploration to all corners of our little island, building miniature huts and skipping stones; picking fruits and flowers as I ran, but always, in the end, returning to the disciplines of these two establishments which were conspiring to make me into a man. Both were very British, and a very British gentleman they sought to make me. That in the end I would turn out to be an American sailor was no fault of theirs – they did their best.

Our home was an eight-room cottage, surrounded by a masonry wall. Fronting it was a well-kept garden in which all the lovely flowers of the island were opened in almost perpetual bloom. Inside life was well ordered; our parents had maxims for all contingencies, and we were expected to learn them well. We learned that there was a place for everything and that everything should be in its place; that we should attempt but one thing at a time, and do that well. Above all we learned those rules which were the most binding of all – the Ten Commandments.

Of course life was too unpredictable, even on a tropic isle, to be everlastingly served by maxims. On the occasions when situations arose for which there were no existing proverbs – our parents improvised new ones on the spot. And their words were always law. Neither mother nor father believed in physical punishment, an unusual attitude in those days. Nevertheless they wielded, benev-. olently but firmly, total authority. They expected us to do what they considered the right thing; a stern glance or harsh word accomplished more than fear or flogging.

Thus our island day was a sweet succession of delightful events and stern lectures when we misbehaved. The mornings began with a walk to the farm, for in addition to his whaling business, father owned a cattle farm with about 300 head of cattle. The cows provided milk for the island, while steers were fattened for sale or slaughter.

My little sister Luvina had an encounter with one of the latter when she was three years old. She was on the front stoop playing when one of the boys passed, taking the cows to pasture. She paid him no mind and started to run. Suddenly a big black steer rushed after her and tossed her up in the air. His horn was driven into her mouth clean through her nostrils before she was rescued. Luvina was rushed to the hospital and my father killed that steer on the spot.

The milk cows were highly intelligent. Each had been given a name and responded to the call of the boys into whose care they had been given. "Labwing heifer, come out," one of the boys would call, and the cow, who had not been a heifer for years, would leave the pen and stand ready to be milked. Queenie, Jeanette, Spreakel, and all the others likewise responded to the call of their names.

After each of us had two cups of fresh, frothy milk, we headed for the beach and a quick swim and bath. Then it was back to the house for a breakfast of hot chocolate, made from cocoa grown in St. Vincent, and freshly baked bread. Well before the appointed hour we were ready for school, which began at nine o'clock.

Education was not free on Union Island, and the only ones to enjoy its benefits were those whose parents could afford to pay two pence a week and provide the necessary books. Thus classes were small and discipline strict. In my case it was doubly strict, since the schoolmaster was James Donowa, my maternal grandfather. While we were on his premises he ruled his charges exactly as a feudal baron ruled his serfs. There were no modern notions of a permissive relationship between pupil and teacher, nor was the schoolmaster loath to punctuate the meaning of a special point with a smack of his hand or a stinging crack across the backside of the recalcitrant student. We studied and memorized relentlessly.

After finishing the primary grades on Union Island, I left for secondary school in St. Vincent. Our family also maintained a home in Kingston, another eight-room cottage on Middle Street, with a magnificent veranda decorated with flowers. Painted white, and topped with a red-shingled roof, it sparkled in the rays of the sun filtering through the leaves of a giant breadfruit tree which covered almost the entire yard. Inside it was always cool and airy, and a wonderful place to study.

At eighteen I graduated from high school in St. Vincent. Had I followed the lure of books I might have proceeded to one of the two institutions of higher learning in the West Indies: Codrington College in Barbados, or Mico College in Antigua. By this time, however, I had begun to learn that there were aspects of life not encompassed in the books in British schools. Mathematics and geography had been my favorite subjects, and I received excellent grounding in them, but history was always a puzzle. All the history in West Indian schools was British history. We learned of Celts, Queen Elizabeth, and Henry VIII, the War of the Roses and the Reformation, the daring and gallantry of Sir Walter Raleigh and Lord Nelson – and very little else. Of castles, lords and dukes, and counts, we had our fill. The glory and growth of the Empire was a part of our daily intellectual diet.

But we were children of Africa, and ·of Africa we learned nothing. It was a "dark continent" with habits puzzling to "our" Western ways. And of West Indian history, the story of our own islands and peoples, also we learned nothing whatever.

Church was little more enlightening than school, especially since James Donowa, schoolmaster-grandfather, was also minister, and my mother the organist. Mother had been something of a prodigy, who at thirteen had won an all-islands piano competition. Now, during my youth, she was the accompanist of the choir and music director. Each Sunday I dutifully took my place as an altar boy, intoned the familiar hymns and listened to the earnest preachments which constituted grandfather's sermons.

Yet there were happier church events – the time of the harvest festival, for example. Harvesting began in August, toward the end of the rainy season. When all the crops had been gathered the people selected the best fruits and vegetables from their gardens, and the finest specimens of livestock. After church the minister would bless these offerings, which were then sold at auction for the benefit of the church. It was always a joy to examine the offerings, and to race around in the festival atmosphere.

Even greater fun was the *maroon*, a picnic of African origin. Once a year, after the harvest, the people of the village gathered at a selected place in the hills, bringing with them as much uncooked food as they could carry. There they would light fires and all day long prepare their viands, competing with one another to offer the tastiest dish. When the food was ready grandfather Donowa would pass among the celebrants and bless each dish, and then everyone would fall to, sharing and comparing the victuals.

"Why, Aunt Lou, what a fine calilou* you have prepared," one island matron would exclaim to another. Or someone else, less charitable, might say, "That's some fine jack fish you have there, girl, but if you really want to taste some good one, just step over here and have a mouthful of mine!" Whatever the comments everyone gorged himself at the *maroon* picnic, and if someone said, "Ain't had such good eatin' since last *maroon* picnic day," he merely expressed the sentiments of all.

After food came the song and dance, when the rhythms

* A stew of okra, other greens, and crabmeat.

of distant Africa would break through the prim decorum of British habit. Many of the older residents retained Africanisms in their speech. I knew one old lady who spoke almost no English and used the broken remnant of her African tongue, yet most of the other islanders understood her.

Both young and old danced the African dance, the *bongay*, to the beat of African drums. Some of the others, especially youngsters who had visited cosmopolitan Trinidad, disdained the old dances and preferred waltzes, paseos, chardis and lances, but the dominant spirit of the *maroon* picnic was always the intricate, high-spirited dance of Africa.

Aside from the harvest and the *maroon* picnic, the most notable holidays on Union Island were Christmas, New Year's Day, Easter, King's and Queen's birthdays, and Emancipation Day, August 1st. On these days athletic games were the rule and I gloried in them. Cricket, of course, was the national game, and I developed an island-wide reputation as a cricketeer. Boat racing, swimming, donkey and horse races were also popular. Particularly fascinating were the horizontal and vertical pole races, in which prizes were hung at the end of a greased pole. To scale the vertical pole, 35 feet in the air, or to make one's way to the end of the horizontal pole, placed on top of the jetty over the water, required more than moderate skill. But at the end, for the few who persevered, there was always a ham, a slab of bacon or some other prized edible. Rounders was another favorite game. The same rules applied as in American baseball, except that the rubber ball was batted with the hand rather than a stick.

My penchant for sports and for taking the lead in almost any new venture almost became my undoing on one memorable occasion. A group of us was standing on top of a high hill watching father's men, who had just captured an unusually large whale. We watched them through a telescope as they towed it to Frigit Rock and windlassed it up on the beach. All of us wanted to go over and see the big whale, but this required crossing a dangerous stretch of water. I sought to persuade the others to join me but none would take the chance. I ran down to the beach, jumped into a rowboat, and set out alone.

Halfway across I was completely tired out. The oars became heavier with each stroke, the current was contrary, and it soon became apparent that struggle as I would I could make no headway. The little craft began to drift and there seemed to be no way I could change its direction. For a time I reconciled myself to the drift, hoping that after a brief respite I would have strength enough to bring the boat back on her course. But each time I tried anew the oars were heavier than ever.

Gradually the realization dawned that I was no match for the powerful current, and panic displaced determination. The boat had now drifted several miles from Frigit Rock, toward the open sea. I decided that what little strength remained could best be spent in cries for help, and at the top of my lungs screamed in all directions, praying the wind would carry my voice to some nearby voyager.

Half an hour later two sturdy fishermen in a boat much like my own heard my cries, took me in tow, and rowed me back to shore. There my companions who had refused to join the venture met me with howls of derision, and my usually gentle father gave me the beating of a lifetime. Thus ended my first seafaring expedition.

While this experience served to dampen my enthusiasm for a time, it did break the monotony of island life where there was little communication with the world. There was no newspaper on the island, no telephone or telegraph. The only events which disturbed our lives were the unpredictable arrivals of the mail boat from St. Vincent or adventures of our own contrivance. The boats that visited Union were seldom motorboats, and thus their schedule could never be precisely forecast. But their arrival, with provisions for the few stores on the island and the rum shop, was always an exciting event.

The rum came from St. Vincent in 25-gallon casks, which father bottled for sale. One of the principal habitués of the rum shop was father's own brother, Uncle Johnnie. He was the pleasantest of men, always ready with a kind word for a friend or neighbor and dedicated to doing good turns. He liked his rum as much as anyone, and when the cask was empty would refill it with a few gallons of water and seal it up for three or four days. Then one night he would open it up and start doing an American jig, a favorite divertissement which drinking invariably provoked. Finally he would lay right down on the floor with his mouth against the dripping spigot, and the news would flash around the island, "Uncle Johnnie's drinkin' the cask water again."

Perhaps the biggest event of our childhood came one day in the late '90's, I think it was. Grandfather had been carrying on a campaign to get the people to come to Sunday service. He was battling against long-entrenched custom, for the islanders habitually went to their gardens on Sunday morning to select fruits and vegetables for Sunday dinner.

Since this interfered with church attendance, Grandfather considered the custom "labor" and reminded them of the Biblical injunction, "Six days shalt thou labor and do all thy work, but the seventh day is the Sabbath, and on it thou shalt do no manner of work." One day grandfather happened to be consulting the Bristol Almanac and discovered that an eclipse of the sun would be visible from the island two Sundays hence. The next Sunday he told the congregation that if they persisted in going to their gardens on the Lord's Day God would spread darkness over the land.

Grandfather had pleaded, cajoled and threatened so often that the people did not believe him. The following Sunday most were right back in their gardens when the service began at 11 a.m. The sun was bright in the sky as it can be only on a late West Indian morning. But before midday the moon moved into its prescribed position and darkness began to spread over the island.

The terrified islanders rushed toward the church from all parts of the land, and fell on their knees before Grandfather and implored him to pray to God for forgiveness. Grandfather agreed – provided they would come to church faithfully from that moment on. He had no more trouble – each Sunday the church was packed.

2

When I returned from St. Vincent in 1904, at the age of eighteen, I had other interests than fun and mathematics. Back on Union Island I met once again a favorite of my early school days, Edith Mulrain, a lovely girl a year older than I, but clearly fond of me. Edith's father was dead, and she was partly responsible for the support of her family. She was very good at sewing and crocheting, took piano lessons from my mother, and was my ideal of a wife.

Sometime after I came back from secondary school we became secretly engaged, a state of affairs that worried us both, and finally Edith persuaded me to write to her mother, asking for her hand in marriage. Mrs. Mulrain discussed the matter with Edith, and we were disappointed to learn that she considered us both too young – and me too untried in the ways of the world to make a stable husband.

My spirit was not crushed. "I will go away for three years and make good," I told Mrs. Mulrain. "When I come back, if Edith will wait for me, I will claim her." Both Edith and Mrs. Mulrain agreed, Edith because she sincerely loved me, and Mrs. Mulrain, I suppose, because she saw no greater prospect for Edith than one of the Mulzac boys.

Now I faced the real problem: to "go away and make good" was easy to say, but where was I to go? And *how* make good? Few of the boys on Union Island ever left at all, and those who did never returned. Of two things, however, I was certain: first that I must get away, and second, that when I did I would have the courage and wit to deal with the world as I found it.

From time to time I discussed my future with father, who was eager to send me to higher schools to become an engineer. But to me the world was a fascinating and mysterious myriad of lands waiting to be known and explored. Nothing appealed to me less than four grueling years at college when distant ports, new faces, and thrilling adventures beckoned. There would be time enough later to settle on a career. If I felt that way, father agreed, then the best place for me was at the shipyard. After an apprenticeship learning how to *build* boats it would be time to consider sailing them.

For the next twelve months I worked in the shop on the waterfront at Frigit Rock, learning to shape the huge beams, fit the struts and supports, and lay the wood skin of the sturdy vessels, to sink the masts and rig the braces. Of the vessels we built during this time I can remember well the *Spartan, Ocean King, Lady Osprey, Wanderer, Wild Rover* and the vessel I was to come to know better, the *Sunbeam.* Finally, having built my first and very own small boat, I decided I was ready for sea. I reported my desire to father, who had already sensed my restlessness. "All right," he said, "you can go aboard the *Sunbeam* with your brother John. It's the best way to learn deck work and navigation."

The *Sunbeam* was a 90-ton schooner engaged in the island trade, and John was a most efficient master. In later years he was noted throughout the British West Indies for his skill. He could take a vessel into virtually any port in the Leeward and Windward Island groups without charts or marker buoys. He was also, like most men who have learned their skills from the ground up, a difficult taskmaster. Virtually from the second the *Sunbeam* reached the heavy ocean swells I became seasick, and John showed no sympathy.

"Get your ass out on deck," he roared when he found me moaning in my bunk.

Barbados was only ninety miles from St. Vincent, usually a two-day run. I was miserable all the way over and all the way back. John threatened to discharge me when we returned, but I begged for another chance and he relented.

On our second trip we took a load of firewood to Barbados, easternmost island of the Lesser Antilles, and the first of Britain's colonies in the West Indies. It was also one of the most densely populated spots on earth. Almost every square foot of land was intensively cultivated to provide food for the population or to grow cane for sugar or molasses which were then exported to Canada. There were, as a result, practically no forests, and the wood and charcoal universally used on the island had to be imported. In later years I was to discover many other examples of the misuse of nature to the detriment of the well-being of the local population.

This time John was determined to help me overcome my seasickness once and for all. As we came into rough seas he ordered me aloft to make up the topsails. "I can't! I'm sick," I cried.

At this John seized a length of rope and shouted, *"Go up!* Go up or I'll beat hell out of you! If you want to go to sea you've got to learn the hard way!"

Fighting off the dizziness from the rocking of the ship and the foul smell of the bilgewater in the hold I mounted the mast. Fear drove away the seasickness, and I have never been seasick since.

During these first voyages I had been signed on as deck

boy. My job was simply to do whatever the master ordered me to, and to learn the seaman's trade. For this I received no pay. By the end of the fifth trip, however, John's tutelage had paid off. I had learned to make up the topsails, rig the gear for discharging cargo and many other bits of sailor's lore, and was promoted to ordinary seaman at the munificent wage of six shillings per month – the equivalent of about $1.50 United States currency at the time.

Gradually I learned by doing, and as the months went by my muscles hardened, my hands grew strong and calloused. I learned to splice rope and wire, make grommets and cringles, and sew sails. Soon thereafter I was promoted to able seaman and drew twelve shillings a month. I was, I thought, well embarked on the climb to fame and fortune.

As we ran from port to port in the Grenadines, and occasionally beyond, I began to study navigation with John, and got that first grounding in the movement of celestial bodies which was to serve me throughout the years. I fixed the approach to our ports of call indelibly in my memory, and to this day, though I have never put into them since, I think I could find my way through the channels at Tyrell Bay, Mustique, or Little St. Vincent without difficulty.

But goals once achieved become commonplace. After eight months on the *Sunbeam* a mate's job opened up and I asked John to promote me. He refused. The job went to a more experienced salt, and I sulked. The A.B.'s job was too small for my ambitions. I wanted to sign on an oceangoing vessel and head for Europe, South America, Africa, and the world's more distant ports. Life on the *Sunbeam* began to pall, and though we had many good times, such as the occasions when John played the violin and I the guitar before dockside audiences of as many as a hundred people, I had already set new stars to steer by.

I was not alone in my ambition to escape Union Island for the trackless paths of the sea; several others my own age also wanted to get away. Childhood on the islands was carefree and happy, but for youth growing into manhood what could the future hold? The only respectable openings were in government service, and these were so few and so totally dependent upon knowing the right people that an ordinary youngster could not aspire to them. Even those who won them were doomed to a narrow, dull, underpaid existence as tiny cogs in the British *Imperial* machine. Thus ten of us made a pact: we would leave together and be a long time coming home.

We all left on the *Sunbeam,* March 12, 1907, a few weeks short of my twenty-first birthday. Our girls came down to the jetty to see us off, and we played our guitars, violins, and mandolins in a farewell serenade. The girls cried but we gave our solemn assurance that we would return to marry them when we improved our fortunes, and sweep them off to lands far across the seas. Edith was there, with tear-filled eyes, and I meant it when I promised her to return.

That night we left for Barbados and two days later, with the southeast trades giving us a brisk assist, put into port at Bridgetown. As the *Sunbeam* discharged her cargo, one by one my companions made their private arrangements and either bought passage or signed on ships bound for lands of hope. Three days later all were gone, and I was sitting disconsolately on the deck. John was in town negotiating a cargo for the return trip.

A shadow fell across me on the deck, and I glanced up into the twinkling blue eyes of a tall man with blond hair. "Do you know anyone who wants to go to sea?" he asked.

Fortune of fortunes! Anxious not to betray my eagerness I said laconically, "I might. Where's you bound?"

"America first, then Europe. I'm the master of a 500-ton barque, the *Aeolus,* anchored outside. I need an ordinary seaman."

I could no longer restrain my enthusiasm. "I'm your

man," I said quickly. "I'm mate on this ship and I deserve more than an ordinary's rating, but I'll take it just to get away from here." Of course I was not the mate, but I thought it better to put up a good front. The captain, whose name was Granderson, sensed the effort.

"Are you on your own?" He seemed suddenly struck by my youth.

"I'm twenty-one and I can go."

"All right. We sail this evening. Get your things. I'll wait and we'll leave in a boat together."

An hour later I was walking the decks of the *Aeolus,* waiting impatiently for the command to hoist sails and get out of Bridgetown before John should learn of my departure. But it was not to be. From the bow I watched a small boat approach and a few moments later John's lanky figure clambered over the side. My brother's crew had told him I'd left, and he was a mad captain. I knew he thought duty came first and regarded me as a deserter. But I knew also he loved me and wanted me to succeed.

Now his flashing eyes and steely voice betrayed no hint of kindness. "Is this the way you're going away — without a word to anybody? Shall I go back and tell Dad-Sonny that you left without a word? And how am I to man my ship?"

I begged John to let me go. I was nearly twenty-one years old, I reminded him, and was determined to make my own way. If I did not go now, I warned him, I would go later anyway. Union Island could not hold me. As for Dad-Sonny and mother, I pleaded that he give them my fondest farewell, and assure them I would write often. I was alternately conciliatory and threatening, beseeching and cold, and gradually John relented. I realized later that he was prepared to give in, and that his show of anger was largely demanded by his role as captain and older brother.

Captain Granderson appeared and I introduced the two men. John asked the Norwegian to take good care of me and Captain Granderson promised he would. With that there was little left to say. In a moment, after a parting handshake, John was over the side. He poised for a moment at the gunwales, then said, "Good luck, Hugh," and waved and disappeared. He was a fine, sensitive and loyal brother, from whom I learned so much that was to stay with me throughout my life.

That evening we sailed for Wilmington, North Carolina, and as soon as we were at sea the broad-shouldered Norwegian from Kraagerow took me to his cabin and signed me on the articles at three pounds sterling and two shillings per month – abouth $12 United States currency. I was overcome with my vast good fortune.

Two Danes, a Swede, an Irishman, and five Norwegians made up the balance of the crew, and from them I began to learn new chores. None of the duties was beyond me. We painted most of the day when not at the wheel. Watches were, as was the custom in those days, four on and four off. As "ordinary" I was also sent up to make up the royal and the topgallant sails, and while I was higher above the deck than I'd ever been before it didn't bother me at all.

I learned another important lesson, too – the ethics of the sea. Captain Granderson, it developed, was more than devout, he was actually a licensed roving missionary. Our second day at sea he asked me, "Did you go to church at home?"

"Oh, yes, sir,' I replied, "I was choir boy and altar boy, and my grandfather was the minister and my mother the organist of our church."

"Good! You may come to my cabin every Friday and Sunday morning. We have prayer meetings, and I'm sure you'll feel at home."

Later in the fo'c'sle I told the others about the captain's invitation and was shocked at the reaction. "Don't get mixed up with that son-of-a-bitch," one of the A.B.'s snarled. "His religion's going to jinx this ship. We'll have bad weather the whole trip. Don't have anything to do with him."

I had never heard such blasphemous language before, and was surprised to discover there could be such a difference of opinion about matters I'd always taken for granted. In my bewilderment I went back and told the captain what the men had said.

Captain Granderson was furious. He went forward at once and lit into the men. It was bad enough, he said, that they were infidels, but to turn a young boy against his faith was too much.

The instant he was gone the crew members lit into *me!* "So, the captain's tattler!" they accused. "Well, you don't sleep in this fo'c'sle. If you do your fine captain will be missing you in the morning."

The others were old timers and their words and manners were frightening. There was no place else to sleep. The fo'c'sle was in the forepeak, with six bunks – two tiers, three high each – on the port side and six to starboard. Bravado, I figured, was the best way out. "Now look here," I said, fingering my sheath knife meaningfully, "this is my first deep sea trip, and I may have a lot to learn, but nobody's going to run me off this ship. I'm going to the prayer meeting with the captain and if anyone tries to throw me overboard you can bet there'll be more than one going over."

That night I slept in the fo'c'sle and I woke up in the morning in my bunk. From that time on the men swore and threatened but did no harm. And I learned not to tell tales to the captain.

Sailing past the Leeward Islands we picked up a nice southwester and set all sails to take advantage of it. We also took advantage of the weather to put out fishing lines. Soon we were in the thickest school of dolphin I'd ever seen. As soon as we dropped a hook with a piece of rag tied to it for bait a big one would strike. We caught over sixty dolphin that day, some weighing up to one hundred pounds. There were no ice boxes aboard the *Aeolus,* of course, so after a great fish feast we salted what was left and had fish, fish, *fish* all the way to Wilmington. Dolphin meat is as sweet as any, but in the following two weeks I had more than my fill.

We arrived in Wilmington on a Friday morning, three weeks out of Barbados. This was not "Old England" of storybook fame, but it looked impressive to me. It was the "New World," the sailors said, a land of fabulous wealth and unlimited opportunity.

As we docked Captain Granderson told me, "Now when I go to town, Hugh, I'll find out where there's a good Protestant Church. On Sunday we'll enjoy a real service, so get your best clothes ready."

In the haste of my departure from Barbados I had failed to bring my best suit, but when Sunday morning came I passed Captain Granderson's muster, and six of us – the deck boy, Johnny, the sailmaker, bo'sun, chief mate, and Captain Granderson set out for the church.

The bells were ringing when we arrived, and we started in. The captain went first, followed by the others, and I brought up the rear. Just as I started to enter a long arm stretched out to block my way, and I looked up into my first leering southern face.

"Where you goin', boy?" a voice asked.

"Why, I'm going in to church," I replied.

"Oh no you're not . . . not *this* church!"

"Why not?" I asked, "what have I done?"

"Oh no," the man replied, "oh no, no, no, no, *no!*"

By this time Captain Granderson had become aware of the delay and returned to the door to see what was the matter. "This boy's with me," he explained, "I've just brought him from Barbados in the West Indies . . . he's a very religious boy. His grandfather's a minister of the gospel."

"That don't mean nothin' *here*," the man at the door replied.

"Now see here," the captain persisted, "my name is Granderson. I'm the captain of a barque out in Wilmington harbor, the *Aeolus*. In addition to that I'm a missionary minister." He removed his badge from his pocket and said, "See. This is a missionary's badge. In every country I go to I'm usually asked to preach in the local churches. Why, in God's name, can't my crew join me at your service?"

"Can't help who you are, captain, the boy can't enter. This is North Carolina!" Then he weakened a little and said, "Wait here a minute."

A short time later he returned with the curate, and Captain Granderson again made a detailed explanation. The curate was sympathetic but said, "The trouble is that this is not the church's doing, it's the law of the state. The North Carolina law forbids the mixing of congregations."

"What about heaven," countered Captain Granderson, "when we die and go to heaven is it the law there too?"

"I don't know about the laws there," said the curate, "but we have our own down here and they have to be obeyed."

While we stood there the service got underway. The congregation rose to sing and the words of the captain and curate merged with the strains of the hymn, "O God Our Help in Ages Past." The music apparently inspired the curate.

"I have it! You can all go in and sit down and the boy can go up in the balcony."

"Oh no," cried the captain, "that won't do! If he can't sit down here with us we'll go up and sit with him. We'll *all* sit in the balcony. Up we go, my lads, all together!"

By this time I was sick with anger and humiliation. "Oh no, not me!" I exclaimed, "I'm not going anywhere. These people are not Christians, but savages!"

Now the Captain was adamant. "Come on, my boy. We'll all go up together and after the service I'm going to do something about this." But our day was spoiled. The service seemed sour and hypocritical, and when it was over we all returned to the ship. Whatever Captain Granderson could do he had done. I returned straightway to my bunk and wrote letters to Dad-Sonny and Edith, explaining the barbaric custom of our northern neighbors. Though much had happened since I left Union Island there was not a word about the crew, the seas, the dolphin, and very few about the fine captain. There were just hot and tear-stained words about the church in Wilmington, North Carolina, and about a word I had learned for the first time – segregation.

Throughout our stay in the United States I did not go ashore again. Discrimination was a new experience for me. There was none in the West Indies, or even any concept of slavery. There was class distinction adopted by the West Indians themselves based on the white man's pattern. "If you are not as rich as I am you may not live in my neighborhood." But rich and poor, colored and white used the same beaches, patronized the same stores, and certainly attended the same churches. There were no elaborate rationalizations calculated to establish the natural superiority of one race over another. I was happy when the holds of the *Aeolus* were filled with resin, and we set sail for London. What I had seen of the "New World" was more than enough for me.

Our trip across took fifty days, most of it engaged in a furious battle with the sea. Gale followed gale, as the Atlantic seemed determined to add the *Aeolus* to the incalculable store of treasures at its bottom. My experience with a square rig ship had been limited to the trip up from Barbados, and now I had to learn real seamanship in a hurry. The other crew members were all veterans of the Atlantic, and I was determined to keep pace with them. For days we sailed under upper and lower topsails and storm trysails, reducing the target for the angry winds. Even though the winds were northwest, pushing us most of the time, we stayed under water practically half the way. No scuppers ever built are large enough to handle the mountains of water that come crashing over the bulwarks in heavy weather. Day and night the decks were awash. We slept in oilskins and seaboots. Each wave was bigger than the last and I wondered if the next would end my brief seafaring career in the middle of the Atlantic.

Forty-five days out of Wilmington we sighted Land's End, the southern tip of England, and the weather suddenly turned clear and beautiful, and the sea placid. As we swung into the English Channel Captain Granderson gave orders to hoist the pilot flag and signal for a tugboat. All hands were ordered on deck and we took in all sails, making them snug on the yardarm, for it was the practice to tow sailing ships through the capricious Channel. I was at the wheel when the tug pulled alongside, made fast, and the pilot came aboard. He instructed me to steer directly behind the tug and not let the ship's head veer away from the mast of the tug. Then the pilot and Captain Granderson decided to go forward to inspect the hawser and make sure everything was well secured.

I had never sailed the Channel before, of course, and didn't know how treacherous it could be. Thus, a moment after the two had gone forward I stared in disbelief at the heavy fog bearing down on us from the northeast. I realized that when it enveloped us I would not be able to see the mast of our tow anymore, and thus quickly took a compass bearing so I could hold to our course.

Seconds later the white shroud rolled in and swallowed up the tug, and then moved quickly upon the *Aeolus*. Pleased with my forethought I held to my course. What happened then was never precisely ascertained. A moment or so later I heard Captain Granderson's voice through the dense fog, "Hard-a-port! Hard-a-port!" I turned the huge wheel over as fast as I could, and the Captain appeared at my side suddenly and helped me hold her over, but it was too late. There, coming out of the impenetrable mist was a huge barquentine bearing straight upon us!

Every piece of sail was drawn, and with a 10-knot wind on her beam she was kicking up the foam on her bow. She struck us with a mighty crash, tearing away our starboard anchor, her mighty yards sweeping over the *Aeolus* like a gigantic scythe. Our yardarms splintered like matchsticks; the fore topgallant mast and sails tore away, spars and wood splinters came crashing to the deck. A seaman leapt to the bulwark and stood poised, ready to leap. The Captain and I abandoned the wheel and threw ourselves on the deck alongside a rope locker for protection as the entire superstructure seemed to come crashing about us.

As the barquentine tore past us we could see her port of registry in broad letters on her stern – *Sevastopol*. As if oblivious of her encounter she sailed blithely on, disappearing into the fog from which she had emerged.

Had the *Aeolus* been light we might have been sunk, but loaded with resin we did not receive a damaging blow. However, the topside damage was considerable. We hove to at once, clearing the deck of debris and making what repairs we could. Heavily loaded as we were, the Captain decided to signal for another tug; two of them towed us up the Channel into the safety of the Thames. During the night of June 12, 1907, we moved up the river to London, and came alongside the dock at 9 a.m.

During the next few days we removed the broken yardarms, many still dangling in mid-air, and ordered new ones from the shipyard. On June 14th the crew was paid off, but Captain Granderson kept me aboard for another week to testify before the Admiralty's hearing board. The following week I gave my testimony, and collected my pay – three pounds, four shillings and three pence.

This seemed like a fortune to me, and immediately I bought the two things I most wanted: an engagement ring for Edith, which I sent off to Union by the first mail, and a set of books on navigation. One of them, Norrie's *Epitome*, now worn and dog-eared, remains with me to this day, and afforded me my basic knowledge of ocean navigation and nautical astronomy. This done, I settled back to decide what to do next.

Captain Granderson wanted me to continue with him and the *Aeolus* to Kraagerow, Norway, where the ship would be overhauled and take on new cargo. But this was my first trip to England, the land of dukes and battlefields I had read so much about, and I was loath to leave. The captain had been a fine friend. He had fulfilled his pledge to John to look after me and help me learn the ways of the sea, entrusting me with all manner of tasks so that now I felt like an able seaman. Yet, much as I admired him I secretly resented his guardianship, as I had resented John's. I wanted to strike out on my own, away from those who loved me and were determined to take care of me. Unfortunately the engagement ring and the fifteen shillings for the nautical books had reduced my proud fortune to ten shillings. Nevertheless I resolved to leave the ship. I told Captain Granderson of my decision and he did not contest it. I packed my seabag, shook hands with him and we wished each other well. He stood at the bulwarks as I leapt across to the dock, and that was the last I was ever to see or hear of him for thirty-five years.

For the first time in my life I was free in a strange port, completely on my own. The few shillings in my pocket did not worry me. I was confident I could overcome the minor difficulty of being without food or shelter. I was strong, free and eager to try my talents. I would find my place in the world, return and marry Edith and we would live happily together ever after!

3

Careful checking among sailors around London indicated that the best port in which to catch a ship was Cardiff, so after a few days of seeing the sights – Westminster, Buckingham Palace, the Houses of Parliament and other places famous in English history – I caught the train to the principal shipping center of Wales. A taxi driver at the station spied me at once and offered to take me to a boarding house. This seemed a futile thing to do, for I had only three shillings and sixpence left, but the boarding master said expansively, "Why, that's all right, son. I have a steamer right now, bound for the Mediterranean. Do you want to go?"

While I would have preferred a sailing ship, where I felt at home, the opportunity seemed too timely to pass up. Steamers made shorter trips and the wages were lower, but to visit Mediterranean ports was tempting. I quickly said yes – grateful to my host for taking such an interest in me. My gratitude was short-lived. The boarding master delivered me to the ship and promptly drew an advance note on my first month's wages, two pounds and five shillings. He kept the two pounds, leaving the five shillings to me. It was my introduction to the shipping "crimp," then protected under British and American laws and very well paid for his procuring.

My new home was the *Wolf*, a slow flush-decked tramp operated by the Farragroves Company of London. She was loaded with coal for the British naval base at Malta, and even at her slovenly pace we reached our destination in twelve days, sailing throughout in beautiful weather.

At Malta I drew ten shillings against my pay, and while the other members of the crew set out for their favorite haunts I elected to sightsee. A few hundred yards from the *Wolf* I was approached by one of the ubiquitous guides who haunt the waterfronts of the world. For a shilling, he said, he would show me all of Malta s fascinating sights. I agreed, and off we went.

Our first stop was a Roman Catholic Church, one of the finest edifices in Malta, and I was surprised when my guide led me through a huge door, down a flight of steps and into a gloomy anteroom. "I'll show you a sight you never expected to see," he whispered. He told me to drop a penny in a slot, and as I did, another huge door opened before us, and we walked through a gloomy, subterranean passage until we were confronted by still another door. My uneasiness was slowly turning to panic, and my hand tightened about the jacknife I always carried. My guide sensed my uneasiness and said, "Don't be afraid," and swung open the door. There indeed was a sight I never expected to see – the rooms were lined with shelves and stacked from floor to ceiling were thousands of human bones!

"Oh, no!" I cried, instantly certain that I had been led into a trap. My guide was a fiend who brought his victims here, robbed and murdered them! There some years hence, would come some young West Indian boy to inspect the bones of Hugh Mulzac of Union Island!

Apparently, however, he had no wish to kill me at the moment; he was busy explaining that the bones were the remains of soldiers killed in a war between France and Britain. The French army, led by a woman, had been decimated, and the English had neatly stored their rivals' bones. "There, you see," he said, "they have even made a distinction between officers and enlisted men." Each general's bones were on a low shelf of their own, while the poor soldiers' were all piled together on the highest tiers.

"I didn't come to Malta to see dead Frenchmen," I asserted finally, thinking what poor luck I was having with churches, "I'd rather see some live Maltese! Let's get out of here!"

My guide assented and I let him go ahead, still grasping my knife, until we were back in the sunlight. "You had a narrow escape," I said to him withdrawing my knife, "any more trips like that and . . ."

His face turned white. He backed away, and finally turned and ran, without even collecting his shilling. I saw the rest of Malta on my own.

The *Wolf* discharged her cargo and received orders to proceed to Rumania for a load of grain for Liverpool. Going through the Bosphorus we put in for two days at Constantinople. Every seaman remembers his first "foreign port" vividly, and for me it was Constantinople, for Wilmington and London were, after all, more closely related to our Union Island culture.

Most shocking to me were the veiled women and the abject wretchedness of the people. On Union Island I had been brought up to understand that men were masters of the home, leaders in all affairs, and woman's place was in the home. But nothing prepared me for such a complete denial of their humanity and sex which seemed the object of the veils worn by the women of Islam. That men should build such magnificent palaces and shrines and yet reduce their women to walking shrouds seemed incomprehensible. Equally distressing were the ignorance and poverty of the people and the filth. Human excretion was deposited against walls. The difference in the standard of living between the wealthy and poor was incomprehensible to me. On Union Island sharecroppers lived in mud houses with thatched roofs, while our family had clapboard houses, both in St. Vincent and Union. Otherwise we lived virtually the same, working the same number of hours, eating the same kinds of food and drawing water from the same cisterns. In Constantinople rich and poor lived in separate worlds, and the glaring contradiction made a lasting impression upon me.

It was a lesson that was to be etched even more deeply in our next port, Soulina, on the Black Sea. Soulina was a town of about 10,000 people, with many lovely streets and homes, but here was the same degrading poverty we had left in Constantinople. The *Wolf* had scarcely made fast along the quay when a swarm of barefooted, scantily dressed teen-age girls descended upon us. Throughout the voyage I had noticed the men storing away crackers, cans of bully beef, and whatever else they could steal, and now I learned why. The crew members disappeared with the girls in whatever secluded spot they could find from the bridge to the rope locker, for a bar of soap could win a girl's favors for the whole night.

The longshoremen worked for a pittance. Their basic diet was black bread, onions, and enough vodka to enable them to drown their misery. There are those who sneer at working-class alcoholism, but how much greater their right to get drunk than the cafe society habitués who never do a lick of work their whole lives. The Rumanian dock workers labored long and hard for a few pennies, and if vodka made their suffering more bearable they were at least entitled to get through their dreary days and nights.

Yet, while I had sympathy for them, I could not understand why, with so many Rumanians starving, we should come in for a shipload of grain to take back to the British Isles. I had studied very little economics in school, but I knew that Rumania was one of the richest granaries of the Black Sea Coast. Why then, was the grain they sowed not their own? It was a problem I was not to comprehend for many years.

With the *Wolf's* holds loaded deep with rich Rumanian produce the sailors said good-bye to their girls, and we returned through the Bosphorus to Liverpool. Sailing in the Mediterranean reminded me of the West Indies; every day was like the previous one, with deep blue skies, fleecy clouds, a flat sea, and barely an hour out of sight of land.

"If you stay aboard long enough," an old sailor's saying went, "you'll see every port in the world." Today, when the great majority of the world's ships operate on scheduled, government-subsidized runs, this is no longer true. But a "tramp" was exactly what the name implied: it had no schedule, picking up cargoes wherever they were available and carrying them wherever they were assigned. The *Wolf's* next voyage, it turned out, was to South America with a cargo destined for Colestina, a little town up the

River Plata from Buenos Aires. Another incident however, was to mar our departure.

Traditionally most sailors quit the ship at the end of every voyage. Every vessel is a "rustbucket," a "hungry feeder," and its master a "Captain Bligh." There is always the hope that the next vessel will become a "home," with good food, decent hours, and benevolent mates and engineers. Most of the crew members of the *Wolf,* accordingly, paid off in Liverpool, and accommodating *crimps* supplied new sailors, among whom were five Greeks.

I had decided to remain aboard, at least temporarily, and was in the main deck fo'c'sle making up my bunk when the Greek sailors entered. They took one look at me and stopped dead in their tracks. "What are *you* doing here?" one of them asked.

"Making up my bunk, can't you see? I'm an A.B."

"Oh, you are, are you," he shot back, "we'll see about that!"

He dropped his seabag and stalked out, the others following upon his heels, while I pursued all five.

We went to the captain's stateroom, and they voiced their complaint. "We are not sailing with a *darky* in the fo'c'sle," the leader said. The captain regarded them coolly; I swallowed. Would he be a Granderson, or would he be like the sexton of the church at Wilmington? The matter was quickly settled.

"You have signed the articles, have you not?" the captain asked.

"Yes."

"You understand that Mulzac is a British subject sailing on a British vessel, while you are aliens?"

"Yes."

"Nevertheless, you want to prescribe the regulations under which British vessels shall sail?"

No answer.

"You realize that if you leave the ship I will make an entry in your books, charging desertion?"

"Yes."

"Well then, Mulzac stays on the ship! That's final!"

The seamen returned to the fo'c'sle, picked up their bags and left the ship. They were replaced the following day and the captain turned over their books to the British Board of Trade, marked "Deserter." It was a lesson I have never forgotten. If all masters behaved the same way the world would not be safe for segregationists.

We loaded coal, steel rails and general cargo and then steamed out of the harbor on a course set for Argentina.

Though I had made a complete trip on the *Wolf* I found it difficult to get used to the routine on a steamer. Life was too mechanized and there was too much leisure time. On the four-on, four-off watches on the *Aeolus* and the *Sunbeam* I had little time to myself. On the steamer, however, there was little to do. Aside from standing watch and chipping paint your time was your own, and though I studied navigation and the rules of the road, I felt uneasy away from the job.

This *ennui* crept into my work, too. I was on the wheel one night as we approached the equator, traveling along at about five knots. It was the twelve-to-four watch and the light of a great golden moon cast a glossy sheen on the water, as if laying down a path for us to follow. Nothing aboard stirred. The only sound that broke the stillness was the *tonkety-tonk, tonkety-tonk, tonkety-tonk* of the engines, and the steady rhythm and the glittering, expansive silence of the sea exerted a hypnotic influence upon both the mate and me. I was steering a southwesterly course, and from time to time stole a glance at the mate . . . he was sound asleep!

I relaxed too and began to daydream. Shortly before two I began to concentrate on the moon settling low in the sky. I watched, fascinated as it seemed to let itself down out of the heavens as if by a gigantic handy-billy . . . lower, lower, glittering in the water . . . mixing with my dreams.

The next thing I remember was shaking my head and struggling to focus on the moon's path again. I looked for it frantically, but it was nowhere to be seen. In desperation I wheeled about – and there was the same golden friend directly off the stern! I could not have fallen asleep for more than a few minutes, but in that time I had lost the helm and the *Wolf* had turned 180° around! I inched the wheel over carefully so as not to disturb the mate, and when I had brought the ship back on course I nudged him gently.

"Anything wrong?" he asked quickly.

"I thought I heard the captain."

"Oh, thanks."

The captain, of course, never appeared, and we *tonkety-tonked* steadily on our way toward B. A. I have always been thankful that back in those days we did not have a "tattle tale" – the electronic course recorder which leaves an indelible record of changes of course for the master to inspect. The mate and I would have received a royal tongue-lashing and perhaps even a logging.

On our twenty-eighth day at sea we reached the estuary of the Rio de la Plata, followed it up to its main tributary, the Parana, and taking on a pilot steamed up the river to the little town of Colestina. After discharging half our cargo we moved even further up the Parana to unload the balance and to begin loading giant logs which were to be used for building a seaway and docks in Bremen, Germany.

It was because of our return cargo that I decided to part company with the *Wolf* and seek another berth. As the stevedores loaded the great pilings they would occasionally stick their hands in holes in the logs and pull out squirming snakes. The reptiles were between three and four feet long and the stevedores would casually break their necks and throw them over the side into the river. Sailing with snakes was a detail of my seafaring obligations that had not been specifically spelled out in the articles. It therefore seemed to me that my contract with the *Wolf* was no longer valid. I communicated this to the captain, who laughed and assured me the snakes were harmless.

One morning after standing the night watch I showered and shaved and headed toward the fo'c'sle to get a few hours rest. I flung back the blanket to lie down for a nap – and there curled up was Mr. Snake! That settled it! I waited until evening and took my seabag ashore. The next day I asked the captain for as big a draw as I could get, and three others joined me – Victor Garcia, Albert De Hall, and a Greek sailor whose name I never did learn to pronounce. We didn't know what we wanted to do, but we were united in the conviction that snakes did not make good shipmates. The *Wolf* departed the following day without us.

Fortune usually smiles upon sailors in a foreign port. We had not been ashore more than a few hours when we were accosted by a little old man who asked us in Spanish, "Where are you going?" Albert De Hall, born in Guadaloupe and raised in Marseilles, who had sailed the seven seas many times over and picked up a waterfront fluency in Spanish, Greek, and Turkish as well as his native French and English, became our interpreter. He told the old man we had been thinking of going to Rosario to pick up another ship.

"No, no," he replied, "you must come with me! I have a little place in the country. You can eat and sleep no cost."

Such generosity was not customary, and we tried to find out what was expected of us in return for such hospitality. It turned out that the little old man was a widower with five single daughters.

"When my countrymen come to our place they want to treat my girls as they please," he said. "They have no manners. I don't want them around. But sailors are gentlemen, and the girls have a right to meet good boys their

43

own age. Come! Stay a week or two. If you decide to marry my girls, well, fine!"

Who could refuse such an offer? We picked up our dufflebags and followed the old man to his little farm and five daughters in the hills.

The farm was surprisingly pleasant – and so were the daughters! They ranged in age from seventeen to twenty-eight, and were uniformly attractive. In addition the old man had a good herd of cattle, several horses, and grew all his own vegetables.

The four of us settled down for some weeks. We helped the old man on the farm during the day – and in the evening sang songs, danced and boasted to the girls of our exploits in foreign lands. It wasn't long before we were paired off, and since I was youngest the sweet seventeen-year-old girl fell to me. My Spanish was weak, but there was no mistaking her intentions: she wanted to marry. Before long the others also had propositions and the old man was delighted – he wanted to arrange a quadruple marriage right there!

Victor, Albert, and myself, however, had second thoughts, though our Greek comrade was ready to settle down for the rest of his life. We asked the old man for a few days to think it over and finally told him we felt that we had to move on. He was very upset, and the daughters sobbed throughout the evening of our departure. The kindest thing we could think of to say was that we would be back, a sailor's promise. Then we caught the train to Rosario.

British Consulates back in the old days functioned as shipping halls for merchant seamen, and when we called there we noticed that a barquentine, the *Sound of Jura,* was posted on the shipping board. She was an English vessel, light in ballast, bound for Newcastle, New South Wales, Australia. All three of us signed on the same day. I was glad to be back on a sailing ship – one without snakes at that.

The ship was anchored out in the Plata. When we came aboard she was ready to sail, but the captain was nowhere to be found. A few hours later a small boat put alongside and the worthy gentleman was so stupefied drunk that we had to hoist him aboard in a cargo sling. With the chief mate in command the pilot guided us down the river and out to sea. We dropped the pilot, the Old Man appeared on deck shaky but sober, and ordered us to set all sails. A stiff northwester was blowing, and we were running the eastern down, making for the Cape of Good Hope on our way to Australia!

4

In the old days seamen signed on English ships under articles which specified a scale of provisions. This clause had been inserted to help guarantee a minimum standard of subsistence to prevent the illnesses and malnutrition so common at the time. The shipowners, of course, were quick to use this *minimum* standard under the law as a *maximum,* and like so many standards fixed by political authority it became virtually impossible to change.

Accordingly, each Saturday morning we would go forward to the steward's locker to draw our specified weekly stores, excluding flour and meat, which were issued daily. On the *Sound of Jura* our rations were the absolute minimum required, and with a sixteen-hour workday stimulating appetites of ravenous proportions it was difficult to make these scanty provisions last through the week.

We were only three weeks out of Rosario when even this skimpy scale was abandoned. Of flour, meat, canned goods, and vegetables the *Sound of Jura* had none. "Spiller & Baker's" was our only fare. These were biscuits about four inches square and half an inch thick, made by a London firm of that name and intended, I suppose, only for hogs, the overseas army, and merchant seamen... or possibly as weapons for rock fights. The strongest man on the ship could not break one with his bare hands; we had to whack them open with belayin' pins (heavy iron pins which fitted into the gunwales and to which the braces and halyards were made fast).

When the biscuits finally yielded to our assault fat worms would crawl out. We'd throw them overboard, and devour what was left. From time to time a seaman would "discover" that he had overlooked a can of corned beef that remained from his rations – and the biscuits and corned beef would be put in a piece of canvas and pounded into cracker hash.

We lived like this for twelve weeks. No coffee, no milk, no bread, no jam, no meat – nothing but mouldy biscuits and occasionally a mouthful of cracker hash. Most infuriating, the steward told us that the captain's cabin was provisioned with more food than any one man could consume. For days we dreamed up ingenious tricks to get the captain out of his quarters long enough for one of us to steal in and capture a few rations. We never succeeded. Then we concentrated on his fat little dog; whistling, dancing, making dog noises and rolling our eyes with intimations of secret delights in store for him if he would but venture down off the poop deck, but we were thwarted once again.

At the end of our twelfth week we sighted Tasmania and crowded all sails through Bass Straight. Two days later we docked at Newcastle, in New South Wales, a starved and bitter crew. As soon as the ship docked we headed for the Board of Trade to report the captain. No crew member would make the return trip on that starvation ship, and we demanded that we be paid off and recompensed for the provisions owed us.

The Board of Trade readily assented – in part. That is, all the men were to be paid wages and penalty except four – the four of us who were colored. The Commonwealth of Australia, the Board reminded us, forbade non-Caucasians from staying on the island continent; we could remain only if the captain posted a bond of one hundred pounds sterling on each of our heads to cover the cost of deportation, if necessary.

The Australian law seemed more offensive to me than even the customs of the United States. In the United States, true, I had been segregated in a Wilmington church, but at least I had had access to the streets! Further, we four were British subjects in a British land, while the others hailed from many different nations. However, they had all they needed to land under Australian law – white skins. We protested this discrimination without success; without bonds we would be returned to the ship. Finally the captain agreed to post the bonds and we were allowed to leave the ship.

We soon learned that the government policy was held in contempt by the Australian people. Though we were kept under surveillance we went all over town and were treated warmly wherever we went. Occasionally I entertained on the guitar and Victor danced. Part of our popularity was reflected glory, for an American colored man had arrived in Australia at the same time – Jack Johnson, who fought Tommy Burns on June 1, 1908, for the heavyweight championship. When Johnson won, the four of us rose mightily in the esteem of our hosts.

After twenty-five days the Board of Trade called us in and offered us berths on the *County of Linlithgow*, a full-rigged fourmaster loading coal for Coquimbo, Chile. The *County of Linlithgow* was the largest ship I had ever boarded. She was nine thousand gross tons and carried a stump topgallant mast.

Big or not, two days out we discovered we were on another starvation ship. Breakfast was *bogu,* an unbelievably coarse oatmeal with a little brown sugar sprinkled on top. There was no canned milk on board. Black chicory served as the noontime coffee, and at five p.m. we were treated to a tiny piece of salt meat and chili beans. Fortunately, with all sails set we could make up to fifteen knots and thus suffered this fare for only forty-two days, arriving in Coquimbo July 18.

Again, there was no thought of staying with the ship for another trip. Victor and I separated from our comrades and went down to Valparaiso. There I caught the *S.S. Puna*, a coastwise combination freighter and passenger vessel operated by the Pacific Steam Navigation Company, trading along the whole coast from Peru to southern Chilean ports. I was the only English-speaking member of the crew.

The *Puna* remains distinct in my memory for one event in particular. On one trip a Chinese passenger boarded in Valparaiso with passage to Callao. From his appearance and demeanor one could guess he was a rich man, an impression confirmed by the impressive number of suitcases and boxes that were delivered to his stateroom. Two days later he was missing. A search of his quarters, engine room, and obscure places from the forepeak to the shaft alley failed to reveal a single trace of him.

While the search was in progress the smokestack, rising from the boiler room right past the bridge, began to give off a peculiar odor. The captain called down to the engine room to ask what was burning. The engineer on watch investigated – and raked the poor, dismembered body of our rich passenger from the furnace. The crime was quickly traced to the firemen, who were turned over to the police in the next port.

My luck with ships had been uniformly bad, and now it was to continue bad ashore. I paid off the *Puna* with one pound, ten, not enough to keep me very long. Happily, I ran into a Mr. Thompson who maintained a boarding house where a number of other West Indian sailors were staying. We were all in the same boat, and equally penniless. We decided to roam the streets of "Valpo" playing the guitar and singing for pesos, and for a week or more earned enough to pay Mr. Thompson for our board and room.

One night, however, a swarthy fellow approached us on the street and after listening awhile said, "Do you mind if I show you how to play our Chilean songs?"

Eager to learn, I put my guitar in his hands and he was off like a flash! We chased him and sought him out in every hide-away for over an hour but never saw him or the guitar again.

Luckily the following day another full-rigged English ship, the *Durbridge,* was signing on a crew. She was loaded with saltpetre in 150 pound bags, destined for Hamburg, Germany. She carried twenty-two men before the mast, plus three apprentices, a boatswain, boatswain's mate, and sailmaker. The captain's wife, as was the custom, also was aboard.

We weighed anchor that night and sailed for the Horn. Fourteen days later, just at dawn, we sighted our first white mountain, looming out of the mist a few points off the starboard bow and about a mile away. A cool wave of air swept over the ship; we changed course at once, and that was the beginning of one of the worst times I have ever had at sea.

A heavy southeast storm came up a few hours later. All hands were called on deck to take in and make fast the sails. There was no steam on the *Durbridge,* not even to hoist the sails. The barometer fell throughout the morning, the seas continued to rise, and by noon we were in a full-fledged Antarctic storm. Icebergs lined the starboard side, like one great continent of ice, and the temperature plummeted way below zero. Try as we might, we could not get the sails in – they were frozen stiff as boards! Dusk fell early in the afternoon, and as the wind drove to gale force – sixty-five miles per hour – hail stones began to pound us up on the masts and yardarms, breaking the skin of our knuckles, in minutes mashing our hands and fingers into bleeding pulp. It was so dark on the yardarms that you could not see a man two feet away, or even feel him through your senseless, frozen fingers. Nor could you hear him, though he screamed at the top of his lungs, for the roar of the winds and the thunder of the sea, breaking over the bow, drowned out every sound!

For two hours at a time we stayed aloft trying to bend the stiff sails, most of the time simply holding on for dear life as the frozen canvas blew right out of the ropings. The descent to the deck, sometimes seventy-five feet down ice-laden rattlings was extremely hazardous – nor was there warmth on deck – no fire, no blankets. We broke open the hold, cut open the saltpetre bags, sewed them together and huddled under them for two hours till it was time to go up again.

At midnight we discovered two men missing and searched the vessel. They were nowhere to be found. We knew they could not survive aloft even if, perchance, they had lashed themselves to the mast. We assumed they had fallen from the yardarms into the sea.

Dawn gave us part of our answer: the body of one of them, a cheerful, friendly 200-pound Irishman named O'Brien, was lying across a capstan. Presumably the wind had broken his grip on the yardarm and cast him to the deck. We sewed him up in canvas and gave him to the sea. The other missing sailor, an old salt named Teddy, did not receive even this attention. We never saw him again, and could only assume he had fallen overboard.

Morning brought no end to our ordeal, or the following morning or a week of mornings. We fought the gale for twenty-eight days trying to round Cape Horn. The only way we could make any progress was by hoisting canvas, yet when the storm increased it had to be taken down again. The blizzard was relentless, as if Antarctic demons had marked our ship for extinction and would not let us go. We lived virtually underwater day after day. It was impossible even to get dry. Each day the captain gave every man a jigger of rum, for without it we couldn't have gone aloft at all. Big as the *Durbridge* was she tossed like a cork in the water, buffeted by wind and sleet, hail and sea; and we drove ourselves drunkenly, like punch-drunk fighters, going through our duties in sheer desperation to save our lives, losing track of the hours and even days.

On the 25th of October, 1908, we finally rounded the Cape and hauled up to the northeast where a new calamity awaited us – the doldrums.

It is impossible to tell what conditions of weather can drive you more quickly to distraction – the hazards of a gale or the tortures of the doldrums, where northeast and southwest trade winds create a zone of calm, and for days on end nothing moves. We sailed on a sea of alternate calm and squalls. For days no wind blew to move us or to carry away the oppressive heat rising from the steaming sea. Then suddenly, from nowhere, a gust would descend upon us threatening to capsize the vessel. Sometimes there came a gigantic clap of thunder, like a stage effect, warning of doom – and as quickly as it had arisen the threat would subside. We would unbend the storm sails and rebend the summer sails, anxious that our canvas should not blow away – and the next moment would bring an ominously calm and motionless sea in which we begged for even a breath of wind to carry us on our way.

The *Durbridge* drifted for two months in the doldrums. Our food and water began to run low. There was little left to eat but hard tack, dried potatoes, and "Harriet Lane."

"Harriet Lane" was a girl whose name had been given to a kind of canned meat which was one of the main staples of every British ship. She had been an employee of a big meat-packing firm in London, and in her haste to make the company's exquisite offering ready for sailors' palates had lost a finger one day in a machine. She mourned the loss, not only of the useful finger but also of the ring that graced it. But neither ring nor finger was ever found in the meat-packing plant.

Eight months later, however, a sailor on a ship at sea opened a can of meat and there, ring and all, was Harriet Lane's finger. The British Board of Trade launched a widely publicized investigation, and from that day forward cans of meat have been known as "Harriet Lanes" to British seamen.

Day after day we drifted. Water was carefully rationed and the handouts of food became skimpier each week. Then one afternoon the sun, which had been scorching us without mercy, gave way to a sudden squall. We stretched a topsail from port to starboard, cut a hole in the center, and organized a bucket brigade. When the rain struck we were ready, and filled every tank on the ship. The food shortage was not so easily solved, though we dragged lines twenty-four hours a day. Tempers grew short and fights broke out, and though never a belligerent type I had a dispute of my own.

The *Durbridge* carried three apprentices on deck. Shortly before leaving Valparaiso the second mate had fallen ill, and the chief apprentice had been promoted to take his place. He was a boy of nineteen, and happened to be on my watch, the twelve-to-four. One morning as I was being relieved I gave the man who relieved me the course, as usual, "East Northeast." He acknowledged the transfer of the wheel, and I turned to the mate and gave him the course, "East Northeast." There was no reply and thinking he might be dozing I repeated more loudly, *"East Northeast."* Again there was no answer. I shrugged and began to walk away. The mate called me back. "What was that course again?"

"East Northeast" I repeated a third time.

"Don't you know how to give a course yet?" the nineteen-year-old apprentice snarled, "East Northeast, *sir.*"

"I will not say 'sir' to *you,*" I shot back, and walked off the poop.

The following morning the captain called me to his quarters, accused me of being insolent to the mate and logged me two days pay. I repeated I would not say "sir" to such a young upstart. We both knew very well that the Board of Trade would not sustain the log when we got to port, and the captain himself lifted it a short time later.

A few days after the squall the weakest of winds came out of the south, permitting light sailing, and held for three weeks – long enough to get us out of the doldrums. The rest of the voyage was almost a picnic compared to what had gone before. On the dog watch, from four to eight in the evening, we turned to sports on deck – boxing, wrestling, horse shoes, throwing rings, and other games. We made articles out of the material at hand – manila rope – and turned out rope-soled slippers, mats and belts, with plenty of time to spare. I enjoyed dyeing the rope and fashioning intricately patterned mats for friends back in England.

An important part of a seaman's job in those days was to know how to knot and splice rope. Rope provided our lifeline as well as our pastime, and one such day I received a brief and memorable lesson from the mate. He had given me a particularly difficult splice to make and came upon me as I was having trouble. "Johnny," he said, "always serve the reverse way." Then, suiting word to deed as he showed me, "Worm or parcel with the lay, then turn your ass and serve the other way." The advice worked when I applied it and the job turned out beautifully.

Eventually we sighted Land's End, called for a pilot and drove for the English Channel. We soon learned that we had not had our last adventure, for with all the savagery of a hurricane a heavy northeast storm came down upon us. I was off watch and sound asleep when the storm struck, and through the din heard the bos'un shout, "All hands on deck, all hands on deck." We hurriedly donned our oilskins, and rushed to clear braces and halyards that were drifting overboard. My watch had taken the mainmast, and I was struggling to free some braces from the scuppers, my back to the bow, when a gigantic wave, I was told later, poured over the deck and hit me from behind!

The *Durbridge* rolled with the wave, her starboard gunnels under the water, and I went spilling and tumbling over the side! When I finally fought my way to the surface the *Durbridge* was 30 feet away. I struck out for her furiously as another great swell hit the ship again, rolling her toward me and as it passed under cupped me neatly in its curve and washed me back aboard deck! Never before or since has nature worked its wonders for me with such perfect and fortuitous accuracy.

The old chief mate was not so lucky; the wave that hit me smashed him between the winches, and it was some time, working between the huge waves that kept piling over the bow, before we could free him.

Finally the storm subsided and we drove through the Channel to Hamburg, arriving there January 20th, 1909, over five months out of "Valpo." Our sails and ropings were icebound, the decks a solid sheet of ice. It was a happy night when we paid off, especially when the captain, in a rare gesture, gave us a few extra shillings toward the cost of our trip back to England. It was my first trip to Germany, but I couldn't have been less curious about a foreign land – my only thought was to get back to England as fast as possible. I caught the Grimsby boat that evening and will never forget the platter of ham and eggs the waiter placed before me on that little steamer. It was finer than any meal I had ever had.

One of the many advantages of sea life is that you have plenty of time to think. And by "think" I do not mean that occasional moment of frustrated concern which landlubbers bring to their problems. It is impossible for any reasonably sensitive human being to stand at a ship's wheel for two hours a watch, three times a day, week in, week out, in the radiant beauty of a starlit night or surrounded by pure, exquisite colors of a dawn or sunset at sea, without giving some thought to the world around him, his own past and the future of both it and himself.

I had been going to sea now, for two years. I was a good seaman. I was lithe, strong, capable in deck work, an expert helmsman, and I learned fast and well. I was nearly twenty-three years old, and had seen a good part of the world. But where was I going? What did I want? I had told Edith, "I will go away for three years and make good." But I had already been away two years and I hadn't a farthing to my name! *How* was I to make good ... and *when*? Clearly, sailing as an able seaman the rest of my life would bring me no fortune, nor Edith either.

Though it was the middle of winter and a mild blizzard was blowing over the North Sea, I walked out on deck that evening as we crossed the Channel, trying to decide what to do when we docked the following morning, where to go. It was time, I resolved at last, to get on with my career. I would head for the Nautical School in Swansea and take courses in ocean navigation. Then, qualified for a second mate's license, I would steadily climb the ladder, get my chief officer's ticket and finally my master's license. When we docked in the morning I made for the train station and a new life.

Fortune has a way of intervening at propitious moments. In Swansea I grabbed a taxi and when the driver learned where I was from told me he had a good West Indian friend. Since I needed a place to stay, his friend might take me in. In my brief travels I had discovered that the West Indies had sent its sons all over the world; there were few places you could go without finding a West Indian sailor who had gone forth earlier and settled down. And the taxi driver took me to Bill Boyd, who was not only a West Indian but a native of St. Vincent.

Bill took me in and his English wife and children very quickly made me feel at home. Bill had been away for many years, and I was able to fill him in with news of recent events. We discussed the islands, our boyhood and local personalities far into the night and before long I was filled with a nostalgia for home which gave new urgency to my studies.

The eight weeks at the Swansea Nautical College were solid work. I attended classes all day and studied far into the night. Yet the eight weeks passed quickly, and the prize was worth the effort. Soon after I graduated I sat for my second mate's certificate and passed with flying colors.

I discovered, however, that I had no money left. My months on the *Durbridge* had paid for my education, but out of my ten pounds, seven shillings; four pounds ten had gone to the college and the rest for board, lodging, clothes, books, and sundries.

There was only one thing to do: take jobs on the weekly English coastal boats and save, save, *save*! I stayed with the Boyds between ships, and sailed regularly on the *Demetian, Armorer, City of Cork,* and other local vessels, running to Germany, Holland, France, and Ireland. In each port I would walk the boulevards, visit the libraries and museums, talk to people; and hoard my wages like a miser. I worked on the coastwise vessels for over a year, guarding every penny. By the summer of 1910 I had saved forty gold pounds, enough, I thought, to return and claim Edith. I waited anxiously for a ship to the Caribbean, checking with the Board of Trade officers in every port, and even the shipping *crimps* in case I would be able to "buy" a job.

Before my chance came we were to carry some interesting cargo from Germany. Two great liners, the *Titanic* and the *Olympic* were under construction at the Harlan and Wolf dry docks in Belfast, Ireland. Most of the gear for these ships was cast in Essen, and was brought over by the weekly coastal steamers, especially the *City of Cork.* On one of my last trips we loaded on our afterdeck part of the rudder case for the *Titanic.*

A few years later, in April of 1912, that rudder case

was to go to the bottom in one of the greatest marine disasters of all time, claiming some 1500 lives. Such are the ways of the sea – and of men. On the *Durbridge* we could round the Horn, lie becalmed in the doldrums and fight through the English Channel with the loss of only two men. But the world's most modern liner piled up on an iceberg!

My waiting paid off in the summer of 1910. The *Port Kingston,* a Royal Mail steamer, was leaving Bristol for Jamaica, British West Indies, and had an opening for an able seaman. I decided to take her, for in Jamaica I would have no difficulty finding a ship for Trinidad and, eventually, to St. Vincent. Before we left Bristol I splurged on gifts – a wedding ring for Edith, a variety of presents for my mother and Dad-Sonny, and an inexpensive violin for myself, for I had also enrolled with the Venice College of Music for lessons on the violin. To these my friends in Swansea, eager to aid the native's return, added a handsome walking stick with an initialed silver band.

Thus equipped, I buried my forty pounds in the bottom of my trunk, boarded the *Port Kingston,* and nine days later arrived in Kingston, Jamaica. There I was irked to learn that the ship that was to take me to Trinidad and St. Vincent had departed the day before. I would have to wait thirteen days for her return. No disappointments in life seem so great as those which intervene on the very eve of an accomplishment. Nevertheless, reconciled to the wait, I paid off the *Port Kingston,* and took a room in St. Mary's Hotel, one of the least expensive hostelries in Jamaica.

For the first several days I barely left my room, anxious not to be bilked of my fortune. Neither high living, tourist ventures, nor ordinary comforts were to jeopardize my return to claim my prize. But one night I decided to take a walk, locked the door and embarked on a leisurely stroll around Kingston. I did not drink, smoke, or have a weakness for night spots, so at about 9:30 p.m. I returned to the hotel – and a thoroughly pilfered room! *Everything* was gone – trunk, baggage, money, violin, gifts, wedding ring, all were gone! All that remained was a sextant and an enlarged photo of myself. The forty shiny gold pieces – a lifetime's savings and a bride's ransom, these too were gone. In the few hours I had been walking the streets of Kingston the sextant, picture, and the clothes on my back had become my only possessions. I called the manager, who called the police, and together we searched every room in the house. Nothing was to be found. The police suggested that I get a lawyer, and the following morning I stopped in at the first barrister's sign I saw. He wanted a twelve-shilling down payment to take the case, and I was stymied – all the money I had was in the trunk.

To return to St. Vincent and Union with only forty pounds and a second mate's license would have been a meager enough accomplishment, but to return *penniless* was unthinkable! I decided I would not return. I sold the sextant to get enough money to live on until I could catch another vessel, mailed the photograph to Dad-Sonny and wrote a long letter to Edith. I told her what had happened, what I had decided; and begged her to wait just a little longer. Before I left Jamaica she answered: she did not believe my story, but she would wait a little longer. With all the resolution I could muster I put my misfortune out of my mind and scoured the waterfront for a job. Before long I landed an opening as second mate on the Norwegian freighter *America,* running from Jamaica to Baltimore with bananas. At last, I thought, I'm on my way – sailing on a steady run as second mate. Within six months I could save enough to return to St. Vincent in dignity. I applied myself to the job as no one has before or since. Unfortunately, at the beginning of the third trip the *America* was tied up in Baltimore, the crew paid off, and I was jobless.

No one could have been less anxious to be stranded in the United States than I was in 1910. Though three years had passed, the experience of the little church in Wilmington was still fresh in my mind. But I had little choice. The British Consulate could do nothing for me. The depression of 1911 was setting in, and jobs were scarce. I applied for a job at the Merchant and Miners Steamship Company, only to be told that "We hire niggers only in the steward's department." From one pier to the next, one shipping office to another, I made my way week after week, month after month. Finally, as things seemed hopeless, Captain Diggs, a friendly old shipping master I had come to know, steered me to a job as sailor on a magnificent six-masted schooner, the largest in the world at that time, the *Edward J. Lawrence.*

The *Lawrence* hauled coal from Curtis Bay, Baltimore, to Portland, Maine. Besides her master she carried a first mate, second mate, boatswain, steward, and six men before the mast. These six were all West Indians, and the reason quickly became obvious: no white men would take such a job for $25 a month. The *Lawrence* was a mankiller. She would take from five days to two weeks getting north to Portland, depending upon the winds, discharge in two days and head south again. The wind and cold off Cape Cod were brutal and the big sails froze stiff in heavy weather. Trimming sails was a job that made you want to take to your bunk for several days, but there was no rest. She carried a German skipper, Captain Kraeger, who drove us mercilessly, for he knew there were twenty men in port looking for jobs for every one of us who would quit. Trade unionists today who think there is something new about the "speedup" should have sailed this remarkable ship.

I stuck with the *Lawrence* for three trips until my hands were raw and bleeding from making up her sails in New England storms. To this day I do not understand how human beings could have survived those twenty-hour days under this autocratic skipper, whose only rule was *"work."* I signed off angrily when I could take no more, but not without telling the whole crew that only animals could live like this. Then I was back on the beach.

Necessity is the mother of invention, and of careers, too. A West Indian in the United States quickly learns that he is meant for menial labor. The instant I presented my black face to an employment office window my job opportunities were limited. I could pass coal or load lumber on the docks, I could sail as messman or utility aboard a ship, but the deck gangs were white as lilies, and there were no permanent dockside openings for colored people. Many of the clerks seemed to take it as a personal affront that I should even inquire about deck jobs, and of course I never even hinted that I carried a second officer's ticket.

I eked out a living through 1910 and 1911 catching a ship here and there, and haunting the shipping company offices. One day I saw several vessels at the Locust Point shipyard being readied for sea. Conditions in Europe were daily becoming more tense, and France and England were already demanding cargoes. These ships, however, turned out to be banana boats being put into commission to replace vessels with more urgent duties. Again I was told that the only openings for colored applicants were in the steward's department – and to get one of these it would be helpful if I painted out the passenger quarters for two weeks, without pay. Who could argue? I took the job, finally signing on as second cook, not a bit disturbed by this misrepresentation of my talent. To claim that I was a competent cook seemed a paltry deception compared with the hypocrisy of men who not only refused to honor my second mate's certificate, but required me to buy the job with two weeks' free labor! I borrowed a dollar from the steward and bought a cookbook which I intended to study during the trip, and went aboard the *Brookline*, a United Fruit Company ship that was flying the British flag, and carrying bananas between Jamaica and Baltimore.

The *Brookline's* new chef, I discovered when I signed

on, was a heavy drinker. With thirty-five passengers aboard he chose this moment to knock himself out, and did not show up at sailing time. As the ship was ready to sail the steward came to the galley and said, "We're lucky to have a qualified man like you aboard, Mulzac. You can handle it, can't you?"

"I never sailed cook before in my life," I said frankly, "but I'll try."

The steward shook his head in despair. "Well, do the best you can. I'll help you."

The *Brookline* pulled into the Bay and I went to work in my first steward's department job – as chief cook on a passenger vessel! Our first menu was to be beef broth, broiled mackerel or sirloin steak, french-fried potatoes, green peas, lettuce salad, ice cream, tea and coffee. I had no idea how to begin and turned hopefully to my brand-new book. All the directions were there and I followed them to the letter. I threw some large bones and pieces of meat into a pot to begin the soup, and took a large piece of beef out of the icebox for the steaks. I hadn't any idea how this should be cut and sliced away in any direction, intent only upon cutting off slabs that looked like steaks.

By this time we were heading down Chesapeake Bay, and heavy winds gave us a steady roll. Before long an A.B. popped his head in the galley and said "Take it easy, chef, there'll be mighty few customers tonight." Nothing could have pleased me more. This took care of the passengers, but the crew was another matter. The roughest sea did not alter an A.B.'s appetite, except possibly to increase it. At 7 p.m. the plates began to pound in the crew mess, and I tossed the blackened slabs of beef and a few tasteless potatoes on the plates. When these delicacies were served the din grew louder than ever, and for a while I thought I'd be stretched from the yardarms, but eventually their anger died out and the ordeal came to an end.

All night long I memorized the cook book, writing

down recipes for soups and salads and studying diagrams of the cow, learning the various cuts. Who could have imagined so many different desserts had been denied the sailors of the *Sound of Jura* and the *Durbridge?*

The next day I began to put instruction into practice, and had not a second's rest from sunup to sundown. While it was easy enough to follow the book's directions in the preparation of a single dish, timing the dishes so they would be ready simultaneously could be learned only by practice. I had the dessert ready long before the soup, the potatoes were cold before the meat was done. I worked even between meals, when veteran craftsmen would be resting, for I needed time to make errors and correct them before my thrice-daily encounters with the stove.

The help which the steward promised was, of course, never forthcoming. He knew even less about cooking than I did, and I was alone in the galley with my inexperience. Nevertheless, after the first night's fiasco the meals gradually became acceptable and good enough so that when we returned to Baltimore the steward kept me in the job and hired a second cook to take my old place.

I stayed aboard the *Brookline* for six months, until the banana season ended. Remembering my earlier encounter with the Merchants and Miners – that "niggers" were hired only in the steward's department – I went with my *Brookline* discharges and was quickly signed on the first of a number of M & M vessels. I sailed on them as chief cook for more than a year.

There is probably not a merchant seaman in the world who has not considered quitting the sea and settling down some place in a vine-covered cottage with a loyal wife and a flock of chickens in the yard. After a year of sailing with the Merchants and Miners as a cook my dream of becoming a captain seemed more unattainable than ever. I began to wonder if the dream were a false one, a childish notion. Surely it seemed romantic, if American steamship operators would not even permit colored people on deck, to seek to sail as an officer! These ideas began to take root, and late in 1913 a chance meeting with a childhood friend, Reginald Crosby, from St. Vincent brought them to full flower.

I met him one day on Gay Street in Baltimore and over a drink we reported on what had happened to us in the years since we'd last met. Reginald was leaving the following day for Chicago, and when I told him I was a good cook he insisted I join him. I was tired of the sea, at least of sailing as a cook when I had a second mate's license tucked away in my breast pocket, and I agreed to go.

Reginald turned out to be right about Chicago: there were dozens of jobs. The first agency we approached placed us, Reginald in a Loop hotel, and me in a girls' school, the Gerton Academy, in Winnetka.

The Gerton school was a large, private institution with an enrollment of more than seven hundred girls. The principal was a Mr. Cook, and his mother, Mrs. Cook, was in charge of the domestic science courses, the dining room and the kitchen. When I appeared before her Mrs. Cook was obviously disconcerted. "Oh, a *man*!" she cried, "Why did they send a *man*? Men can't cook, and besides they're not clean!"

Sometimes it seems to me that I have devoted my whole life to fighting other people's idiosyncrasies and prejudices. This time, however, it was not that I was colored that bothered Mrs. Cook; it was than I was a man. I could not change my sex any more that I could change my race, but the solution to the problem, I knew, was the same in either case: if Mrs. Cook could just be induced to put up with me for a while I knew everything would turn out all right.

"If madame is not satisfied," I said airily, "I suggest she call the employment agency and tell them so."

Madame did, and was told that there were absolutely no women cooks available, a fact I had ascertained beforehand. Mrs. Cook thereupon decided that I could stay on the job until she could locate a suitable woman.

The subsequent course of events can easily be anticipated by any man who has ever gone to sea. The kitchen was a mess. Grease and filth had accumulated all over the oven and on top of the stove; the ice boxes had not been cleaned in months; the pots and pans had a quarter-inch of rust and crust around the rims. I surveyed the kitchen and called Mrs. Cook.

When she came I said indignantly, "You say men are dirty, but look at this!" I ran my finger down a wall which had not been cleaned since Christ was born. "No man would have left a galley in such a condition." I walked around the kitchen gingerly, as if the dirt were ankle deep. "I can't work in such a filthy mess," I said, "it's impossible!"

Before long Mrs. Cook was begging me to take the job and I finally agreed, providing she would send me two helpers *at once* to put the galley in first-class shape. Two men were sent in from the school's own farm, and after several hours work we had the kitchen sparkling clean.

The next day I started to work. Mrs. Cook's instructions were explicit: "Never prepare a particular salad, soup or dessert oftener than once a month," she said. "Whatever you prepare today, don't prepare it again for thirty days. I want thirty different menus!"

My conscientious hours with cook books on the *Brookline* and the Merchants and Miners ships began to pay off. And in Winnetka, instead of having to rely upon canned and dried provisions I had access to the finest stores, plus the school's own farm, a never-ending source of fresh eggs, cream, butter, milk, and vegetables.

The payoff came at supper the following night. The astonished girls, having enjoyed a fine breakfast and lunch sent a delegation of about twenty to the kitchen to congratulate me, insisting it was the best supper they had had at Gerton Academy. Mrs. Cook was not so immediately impressed, but about a week later came to congratulate me and to say that she thought I'd do.

Before long the domestic science teacher asked me to visit her classes once a week to instruct the students in the preparation of special dishes. "Special dishes" gradually stretched to the point where they were an everyday subject, and I found myself a teacher. But I was young and it was fun. If so many Evanston and Chicago husbands have been happier who knows, or cares?

Everything went well at the Gerton Academy and I might still be there had not a Serbian nationalist assassinated Austrian Archduke Francis Ferdinand at Sarajevo on June 28th, 1914, lighting the fuse of World War I. One did not have to be a prophet to know that the spreading flames would gradually involve the United States, and a girls' school in Illinois seemed among the more unlikely places for a seaman to be.

I told Mrs. Cook I must leave. When the word got around a delegation came to beg me to stay. I was greatly moved by this appeal, but the very presence of these lovely, childish, feminine faces underscored one of the reasons impelling me to go. The triviality of life among seven hundred girls never seemed more obvious than when Europe had burst into flames and America seemed at the point of needing its hardiest men. The halcyon days at Gerton were over. Some of the girls wept, and I explained that my departure was only temporary. I would be back when the war was over. The following week I returned to Chicago and entrained for Baltimore.

5

When I arrived at the B & O station I picked up a copy of the Baltimore *Sun*. There was a page-one story on the shortage of skilled maritime personnel; officers and experienced unlicensed seamen were urged to report immediately for refresher courses at the United States Maritime Training School. I had not forgotten my earlier difficulties, but now the country was faced with a gigantic mobilization, and though war wouldn't come for three more years I thought United States shipping interests might even put a colored mate on the bridge.

The following day I went to the customs house and made my way to the third floor, which housed the school, and started through the door. An elderly guard thrust out his arm to bar my way. "Where are you going?"

"Why, to make an application," I said.

"Not here," he said, "*you* make applications on the second floor."

"The sign said officers should come up here."

"Officers! We don't have colored officers. You belong down below."

I had a sudden urge to punch the old man right in the nose. "Don't you know we're trying to help our allies win a war?" I seethed, "The country needs every man it can get!"

The old man's eyes hardened, and he spat into a cuspidor. "Won't ever get so bad we'll need you, boy. Go on down below."

I thrust the old man aside and walked through the door. He followed, shouting that I had assaulted him and calling for the police. In the confusion I told the clerk what I wanted, and was quickly ushered into the office of Mr. Lindau, who was in charge of the school. I told him that I was an experienced seaman with an English second mate's certificate, that I had received my first citizenship papers, and that I wanted to go to sea.

"You're just the kind of man we want," Mr. Lindau replied, "Wait a minute. I'll take care of things." By this time the police had arrived and Mr. Lindau assured them nothing was wrong. When he returned he ascertained that I was qualified, enrolled me in the school, and gave me a letter to the Steamboat Inspector. There I was put through a preliminary examination and given an American "red ink" certificate in exchange for my British certificate. The "red ink" certificate was a temporary document issued to non-citizens for wartime service, so-called because across its face the inspectors wrote "Foreign and Ocean Going" in red ink. It was understood that at the end of the war the holder would be automatically eligible for United States citizenship and an unconditional license.

With my red ink certificate I was assigned to my first job as second mate aboard the S.S. *Riswick*. I went aboard that afternoon and handed the captain my credentials. He looked at me, stared at the assignment slip, looked back at me, *harrumphed* and finally said, "Well, I just don't understand. *We have* a second mate."

"They got the order on the telephone," I said.

The captain was not at all perturbed. "I didn't send for one, I tell you," he said again, and turned away, ending the conversation.

I went down on the dock and called the officer who had sent me out. "Why did you send me out here?" I asked. "They've already got a mate."

"Oh, he called for a mate, all right," he replied, "and he's going to take one, and that one is going to be *you*. Let me talk to him."

I went back aboard and got the captain. They argued back and forth, and I listened as the captain insisted he hadn't called for a mate. Finally he said he would come right down to the office, hung up, and left the ship. He returned an hour later, cold as a piece of steel. Without saying a word to anyone he gathered his belongings, stalked away and disappeared into a taxicab.

The following morning a new skipper came aboard, and at 1 p.m., when the *Riswick* pointed her bow toward the Chesapeake, I was on the bridge as her second officer. On the return trip, our chief officer having been left in France, I was promoted to chief mate.

And thus began my war career. From 1914 to 1918 I sailed on four vessels as a deck officer – the *Riswick,* the *Waken,* the *Millenocket* and the *Pasadena.* Despite the fact that until April of 1917 the United States was not technically at war with the Central Powers we traveled in convoy and had many brushes with German U-boats. My closest call came on the *Waken* – a wooden steamship carrying general cargo to Cherbourg – when a plane dropped a bomb twenty yards off our stern. There were few "incidents" during these years. In times of crisis most men have a way of overcoming their prejudices and except for an occasional sidelong glance or a muttered epithet there was little discrimination.

An event of major personal importance, however, took place in 1916. I got married. I was thirty; Edith was thirty-one, long after an island girl should be a mother – and Edith, it turned out, was. Her letters had become more plaintive and finally despairing; then they had ceased altogether. There was a two-year lapse in our correspondence. But one morning when I returned to Baltimore there was a letter awaiting me, in answer to one of mine. Edith was married, and had a son. She had waited as long for me as she reasonably could, and was happy with her husband as she hoped I would be eventually with another girl.

After the initial shock wore off I began to understand. Edith had waited for me from 1907 until 1913. She could not be expected to wait forever, and had wed another childhood friend.

During this period I was living at the rooming house of a Mrs. Moore when I was ashore. Mrs. Moore, an adroit business woman with interests in everything from a second-hand furniture store and truck rental service to a real estate office, was very perceptive. She noticed, this trip, that something was troubling me, and under her cross-examination I finally spilled out the truth.

"Why Hugh," she exclaimed, "I'm surprised at you!

There are millions of girls in the world. You've been at sea so long you've forgotten. If you lose one then look for another!" As a matter of fact, she went on, I didn't have to look very far: she had a lovely daughter who was attending a girls' school in Philadelphia, and the next time Sadie came home she would introduce us.

On my next trip into Baltimore Sadie was home. She was extremely pretty, and from that time on, between trips, we saw each other steadily. Though she seemed a little *too* fun-loving to me, and I, I'm sure, a little staid to her, we enjoyed each other's company. Headstrong and in love with love was Sadie, and rejected by Edith and anxious to settle down was I; Mrs. Moore couldn't have been more pleased when we told her we had decided to marry.

Virtually from the first moment on Sadie and I had trouble. It is easy enough to overlook minor disagreements when you are courting, but it is much more difficult when you are married. Sadie and I had many differences, but the major one was her former roommate, Irene. They had been constant companions in school, and Irene seemed to consider that I had taken Sadie away from her. When I shipped out Irene moved in, and while I was at sea Irene was busy persuading Sadie that she had made a mistake, that she was too young to settle down. This unhappy state of affairs continued throughout the war. Several months after we were married Sadie became pregnant and to Irene this was adding insult to injury. We had many bitter exchanges during which Sadie was torn between her old friend and her new husband. Her old friend won out. One day when little Elaine was about a year old I returned to port to find no Elaine, no Sadie, and no Irene.

Mrs. Moore and I finally located them and months of patient argument proved fruitless. Sadie would not return without Irene and I was adamant – I would not have Irene in the house. The court awarded Elaine to me.

My first marriage ended in divorce a few years after it

was consummated, and I understood more clearly than ever the folly of not having claimed Edith when I could.

In World War I as in World War II one of the rewards for service in the United States forces for non-citizens was permission to apply for United States citizenship. Having sailed on the bridge during the war years and with every expectation of being able to continue my career in the United States Merchant Service, it was a glorious day, December 9, 1918, when I was awarded full citizenship I can't recall that I ever made United States citizenship my goal exactly — I suppose the step followed more or less naturally from the fact that I had been in the United States when the war began and was assigned to an American vessel. Yet I was immensely proud and pleased. At thirty-two the attractions of the nomadic life had begun to pall; I wanted a "home port" to return to and a nation to call my own. A kind of identity came with my citizenship papers, and from 1918 on I wanted to become integrated more with the life of this promising country — if only it would let me.

An almost equally auspicious occasion took place barely two weeks later. I sat for my master's license.

The time limit for sitting for your master's ticket, after notification, is five days. Baltimore's chief inspectors at that time were Captain Edwin F. White and Captain Dunn, both rough, tough masters of the old school, and both sympathetic to my problem. Two days after notification I appeared at the Steamboat Inspectors office, ready to sit for my license. Captain White took me aside.

"Listen, Hugh," he warned, "you'd better study up a little before you take the examination. We're very strict here. If you don't pass you'll have to wait a whole year. Why don't you take a refresher course in the school and come back later?"

"I've been studying for eight years, Captain," I said, "if I can't pass now I'll never be able to!"

He shrugged and swore me in, and then handed me the

questionnaire at 11 o'clock in the morning. At 4 p.m. papers were picked up and we were told to return the following morning. I had almost finished, and at 9 o'clock the following morning was back in place at the table. By 11 o'clock I had completed the test and turned in my papers to Captain Dunn.

"What's this?" he asked, "you aren't finished?"

"Yes."

"Better go back and look 'em over again, Hugh," he advised, "I'd hate to have to turn you down."

"But I *know* all these things, Cap," I protested, "I've known 'em for years. I just never sat for an examination before. Look 'em over."

Captain Dunn took my papers, pulled the answers from his drawer, and went over the questions one by one. From time to time he'd look up at me, as if he couldn't understand how I'd done it. Before long he had worked through all fifteen sheets, dealing with such subjects as navigation, rules of the road, deviation and variation of the compass, chartwork, meteorology, ship construction, nautical astronomy, and general seamanship. When he came to the end Captain Dunn stood up and extended his hand.

"How long have you been studying navigation?" he wanted to know. I told him, and then said I could have passed the cooking and wireless examinations just as easily.

"I had no idea of it," he said simply, "I thought you were a war sailor."

When Captain Dunn had finished with me he took me to Captain White who was equally flabbergasted. "What examination did you give Mulzac?" he asked. "How did he get through it in seven hours?"

Captain Dunn showed him the papers, and Captain White never said a word. He simply looked through them and led us back into the examination hall. Standing before the hundred or more men, many in Navy uniforms, Captain White said, "Aye, you fellows, look! Some of you have been sitting here for five goddamn days and can't get your second mate's license, and here's a man came in yesterday and got his skipper's ticket! I oughta make some of you pay rent for your seats!" In front of the whole assembly he spun and shook my hand. "You did fine, Mulzac, *fine*!"

The next morning a page-one story in the Baltimore *Sun* reviewed my achievement. My score, it turned out, was 100, and I had not only finished the examination in record time but was the first colored seaman in Baltimore history to sit successfully for his license. Captain White, I learned later, had notified the paper. Though my earlier years, and my later life, were to comprise a virtual history of segregation and discrimination in America, it is only fair to point out that hundreds of intelligent, fairminded Americans gave me boosts up the ladder. The shame of America is not that it doesn't have enough people who believe in equality, but that they are so often silent. If they were to speak out more frequently, and more emphatically, they would discover that many millions of their countrymen feel exactly as they do, but are also frightened by the race haters. Captains Dunn and White were not.

A few days after I had sat for my license I was assigned to the *Pasadena* as chief mate. We were loaded with grain for Finland, for the allies had decided to press the war against the infant Soviet Republic. At this time, obviously, I had no political convictions worthy of the name; I was happy enough to be an American and a first mate. The war was over, and we no longer had to proceed in convoys. We took the northern route around the coast of England, into the North and Baltic seas for Helsinki.

Finnish men were at the front and to our surprise we discovered that all the stevedores were women. Most had never seen a black man before, and some could not help staring at Stanley, a dark-skinned messman, and myself. One of them, just a girl, took her handkerchief and tried to wipe the blackness off Stanley's face. He resented her gesture and shook her off, but it was obvious that she meant no harm; she had never seen a black man before.

When the *Pasadena* returned to New York she was sent to dry dock and the crew paid off. I dreaded the prospect of being on the beach again, so I headed straight for Baltimore to register at the United States Shipping Board office and then, as a second thought, made application for membership in the Masters, Mates and Pilots Union at the same time. I had been turned down earlier, and now was rebuffed again, for there was a clause in the MM&P constitution prohibiting colored sailors from membership.

My experience with trade unions up to 1919 had not been good. I had joined my first one in Liverpool in 1909, the Firemen and Sailors Union. There was no problem of prejudice there – the union officials took a colored seaman's money as readily as a white man's. In return they gave us the same protection – none. Whatever the conditions on the ships, no delegate ever came aboard, no complaint was ever acted upon. The union's service began and ended with collecting dues, marking the sailor's book and providing him with a neat little cardboard envelope to keep it in.

In the United States the problem was different. Whatever services the unions provided I had no way of finding out – their doors were barred against me.

At the United States Shipping Board office, however, the doors were open, and I entered them three or four times daily. There, sitting behind a desk, was Captain Haynes, a conservative Virginian. Each day calls would come in from the operators and Haynes would beckon to one of the men sitting around the hall – any man, it turned out, but me.

One day I was sitting next to a big Norwegian who had come in a few days earlier from Buenos Aires. A call came in for a second officer, and though he had only a red ink certificate Captain Haynes signaled to him to come to the desk. After two months of waiting I was not in a very good mood, and accompanied the Norwegian to the desk as Captain Haynes began writing out the assignment slip. "Look here, Captain," I said, "I've been sitting here for two months with a master's certificate, while this man has just come in and the best he can show is a red ink second mate's license. What's the idea?"

The captain was not disconcerted. "Look here, buddy," he said, "as long as there's a white man in this hall you'll never ship out'a here!" There have been few occasions in my life when I've really lost my temper, but that was one. I had been hoping that what I suspected was not true, but Haynes' brutal words made my degradation "official." I called him every profane word in the sailor's lexicon, without sparing his kinfolk for several generations back. Somewhere in the middle of this outburst Captain Haynes decided to throw me out, but this proved more than he could manage, and no one else in the hall seemed willing to help him. Eventually I ran out of threats and deprecations, sat down to recover my composure, and finally stalked out, never to return.

The war was over and so, obviously, was the policy of shipping colored seamen on the bridge. For several days, I sat at home miserable and resentful, trying to figure out what course to follow. There were several open: I could put up a political fight for a job on the bridge, I could sail in the steward's department, or I could say to hell with the sea and get a shoreside job as chef, probably in a Baltimore hotel.

I had begun to understand that discrimination was not only *my* problem, but a fight of the whole colored race – and of whites too, for that matter, though precious few seemed to realize it. For years I had worked as an individualist – indeed, I had been at sea too long and on too many ships to fight in any other way.

But now, I thought, conditions were different. I was a citizen with a permanent residence; I was a master, with skills and experience that had taken a number of years to acquire. Yet, each time I scaled one barrier another stood in the way – the same barrier which prevented so many other Afro-Americans from realizing their talents. No one of them, nor I, could scale these barriers alone; the degradation of a whole people needed the whole people to fight it.

I went down to the neighborhood YMCA to get the name of the local head of the National Association for the Advancement of Colored People. He turned out to be Reverend James L. Diggs, pastor of Trinity Baptist Church. I went to see him at once and unfolded my story. Reverend Diggs picked up the telephone and put in a call to the War Shipping Administration in Washington, and reaching a responsible admiral, related my story.

The admiral listened, and when Reverend Diggs had finished, assured him that the United States War Shipping Board certainly did not believe in discrimination. As a matter of fact, it urged all of its offices to give colored applicants jobs – in the commissary department! With that he hung up.

I thanked Reverend Diggs for his efforts and left. Out on the street I took a deep breath of fresh air and decided that my maritime service was behind me. I would forget all about sailing and look for work ashore.

A few weeks later, still casting around for something to do, I happened to be walking down McCullough Street when I saw some men wallpapering a shop. I stood watching them for nearly an hour. It looked like an easy job, and I thought I might as well give it a try. I bought two rolls of the cheapest paper I could find, a brush and some paste, all for $3. That night at home I started to paper the ceiling. When I had finished and it looked reasonably good, I decided to launch my new career.

The next day I went door to door soliciting jobs. Before long I found a lady who wanted a back room papered. We agreed on a price of $5 and I went to work. When I finished she was so pleased that she called in a neighbor and the neighbor hired me to do two rooms in her house. With the profits from these two jobs I bought a couple of ladders, tables and other equipment, and began wallpapering for a living. I was neat, thorough, fast, and cheap, and most important of all, I understood very well how to butter up elderly ladies. Before long I had as much business as I could handle. From time to time I'd look wistfully at my master's certificate, but as business grew thoughts of returning to sea receded.

Not only thoughts of business prospered but those of love. Before the war I had met a woman from Jamaica, Miss Bayse, who had been a passenger aboard the *Brookline*. We happened to meet on deck one day, and discovering I was the chef she complimented me on the food. One thing led to another. She learned I was single and said, "I'm coming back from Jamaica soon. Maybe I'll bring a girl for you." Since this was shortly after I had had the bad news from Edith, I said this was a fine idea.

Some time later Miss Bayse was again a passenger on the return voyage and sure enough had a lovely young girl in tow, Miriam Aris. We were introduced, but in the meantime I had met Sadie. As I have related, we were subsequently married and divorced and the years intervened. But now, in 1920, I met the young Jamaican girl again, and we began to see each other regularly. One night at the theater, during intermission, she said casually, "Well, I knew you wouldn't stay married to Sadie . . . she wasn't the kind of girl for you."

"What do you mean? Who *is* the kind of girl for me?"

"*I* am the kind of girl for you," Miriam replied firmly. She was perfectly right. We were married on September 30, 1920, and were united for twenty-eight years.

With a new bride, a child on the way and my wallpaper business booming thoughts of the sea faded away – until once again my career was changed by a chance sidewalk meeting. I was walking along Druid Hill Avenue on my way to a job when I bumped into an old friend from

St. Vincent, Billy Rose. We greeted each other enthusiastically, but it was not old times that Billy wanted to talk about. "What do you think of the Back to Africa movement?" he asked.

"The *what*?"

"The *Back to Africa* movement! Haven't you heard about it? It's the greatest thing that's happened to the race in years. There's a fellow in New York organizing it – his name is Marcus Garvey. Everyone's joining it. They have their own newspaper, the *Negro World,* and their own steamship company, The Black Star Line. You're a seaman, aren't you?"

I told Billy that I was not only a seaman but had my master's license. "Why, then, it's just the thing for you! Garvey's advertising for colored officers! Come on, I'll show you!"

I followed Billy to the YMCA. Sure enough, an appeal for colored officers and seamen was in the *Negro World*. Billy's excitement began to seize me, as the hope of sailing on the bridge came alive once more. Maybe this was the answer, the *only* answer to Captain Haynes, the shipping operators, and all the War Shipping Board admirals – a whole fleet of ships owned and operated by black men!

Billy volunteered to write to Mr. Garvey and tell him all about me, and of course I assented. Three days later I received a telegram from Garvey himself, inviting me to come to New York and join him in his steamship business. I pretended to think twice about the offer, but of course my mind was already made up. Wallpapering had brought us modest prosperity, and a number of customers were waiting for me to fulfill contracts. But the opportunity to go to sea again, combined with the demands of race pride, was overwhelming. I caught a train the next day for New York and my first encounter with Marcus Garvey, president general of the Universal Negro Improvement Association, and president of the Black Star Line.

6

The events which drew me to the Garvey movement in 1920 were also attracting millions of other colored men and women. Chief among them was the outrageous discrimination to which they had been subjected during the war, both in the Army and in civilian jobs. Though Afro-Americans constituted only ten percent of the population of the U.S., they contributed thirteen percent of the soldiers. President Wilson had promised that "with thousands of your young sons in the camps and in France, out of this conflict you must expect nothing less than the enjoyment of full citizenship rights – the same as are enjoyed by any other citizens." However, he lifted not a finger to halt the vicious murders and pogroms which raged through the South when the troops returned home. The spectacle of black bodies dangling from southern trees or burned on the stake was commonplace – their bones and the chains that bound them often distributed to the mob as souvenirs. Afraid that U.S. colored troops would learn too much from French democracy, the Army issued its notorious Order No. 40, forbidding colored troops to associate with white women, and Wilson sent Dr. Robert Russa Moton, Booker T. Washington's successor at Tuskeegee Institute, to France to warn the Negro GI's not to expect freedom and equality when they return home.

In the flight from lynch terror and in search of opportunity, colored men and women had begun moving north as early as the second decade of the century. Individuals, families, whole communities gathered their meager belongings and set out for Hartford, New York, Philadelphia, Pittsburgh, Cleveland and Youngstown, Chicago, St. Louis, and Kansas City. Between 1915 and 1920 more than a million colored people found their way to the segregated tenements of the North.

If they were looking for a Promised Land they were doomed to disappointment. In the North factory doors were usually closed to them and most unions rigidly enforced the color bar. They met social abuse, debasement, thwarting of ambition, caricature, and the disparagement of their culture. The government in Washington did not hide its disdain for its colored citizens, and the administrations of Wilson, and Harding's after him, viewed America's racial crisis with deep-seated unconcern.

With the founding of the National Association for the Advancement of Colored People in 1909, and in 1911 the National Urban League, many leading colored intellectuals and professional men and women joined with sympathetic whites to launch an attack upon the political, social and economic proscriptions under which the Negro labored. But against the solid wall of American race prejudice, North and South, progress was painfully slow. The Negro intellectuals enjoyed very limited support among the colored masses. Racial pride had not yet developed to today's political level. Too few colored citizens could go to school. Too few voted, too few were able to free themselves from the daily hardship of earning a living. The honest, dedicated leaders, with few victories to show, could neither attract a militant following nor convince their hosts, however brilliantly their pleas for full citizenship were set forth, that their appeals needed to be answered.

It was in this setting of bitter disillusionment following the War to Make the World Safe for Democracy that Marcus Garvey for a brief time occupied the center of the stage in the unfolding drama of the black man's struggle. Garvey had been a teacher in his native Jamaica, and in 1914, at the age of forty-seven had founded the Universal Negro Improvement Association. In 1916 the Association's headquarters moved to New York, and aided by the heavy Negro immigration from Puerto Rico, Haiti, Cuba, and the British West Indies, by 1921 had 418 chapters with a membership alleged to total more than two million in the United States alone.

The objective of the UNIA was to redeem the continent of Africa for Africans "at home and abroad." That mighty "dark" land had been the chief prize of the Western Powers following World War I, and if its vast natural and human resources were enough to set white men at each other's throats, Garvey reasoned, why could it not also move black men to action?

Garvey envisioned a sort of supergovernment which would unite the peoples of African descent in Africa, the United States, Latin and South America, and other parts of the world and direct their destinies – a Black Zion. He sought to bring these millions of disenfranchised black folk under one discipline "just as the Pope and the Catholic Church control millions in every land."

Garvey encouraged colored business and manufacturing enterprises, which were stimulated and guided by African Factories Corporation. He sought to win followers and bind them together through a militant organ, *The Negro World*. He advocated increased trade between the United States, the West Indies, and Africa, under black men's control. The Black Star Steamship Corporation was to be the means to this end.

Garvey was an inspired organizer with a flair for promotion; and he launched his enterprises with the most powerful appeals to black African nationalism. "Help float more ships," read one brochure, "and write the name of the race across the commercial history of the world." "White men have invested in their own propositions and today make millions while crushing the souls of the black men. What white men have done colored men can do," read another. The appeal to race patriotism, the promise of an African renaissance under their own control, and the attraction of rapidly multiplying dollars drew colored folk to the Garvey movement as they had not been drawn by any other since the Civil War and Reconstruction.

When I emerged at the subway exit on 135 Street and

Lenox Avenue many a curious passerby on the crowded street stopped to stare at my master's uniform, for I had dressed for the occasion. But as I made my way toward the UNIA headquarters – or to within a block of it – I discovered a line more than 100 yards long waiting to enter 56 West 135 Street. There were jobseekers and supplicants, stock-owners-to-be and a few hero worshippers who simply wanted to tell Mr. Garvey how proud they were of him for what he was doing for the race. Since I had an appointment, I walked past and up the stairway leading from the first floor to the second, and the second to the third. There in the topmost office was a counter stacked high with bundles of bills of small denomination – the savings of thousands of earnest, hard-working folk who had come to buy five-dollar shares of stock in the Black Star Line.

Off this room was Mr. Garvey's office. As I entered he rose from his desk and gave my hand a fierce shake.

"Glad to see you Mulzac," he said, giving me a piercing look from his deep black eyes set in a fleshy but well-formed face. "Sit down, sit down," he ordered and started to unfold his dream before I had even obeyed his command.

Garvey was a short, stocky man of pure African descent. As he expounded, taking off every few moments in a flight of oratory, his black eyes flashed and his quick fingers drove home each point. At one moment he was wildly castigating white men for their cruelty and hypocrisy, and the next extolling the greatness of ancient African civilizations and recounting the unlimited wealth of the "mother continent."

Throughout our half-hour meeting, during which he outlined the greatest "Back to Africa" movement the world has ever seen, I sat transfixed with awe.

"I am going to make you chief officer of the *Yarmouth*," he said, "but this is only the beginning. You are going to help man a vast fleet of speedy ships engaged in the African trade. Afro-Americans shall come into their own."

"Yes, yes," I assented, entranced by the enthusiasm of this man who was obsessed with what he considered to be the great idea. Before I left I had purchased five shares of stock in the Black Star Line and cherished a clear vision of being commander of a great fleet.

Firsthand contact with one of Mr. Garvey's enterprises a few days later began to undermine my more grandiose illusions. Although a great deal of publicity had attended the "launching" of the first ship in the proposed Black Star fleet, the *Yarmouth* was not a vessel to set a sailor's heart aflame. She had been built in Scotland thirty-four years earlier, and was undoubtedly a fine vessel at the time of her christening, a year before my birth. But she had been used as a coal boat during the war and by the time Garvey acquired her she was something less than seaworthy. Her boiler crowns were in need of repair, and her hull was practically worn out. She could not have been worth a penny over $25,000 when the Black Star Line acquired her for $165,000. To add insult to injury, though she was always referred to as the S.S. *Frederick Douglass* in Black Star publicity, the *Yarmouth* she was and the *Yarmouth* she was to remain till the day she was sold for scrap.

Her career under Black Star operation had not been one to inspire confidence, either. On her second voyage she had been chartered to take a cargo of whiskey to Cuba, just a few days before Prohibition took effect. Mr. Garvey and Smith Green, vice-president, had drawn up a contract without consulting the ship's master, Captain Charles Cockburn; though the cargo was worth in excess of a million dollars they had chartered her for $11,000 — a sum insufficient even to get her to her destination, let alone return a dividend for the poor stockholders.

Unfortunately the vessel had been loaded in such haste

that in heavy weather off Cape May the cargo had shifted, giving her a heavy starboard list. Part of the cargo had to be jettisoned, and the *Yarmouth* limped back to New York under a Coast Guard escort.

It was at this point, while she lay at anchor off the Statue of Liberty, that I went aboard, January 23, 1920. Captain Cockburn, a tall colored man who had sailed the African coast for years and had a British master's license, quickly brought me up to date on the *Yarmouth's* misadventures and his differences with Mr. Garvey.

Still under the influence of Garvey's rhetoric, however, I declined to take sides. My immediate task was clear – to make the *Yarmouth* as shipshape as possible so we could resume our voyage. Not only was she carrying a heavy list, but the ashes from her furnaces had been dumped under the lifeboats, the cargo was topsy-turvy, dunnage was all over the vessel, much of the gear was not in operating condition and her plates were covered with rust.

I called for a gang of stevedores and made the crew snap to. Several days later Mr. Garvey came aboard and was so pleased with the appearance of the vessel that he hinted broadly that he intended to discharge Captain Cockburn and make me master of the vessel. I was anxious not to be put into such an ambiguous position, first because while Mr. Garvey was the boss ashore, Cockburn was the master at sea, but more to the point, since the *Yarmouth* was under British registry, my American license would not qualify me to take command. Also, I was imbued with the spirit of the Garvey movement and had no selfish ambitions. But I was soon to learn it was naive to suppose one could remain neutral in any undertaking involving Marcus Garvey. Wherever he went, whatever he undertook, excitement and controversy followed.

On February 27th we raised anchor and with the ship in as good shape as she had been in years, we sailed in clear weather and arrived in Havana March 3rd.

The *Yarmouth's* arrival had been heralded by Cuban

agents of the UNIA and sympathizers flocked from all parts of the island toward the docks to greet the first ship they had ever seen entirely owned and operated by colored men. They came out in boats when we arrived, showering us with flowers and fruit, but we couldn't let them aboard. We lay at anchor for five days waiting for a berth, and I worked the crew overtime cleaning and painting the ship so we would make a good impression. Finally, however, we moved to dock and were overrun with visitors from dawn until sunset.

Since the charter party's overriding interest had been to get the cargo of whiskey out of the United States waters no arrangements had been made for a Cuban consignee. Normally, the owners of a vessel are protected against delays by a demurrage clause in the contract. But because there was no formal consignee and the operators had failed to insist upon the protection of a demurrage clause in their contract with the owners of the liquor, every delay meant that the vessel lost more money. To the five-day wait at anchorage was added a two-week delay when we tied up because of a longshore strike. Thus, instead of collecting the value of its cargo space for each day's delay, including Sundays, which would have amounted to several thousand dollars daily, we not only lost our expenses and possible profits, but had to pay the maintenance of the thirty-five passengers bound for Jamaica and other Caribbean ports.

Though Captain Cockburn and I were almost constantly occupied with such dispiriting details we found time to enjoy the welcome of the Cuban people, from President Menocal on down. There was a party nearly every night. President Menocal honored us with a banquet at the Presidential Palace and expressed his great pride in seeing colored men make their own opportunities in the field of commerce. Before the evening was over he promised the support of the Cuban government for the ventures of the Black Star Line.

Many other Cuban businessmen and landowners also pledged their cooperation. One particularly influential Senator, who owned several thousand acres of sugar cane, said that he had been shipping all of his sugar by United Fruit Company vessels but would readily switch to Black Star if we would promise him seaworthy vessels and good service. In scores of formal and informal gatherings the officers and men of the *Yarmouth* were feted, and at every one some Cuban businessman promised us his trade. Many bought stock in the Black Star Line.

Finally, after thirty-two days in port, we discharged our cargo in bond and with only passengers aboard left for Jamaica. Again hundreds greeted us at the dock. With no cargo to load or discharge we remained only long enough to repair the boilers and to take on bunkers and stores. Then we left for Colon, the Panama Canal Zone, and the biggest reception of all. Literally thousands of Panamanians swarmed the docks with baskets of fruit, vegetables and gifts. I was amazed that the *Yarmouth* had become such a symbol for colored people of every land.

Back in the 1880's and '90's, when two French companies had begun construction of the canal, several thousand West Indians had emigrated to the Canal Zone and had remained when the United States took over the project in 1904. When Americans succeeded the French as builders, however, they brought with them not only great resources of capital and technological skill, but also that characteristic hallmark of United States civilization – flagrant racial discrimination.

The "colored" and "white" signs which designate public facilities throughout the South were replaced in Panama by "gold" and "silver" signs. The West Indians resented having to buy provisions from the "silver" commissary while their white colleagues purchased from the "gold" store, an indignity that applied even in the post-office! An even more grievous affront, however, was that the "gold" pay envelopes invariably contained more money than the "silver" ones, even when the workers performed the same duties, side by side.

From 1904 on the West Indians had fought this treatment bitterly, defeating an effort to institute segregation on street cars and in theaters. Resentment was at a fever pitch when we tied up in 1920, and thousands were anxious to leave the Canal Zone. We finally agreed to take 500 to Cuba, which was then importing workers for the sugar and banana plantations. The accommodations I hastily constructed in the holds were terribly inadequate, and before we were to discharge our passengers at Santiago de Cuba we encountered many difficulties, including shortages of fuel, food, and equipment, but the migrants preferred risking these hazards to remaining a moment longer in a country where they were not free.

En route to Cuba, again at the insistence of Mr. Garvey, we put in at Bocas del Toro, Almirante, and Puerto Limon, Costa Rica. In all three we were accorded the welcome of conquering heroes. At Bocas del Toro thousands of peasants came down from the hills on horses, donkeys, and in makeshift carts, and by a special train provided by the United Fruit Company, which, since it was going to lose its employees for the day anyway, declared a legal holiday. The crowd on the dock was so thick that when we threw our heaving lines ashore the peasants seized the hawsers as they came out of the water and literally breasted us alongside the dock. In the tumult that followed dancing broke out on the deck, great piles of fruit and flowers mounted on the hatch covers, and UNIA agents signed up hundreds of new members.

Yet it was clear to me that we had no reason at all to be in these ports. There was no cargo to be loaded or discharged. We had 500 passengers aboard to be fed and cared for. The *Yarmouth* was simply being used as a propaganda device for recruiting new members to the Universal Negro Improvement Association. It was a helluva way to run a steamship.

When our passengers were finally put off at Santiago de Cuba the *Yarmouth* sailed for Kingston, Jamaica, for a cargo of coconuts – and to have the boiler crowns repaired again, by this time a routine job. Just before leaving Kingston we received fresh orders from Mr. Garvey: coconuts or no coconuts, we were to depart at once for Boston!

The British government still maintained wartime restrictions on food exports from Jamaica, and it was impossible to secure sufficient provisions for the trip home. Captain Cockburn therefore found it expedient to stop at Nassau and then Norfolk for stores and fuel, and in the latter port new orders awaited us: a UNIA celebration was being held in Philadelphia, and we should put in there for a few days en route to Boston! Orders are orders, even when 700 tons of coconuts for New York are rotting in the hold. We dutifully steamed for Philadelphia.

The UNIA celebrations in both ports were spectacular affairs, with thousands joining the parades. Garvey made impassioned speeches, whipping the people into frenzied support of the association. Luckily he had also scheduled a celebration in New York, so the *Yarmouth* could finally deliver its cargo. The crew of the *Yarmouth* joined the parade, which at its peak started at 116th Street and Lenox Avenue, and stretched down to 100th Street, over to Seventh Avenue, and back up to 145th Street! As far as I am aware it was the greatest demonstration of colored solidarity in American history, before or since.

The coconuts, of course, were rotten. The incensed owners promptly filed a damage suit against the Black Star Line, bringing into bold relief another instance of the company's inefficiency: the contract did not contain any limit upon company responsibility. Further, no one in the office knew how to check damage claims submitted by the owners of cargo, placing the company completely at the mercy of the shipper and forced to depend upon *his* estimate of the value of the cargo instead of its own.

While in New York Captain Cockburn's differences with Mr. Garvey reached the boiling point, and the first break in the solid black phalanx occurred: a Captain Dixon, a white Canadian with English papers, was hired as master. For propaganda reasons Mr. Garvey announced that I had been made master of the *Phyllis Wheatley,* a ship that didn't even exist.

The second voyage of the *Yarmouth,* but for one unusual incident, was virtually a repetition of the first. We were chartered to load fertilizer for Cuba, and after discharging there sailed for Port-au-Prince, Haiti, and another admiring throng. From Port-au-Prince we headed for Kingston and a final commercial debacle.

A Japanese vessel, the *Kyo Maru,* had gone aground on the Serrana Banks, 500 miles South of Jamaica, and for two weeks had been waiting for a rescue vessel to relieve her of part of her cargo so she could float or be pulled off. No ship, however, had been willing to risk this operation. Captain Dixon and I both assured Mr. Wilson, agent for Black Star in Kingston, that we could do the job and advised him to charter us for $45,000. The owners of the cargo, and Lloyds of London, would willingly have paid this sum, for this was salvage cargo with a freight value from three to five times the value of ordinary cargo.

Mr. Wilson, however, was a building contractor who understood even less of the shipping business than Mr. Garvey. For reasons known only to himself, he drew up a contract for $12,000, barely enough to cover our expenses to the Banks and back again. On the strength of this contract we sailed for the Serrana Banks with an empty hold and thirty-two passengers. We got alongside the *Kyo Maru* with little trouble and with the assistance of the Japanese crew loaded 2,000 tons of her cargo in two days. She was pulled off the rocks without incident, and we sailed for New York with only one stop – in Charleston, South Carolina, to refuel and repair the ever defective boilers.

After two such profitless trips, I found myself losing confidence in Mr. Garvey and his business acumen. I decided to make a firm effort to put the line's operations, at least, on a sound commercial basis, and drew up a cargo plan containing detailed proposals for accepting and handling freight by weight and cubic measure, and many other provisions which would assure a profitable cargo-handling operation. I submitted this plan to Mr. Thompson, general manager of the company. He could not have been less interested. With membership booming he could not be bothered with such irksome details.

As it turned out, I was too late anyway – the *Yarmouth* had made her last voyage. Her boilers were beyond repair and in most other respects she was no longer a seaworthy vessel. For a number of years she was laid up at Staten Island, and the transaction which separated her from Black Star ownership was of a piece with all the other dealings which marked her brief career under Garvey's auspices. She was finally sold for scrap for $6,000 to cover her wharfage fees.

The Black Star Line operated two other ships, the *Kanawha* and the *Shadyside,* an excursion boat, and their careers as harbingers of the colored people's commercial resurgence were equally short. Although Garvey boasted that all three vessels were to be placed under American registry and rechristened the *Booker T. Washington,* the *Frederick Douglass* and the *Phyllis Wheatley,* after colored American heroes – and these names were widely used in UNIA publicity – this was never done.

In April of 1922 the Black Star Line collapsed, and with it many of Garvey's other far-flung commercial enterprises. In the court proceedings which followed it turned out that the line had lost nearly $700,000 in the few brief years of its existence, nearly half of it on the *Yarmouth.* It was also revealed that Garvey had kept no books, issued no financial reports. He was found guilty and sentenced to serve a five-year term at Atlanta in

1925. He was pardoned in 1927, deported to Jamaica, and died in England in 1940, broken and embittered.

Throughout the United States, and indeed the world, the impact of the failure of the UNIA and the Black Star Line was tremendous. Everyone wanted to know *why*, and in a series of articles published in the Cleveland *Public Journal and Gazette,* in October of 1923, I tried to give the answers.

First, I wrote, the management was incompetent. Not one of the company's officers had the most rudimentary understanding of the shipping business. Mr. Garvey was a great organizer but a poor businessman. Mr. Jeremiah Certain, the second vice-president, was a cigar maker. The executive positions in the company were staffed by opportunists and relatives from all walks of life except the shipping industry. Ocean commerce, especially in the '20's was one of the most highly rationalized industries in the world. Not only was there a surplus of war-built vessels, and many large and efficiently-run companies engaged in cargo trade, but then as now there was a vast fleet of highly competitive tramp steamers sailing under British, Greek, and other registries fighting for the diminishing cargoes of the postwar world. To compete with such companies effectively meant having good ships, sound capital backing, an extensive network of good agents, and above all, efficient management.

More important, however, the use to which the worthless Black Star ships were put represented the triumph of propaganda over business. The *Yarmouth* lost hundreds of thousands of dollars putting into ports where no cargo awaited, and in being chartered below her worth.

Thus the great and bold dream of colored resurgence ended in catastrophe. For their hard won dollars scores of thousands of humble black men and women received in dividends only a transitory inflation of their racial pride.

Nor was there anything wrong in that; in fact, it was to

be encouraged among a folk so long depreciated. But when the bubble burst as it had to, upon the jagged rocks of incompetence and venality the people were left with their dreams of a bright future blighted. They had no steamship line, no newspaper, no successful challenge to white domination, but had instead only monetary losses, more serious: a deep loss of faith in their own capacities.

What had begun as a great adventure for me and hundreds of thousands of others ended in tragedy and disillusionment. It was difficult to compute the suffering that resulted from this idealism. Thousands had mortgaged their homes to buy Black Star stock, others had sold their furniture and possessions to buy passage to Africa on ships that would never leave port. One man in Cuba sold his profitable lumber business and came to New York to book passage. Dollars evaporated with the dreams, personal ambitions with the hopes and aspirations of a whole people. For a few brief years Marcus Garvey fired the torch that lighted the Negro night, bringing dreams of glory and equality. Just as quickly the torch flickered and was out, leaving us in darkness as before; poorer, sadder, and perhaps wiser . . . who knows?

7

While the Black Star Line still operated its very existence stimulated a number of associated enterprises, including one of my own. Even after my discouraging experience on the *Yarmouth* I still hoped Marcus Garvey's bold plan would succeed. I was caught up with the vision of the "Black Fleet," and saw it as the route to the full development of colored men's talent, job equality at home and abroad, and the renaissance of Africa. The wish becomes father to the thought; looking ahead to the time when there would be a demand for colored officers on merchant ships, late in 1921 I got the idea of founding a school to teach navigation, engineering, and wireless to young aspirants.

I rented three large rooms at 442 St. Nicholas Avenue and invested my meager savings in nautical instruments, charts, blackboards, and other classroom equipment. Then I had two thousand cards printed advertising *Mulzac's Nautical Academy*.

Within a few weeks I had enrolled fifty-two students, most of them eager youngsters aflame with the spirit of the Garvey movement. The big problem was the wide variation in their educational backgrounds. Some were students with considerable education, while others had little or none at all. Since I was the only teacher the courses had to be paced to the abilities of the least educated. All, however, were fired with one outstanding characteristic: they were determined to learn, and at the end of the first three-month term all were making noticeable progress. Most important, all were diligent in attendance until the fifth month, when a dark cloud fell over the entire project: the Black Star Line was declared bankrupt.

The official announcement of what many had feared cast a pall over teeming colored communities throughout the nation. Almost immediately students began to drop out of the school. Two weeks after the April announcement only five students reported for class. The bright young faces of a few months before were now filled with doubt and uncertainty. My school was disintegrating before my very eyes. More than that, here were fifty-two young men with an eager faith in the future and a deep determination to make good. Were their youthful aspirations so suddenly to be snuffed out?

By letter and telephone I managed to reach every student, insisting upon his attendance at a special meeting. All fifty-two responded. When everyone was seated I asked for an explanation of their absence, and one young man spoke for the rest.

"Captain Mulzac," he said, "we can't afford to waste time learning to be officers when there's no future in it for us. The Black Star Line has failed. Even if we get our third mate's tickets, where will we get jobs? No white company will hire us. We think it's better to learn something we can make a living at after we graduate."

As carefully as I could I reasoned against this counsel of despair. If we denied ourselves the opportunity to acquire necessary skills, I argued, then the shipowners could always claim that they were *willing* to hire colored officers – there just weren't any around! It was only when we had a substantial number of qualified colored officers on hand that we would be strong enough to make our voices heard, and win equality of employment.

Well-meaning friends, I conceded, had long counseled me in the same way. "Stop chasing this will-o-the-wisp," they argued, "lower your sights and settle down." If we all "settled down" and accepted jobs as busboys, handymen or janitors, we would constitute a race of servants. If, however, we improved our skills, fought for equal jobs, equal pay and continued our education, the jobs would open up, little by little, and the walls of prejudice would come tumbling down. Besides, I told them, one day there would be white workers fighting side by side with their colored comrades for equality, trade unions of colored and white members, both of whom would understand that only by protecting the rights of the minority groups could decent conditions be won for all. But unless we were qualified how could we hope for better jobs?

My words fell upon deaf ears. "If *you're* qualified and can't get a job what hope is there for *us*?" they asked.

I ended the meeting with an appeal to those who had drifted away to return. About a dozen did, and we struggled through the balance of the term, though it was clear to all that the school was finished. Among those who stayed were Clifton Lastic and Adolphus Folks, who eventually received their licenses.

Thus in June of 1922 I was again out of work. Nor was I the only one. The years from 1918 to 1922 had been marked by an almost unending series of bitter strikes and lockouts, as employers and workers throughout the country sought to resolve their conflicting expectations of the Allied victory. More than ten million workers struck during these four years as big business launched a concerted union-busting program. In the crisis of 1920–21 nearly six million were unemployed, and the AFL lost nearly a third of its membership.

Bad as conditions were ashore they were even worse at sea. There were many reasons.

First of all, governments of the world have traditionally played powerful roles in determining the conditions of waterfront employment. The importance of marine transportation to the national welfare, especially in time of war, provided the basis for this supervision and support which included not only the award of mail, construction and operating subsidies, but the establishment of minimum standards of labor. There are few instances where this long cooperation between the government and the steamship operators has redounded to the seamen's benefit; the "law" permitting flogging, "logging" (deprivation of pay), jailing for quitting the ship, and many other onerous conditions including limited manning scales (the number and ratings of workers to be employed on a ship) minimum fo'c'sle space, etc.

Another factor which has served to depress wages and working conditions has been the understandable necessity of guaranteeing the security of the vessel, cargo, and passengers at sea. The captain of a vessel is absolute lord at sea; his commands cannot be questioned. His early authority to call out the crew to trim sails in heavy weather continued into the era of steam, to the point where there was virtually no limit to the number of hours seamen could be worked. Through the years I have described, from the beginning of the century to 1936 (with the exception of the war years) the two-watch system was in effect – four on and four off or six on and six off, constituting a twelve-hour working day and a seven-day work week. In the steward's department men often worked fifteen hours a day and more without overtime pay. Deck workers were often called out in their off hours to "holystone" the deck, splice rope or wire, or chip paint, on the ground that the work was necessary to the safety of the ship.

An added factor is that shipping is an intensely competitive industry, pitting U.S. operators directly against the vessels of nations with even lower wage and manning scales. Throughout the first half of this century, for example, more than twenty-five percent of the entire British merchant fleet was manned by Lascars from the East Indies who received the equivalent of nine dollars a month.

The disparity between the wages of foreign and American seamen was – and still is – used as an argument to force wage cuts on U.S. vessels. Its meaning, essentially, is that American sailors are expected to subsidize shipping operators with lowcost labor, an argument useful to any manufacturer confronted with tough foreign competition. As anyone who probes the record will discover, these arguments are especially specious in view of the vast government subsidies which enable the companies to turn a fancy profit.

Finally, the oppressive conditions aboard the ships, job insecurity, low wages and the ruthless collaboration between government and employers did not attract able workers and led to a high proportion of irresponsible labor. The social process is two-sided. While on the one hand oppressive conditions drove some men to fight back in self protection, they crushed others into human pulp without honor, spirit, dignity, or will to resist. They became friendless nomads, ranging the waterfronts of the world, drunk, beaten, and incapable of responsible social cooperation. These are not the men of whom militant union fighters are made . . . . The presence of such thousands of demoralized workers, forced to find jobs on ships in the fight for survival, often undermined attempts at union organization, and sapped the determination of honest workers to fight for their rights.

Thus, while the American Federation of Labor was established as early as 1885, and its maritime affiliate, the International Seaman's Union, was founded just ten years later, it was not until just prior to America's entry into World War I that the first rudimentary seaman's "Bill of Rights" was won. The 1915 Seaman's Act, for which Andrew Furuseth had fought many long years in the nation's capital, increased fo'c'sle space from 72 to 120 cubic feet a man, provided hospital and washroom space for the first time, and increased daily food and water rations. Allotments to "original creditors" – the shipping *crimps* who provided the sailors with room, board, and whiskey prior to "selling" them to masters and collecting their wages in advance – were abolished. Laws providing for the imprisonment of seamen for deserting their ships in American ports were also struck from the books, and improved manning scales and safety regulations were established.

All of these conditions, of course, were won under the pressure of the wartime emergency. With some fifty thousand seamen needed to man 2300 new war-built vessels the government had to make going to sea attractive. Indeed, the government had gone beyond even this: it had set up its own all-powerful authority to enforce the new conditions – the U.S. Shipping Board – and put authority behind the Board by appropriating funds for employment centers, the Sea Service Bureaus, in twenty-one domestic ports. No longer were we forced to cross a hiring agent's palm or fall into the clutches of a *crimp;* we simply registered at the Sea Service Bureaus and were sent to ships. This was the agency which had dispatched me to the *Riswick, Waken, Pasadena,* and others.

The end of the war brought swift retribution by the same Board. When the allied victory was secure the wartime fleet was laid up. New vessels coming off the ways were towed directly to the boneyards or sold to operators at a few cents on the dollar. Many were peddled off to foreign companies or to U.S. companies to operate under foreign flags.

In the years after the war thousands of beaten, dispirited workers roamed the waterfront in search of jobs. War workers from other industries gravitated toward the waterfront looking for work while the number of U.S. ships steadily declined. With a surplus of seamen to man the ever-dwindling fleet, the steamship companies and the Shipping Board seized the opportunity to destroy the International Seaman's Union. The Board abruptly demanded that all contracts be renegotiated and called for a return to the six-hour watch, in one stroke increasing the work week from fifty-six hours back to eighty-four (a change which also reduced the number of jobs by one-third!); an immediate reduction of twenty-five percent in the wage scale; the elimination of overtime, and many other conditions which the workers could not accept.

It was a clear invitation to a strike, and there was nothing the union could do but accept. The disastrous ISU strike followed. Thousands of rootless workers, plus the young wartime recruits, made excellent "finks." Vessels put to sea with scab crews under the new conditions while militant sailors marched the picket lines ashore. The sudden onslaught of operators' and government power was too much; the strike was lost, and for thirteen years we never recovered.

It was under these conditions that I had to decide whether to go back to sea. Bleak as the prospects were of finding a mate's job even more bleak was the idea of making paperhanging my career.

I was not the only colored seaman looking for a job. Many others who had sailed during the war also found employers' doors closed to them, and most of us frequented the same Harlem haunts. One afternoon, deliberating our plight, we decided to form an organization and to ask for a hearing before the U.S. Shipping Board. As chairman of the Colored Licensed American Officers, I wrote to Albert Lasker, chairman of the Board, in June of 1922:

> *We are competent officers in our respective grades. ... Since the war most of us have been thrown out of employment and no one will employ us as some claim that other white officers will not sail with us. Therefore we have decided to try to sail collectively if we can.*
>
> *As loyal citizens of the United States we are appealing to you to come to our aid. Out of the thousands of ships that are now sailing the seas under the Stars and Stripes we will be satisfied at present to be able to man one ship.*

Our appeal was never acknowledged or answered, and in the weeks that followed I considered returning to Baltimore and paperhanging. But my renewed acquaintance with the sea had evoked slumbering ambitions. Surely in the world's largest port I could find a job, even if it meant sailing as a cook again. I wrote Marie that I was going to try to ship out once more.

As I have explained, 1922 was a most difficult time to look for work. Wages were falling from the $65 a month paid A.B.'s under the old Shipping Board agreement to as low as $25 – the equivalent of seven cents an hour.

So I counted myself lucky when I applied for a job at the Bull Line office, and was offered the steward's post at $36 a month on the *Beatrice,* running from Baltimore to Puerto Rico on one month turn-arounds, and an occasional call in the port of New York. The Baltimore home port was especially attractive, since Marie and Joyce were still there, and it gave me the opportunity for a little home life. Though I was discouraged that the company's general manager, Mr. Kegin, only smiled wryly when I pointed out to him that I had a master's license, beggars cannot be choosers – colored beggars least of all. I took the job.

A steward's lot on a vessel in the '20's was not an easy one. Even Jesus could not have stretched the few loaves and fishes on the *Beatrice* over the four-week trip. The company put aboard only absolutely minimum supplies. Like all ships in those days Bull Line ships operated under a "two pot" system – one menu for the officers and another for the crew. Officers received eggs for breakfast daily, the crew on Sundays only. By a count of noses the port steward knew precisely how many eggs were to be consumed on a four-week trip, and that was the number put aboard. In the mornings a can of condensed milk and a gallon of water were put on the crew mess table. This was milk for porridge or dry breakfast food. Linens were no problem; there were none. I issued a blue sheet, mattress cover and blanket at the beginning of the trip, and there was a pile of straw on the dock for the sailors to make up their mattresses. Soap and matches were distributed once a week. Fo'c'sles were crowded and cold in the North and sweltering hot boxes in the South. The Company refused even to supply windshoots – metal scoops placed in portholes to catch an errant breeze.

Even under these conditions I probably would have sailed aboard the *Beatrice* for years had it not been for another circumstance – my inability to get along with her captain. The master of the *Beatrice* was a Captain Mumford, descendant of an old Mathews County, Virginia, family. Mathews County is notorious among seamen for having supplied to the waterfront a class of arrogant, backward mariners second to none; Mumford was heir to all the race bias of the Virginia aristocracy. As long as his subordinates kept their places and their tongues in their heads it was possible, if not easy, to get along with him. But inadvertently one day I crossed him; from that day on my trips on the *Beatrice* were numbered.

Although sailing as steward I still had my sights set on a mate's job, and carried a load of books with me. In my free moments I studied navigation and kept abreast of current developments through the latest nautical journals. One afternoon, a few days out of Puerto Rico, I was sitting out on number four hatch cover working out some problems in trigonometry for an International Correspondence School course, when Mumford happened to pass by. The books and papers attracted his attention and he came over to peer at my work. "Let me see that," he said, and I handed him the problem I was working out.

"I never heard of this stuff until I got into the higher grades at school," he said gruffly, "and after that I'd have shot anybody who asked me to do it. Why are you studying mathematics?"

Reluctantly I told him about the ICS course, and his manner changed from inquisitive to stern. "Well, you're wasting your time. I hear you have a mate's ticket?"

"No, I have a master's ticket," I told him.

"A master's ticket! Where'd you get it?"

"Baltimore."

Mumford's face flushed — it was where he had sat for his own. "Well," he said finally, "if you got it in Baltimore it must be good. Frankly I think you're too damned smart to sail on this ship." With that he wheeled and stalked away. Nothing I did after that could please him. For days he was sulking and surly and then, when he could no longer control the rage boiling within him, lashed out with contempt. He was critical of the food, the service, the way the messman made his bed. There was obviously not enough room on the five thousand ton *Beatrice* for a biased white captain and an ambitious colored steward.

I stuck it out for ten trips until I could take his abuse no longer. In the absence of a militant crew I was helpless, so I asked the Bull Line office for reassignment. And that is how I happened to come to the *Delisle* and Captain Zac Cullison.

Like the *Beatrice*, the *Delisle* was engaged in the sugar trade, carrying 24,000 100-pound bags from Caribbean ports to Baltimore every twenty-eight days. Like myself, her master had gone to sea as a boy, and when I signed on he noted that we were of the same age and must have much in common. I was not won over by this initial cordiality, and for several trips "kept my place" as the saying goes, seeking merely to do my job well and build up a good relationship with the crew. I did not breathe a word of my qualifications to any of the officers, and indeed affected great naiveté about deck work.

Gradually, however, I came to know Captain Cullison much better and to understand that his friendliness was sincere. He was an educated and lonely man, and we began to spend many evenings in his cabin discussing ships we had sailed and the ways of the world and of man. Little by little, as each unfolded his ambitions to the other, I revealed my qualifications and goal, and Captain Cullison vowed to help me get an officer's berth.

He tried. After I had been aboard a little over six months he wrote to Mr. Kegin asking that I be promoted to mate. We did not have to wait long for the reply. The next time we came into port Captain Cullison was called to the office, sharply reprimanded, and given a letter stating that the Bull Line absolutely would not entertain the idea of putting a colored officer on the bridge of any of its ships.

When the captain returned he showed me the letter. "Never mind, Hugh," he said. "Some day they'll change their minds ... you'll see."

For several days thereafter I debated whether to quit the Bull Line and try elsewhere . . . but where? What steamship company was ready to erase the color bar? Where would I find a more sympathetic skipper? For every Cullison there were a dozen Mumfords. Besides, with more and more American vessels flocking to the protection of foreign flags jobs were disappearing. I decided to stay where I was, and the *Delisle* became my home for seven years.

When the captain's efforts to secure my promotion became known aboard the *Delisle* my secret was out. The crew approved, by and large, but the officers regarded me as an upstart and competitor, and for several trips our relations were cool. Cullison remained firm. He told them that he would not cease in his efforts to win my promotion, and privately assured me that the first time he was shorthanded in an outside port he would promote me on the spot.

Sooner than either of us expected the opportunity arrived. In San Juan the third officer, suffering from a malady not uncommon among sailing men, had to be left behind, and as we were ready to leave port Captain Cullison called me to his office and asked if I wanted the job. I accepted eagerly, and he promised that when we returned to Baltimore he would plead with the company once more to keep me in the rating.

For two days after leaving Puerto Rico we sailed in beautiful weather, under a deep blue, cloudless sky and on a calm sea. Late in the afternoon of our third day out a brisk northeast wind rose, and gradually increased as it shifted around to the southwest. By nightfall we found ourselves in a violent gale. The sea grew rougher through the night, and the *Delisle* began to labor heavily; by dawn we were making barely four knots, rolling and pitching, with mountains of water heaving over the bow.

Toward six o'clock the ship became very sluggish at the helm and we could hear a knock in the steering engine room aft, above the howl of the wind. The captain called out the chief mate and several A.B.'s and ordered them to rig up a relieving tackle. At seven the job was not yet finished, and I was summoned to the bridge to relieve the second mate, while both headed aft to give the chief mate a hand.

The captain and second mate had barely reached the

poop when from the bridge we could see a towering beam wave advancing on the ship. I ordered the wheelsman to put the wheel hard over, but it was too late. Moving like an express train the sea was upon us, catching us almost broadside. The *Delisle* lurched like a cork, and I turned aft just in time to see Captain Cullison hurled between the bitts and the quadrant of the rudder! As the ship righted the crew rushed to pick him up, and we held the wheel firm while they removed him and brought him down from the poop and made for the deckhouse forward. Then the chief mate rushed to relieve me while I administered first aid.

The Captain's leg was savagely crushed. Blood poured in a steady stream from his shattered knee, and I'll never forget his pitiful cry, "Hugh, *help me!*"

I found a syringe and tincture of steel in the medicine chest, cut away the trousers and underwear which were mashed into the flesh, and pumped the liquid into the gaping wound until the blood clogged and the flow stopped. Then I cleaned the leg with alcohol, fixed a splint and bandaged it as well as I could. Throughout this operation Cullison lay with teeth clenched, gripping the side of the bed and grimacing with pain, but not a protest passed his lips. When I finished I poured us each a stiff drink, and then another, until the suffering Captain gradually passed into slumber from pain, exhaustion, and whiskey.

The chief mate, of course, took command of the ship, wired headquarters to have a doctor meet us in Philadelphia, and as we approached quarantine the following day the doctor boarded in a launch. He examined the shattered limb and praised the emergency treatment; but his verdict was swift. The leg must be amputated. Captain Cullison was carefully bound in a stretcher, carried down the gangway and taken ashore on the tug.

With Captain Cullison gone there was no one to press for my promotion, and a new captain and third mate were sent aboard. Three months later we were delighted to see Cullison hobble up the gangway on crutches. A new wooden leg had been ordered and he was already calling himself "Long John Silver." He was unchanged; his first words to me were *"Well, we did it, Hugh,"* referring to my brief term as mate. Then he told me that he had discussed the accident and my emergency treatment with the Bull Line officials, but they were still adamant – they would not have a colored officer on the bridge.

Thus I spent the years from 1921 to 1928.

Throughout this period Marie and I continued to live in Baltimore. We paid $500 down on a three-story house on McCulough Street and took on a mortgage of $4,500. Ten years later when we sold the house it still had a big mortgage. It was a pretty little brick dwelling of six rooms, with a back yard garden where Marie tended flowers and vegetables. It was a haven for some of my family when they came to the United States from Union. My mother and sister and several of my brothers stayed with us there.

Joyce was born there in 1921, followed by Una in 1923 and Claire in 1925. Marie always gave birth while I was away. I was at sea for three months, at home for two weeks, then to sea again. No wonder the children were shy with this stranger from foreign ports. However, I never failed to bring a present for each one and their expectation of what was in store overcame their bashfulness.

Joyce, Una, and Claire were the envy of other children when they paraded around in Japanese silk kimonos or showed their exotic toys. Joyce was fascinated by a three-way electric light bulb that looked like any other bulb until lighted. First it showed a bud, then a bud with leaves; finally, when the power was on full, a full-blown rose shone forth.

"Is it real?" she asked wistfully. It was intricately fashioned and afforded her many hours of pleasure as she gazed at it in fascination.

Most of their toys were from all over the world, strange and wonderful. But nothing made up for not being a full-time father. At the happy events of childhood I was absent.

"Father, I'm going to be in a silhouette play. Can't you come?" begged Una.

Teeth were cut, birthdays celebrated, graduations held without me. I was not there to bandage a bruised knee or soothe the deeper hurts inevitable with poor colored children growing up in Baltimore. Marie made all the children's clothing from materials I bought abroad, and fed them out of my pitiful wages from the Bull Line.

When I was ashore I helped with the household chores. As soon as I arrived the children would shout, "Daddy, bake us some bread!" Early the next morning the smell of baking bread would permeate every corner of the house and Claire would bounce out of bed without coaxing.

"The smell awoke me," she averred. "It's almost as delicious as the bread!"

During this period, the late 20's, the nation was caught up with illusions of permanent prosperity. Little attention was given to the plight of workers and colored citizens. Periodically the NAACP would appeal to the AFL for cooperation in fighting for equal wages and employment opportunities; just as regularly its appeals were pigeon-holed. The whole country, it seemed, was so busy trying to make a quick fortune that there was no time to consider seriously the economic contradictions underlying the chimera of prosperity, or the real problems of the people. When the bubble burst on October 29, 1929, the spectacle of Wall St. brokers diving out of their windows gave little satisfaction to the workers, and could not make up for their suffering throughout the years.

From year to year we suffered the usual family casualties. In 1921 John, to whom I had said goodbye on the decks of the *Aeolus* fifteen years earlier, died in a hurricane while bringing his vessel, the *Evelyn Guy,* into port.

The ship was lost with all hands. Somehow I had always considered John invincible, and it was a shock to learn that the sea had claimed him. Dad-Sonny followed in 1924, from natural causes, and though I had never seen him after I left Union Island on the *Sunbeam,* we had corresponded often, and after his death I persuaded my mother to come to the United States and live with us.

By 1928, when I had been aboard the *Delisle* more than six years, I was convinced that my future did not lie with the Bull Line, and that however sympathetic and generous Captain Cullison was he could never win my promotion. *I* was the one who had to make it come true. I decided I would make one final appeal to Mr. Kegin, and if he refused I would pack my seabag and look elsewhere.

To my great surprise, while he did not offer me a berth on one of the company's larger vessels, Mr. Kegin had an interesting proposition.

"We've bought a small ship from the Weems Line," he said, "the *Dora Weems.* She'll be running coastwise out of Baltimore. Now, you want to sail as a deck officer. Suppose I offered you the second mate's job in addition to the steward's job? Do you think you could handle them both – with a $10-a-month raise?"

During those days it was the policy of the Bull Line to sign men on in double ratings. The captain of the *Delfina,* for example, also handled the radio operator's job.

Mr. Kegin was delighted to get a steward mate at a substantial saving, and I was happy to "buy" mate's discharges at such a small sacrifice in labor and honor. It should be understood that discharges are the "credentials" of the maritime industry; to prove you are qualified for a certain rating it is helpful to be able to show that you have sailed in it before. Yet the Masters, Mates and Pilots Union would not accept colored men for membership, and there was no way I could come by these endorsements honestly – that is, by shipping through a union hall. Yet, though Mr. Kegin's offer was enticing, and I had already decided to accept it, I could not help saying with light sarcasm, "Well, what about the wireless operator's job . . . I have a radio ticket, too."

Mr. Kegin missed the point completely. He answered eagerly, "Do you think you can handle all three? *O. K!* I'll give you a $50 raise! Just supervise the steward's job, and give most of your attention to the mate's job and the radio room."

Nonplussed, I signed on the S.S. *Dora Weems* in all three ratings. In recent years, of course, this would be impossible. The shipping commissioner would forbid it, the unions would forbid it, and I would refuse to do it. In 1928, however, if this was the only way I could batter down the barriers separating colored men from officers' jobs, well, then, this was the way it had to be!

The *Dora Weems* was assigned to run between Bangor, Maine, and Tampa, Florida, hauling potatoes. I worked around the clock. In the morning I opened the key and performed as many of my steward's duties as possible in the vicinity of the radio room until I went on watch at noon. At four I would open the key again and take and receive all messages until 8 p.m., when I doled out stores for the following day, then caught a few winks until midnight when I had to be back on the bridge.

Periods of such intense activity have a tendency to blur in one's mind, as if the brain has a cut-off switch, so that when work becomes too hard one becomes insensitive to it. The day-to-day routine of the *Dora Weems* is lost to me, except two incidents, both of which occurred in Tampa. Both symbolize the low state of democracy for America's colored citizens.

The first took place as a result of my discovery one day that my master's license, good for five years only, was expiring. If I did not have it renewed before we left Tampa I would have to sit for the examination over again. I went to the Steamboat Inspector's office to take my physical. It was two in the afternoon when I entered the office, and a pretty young girl looked up at me in amazement. "What do *you* want?"

"I want to get my license renewed," I replied.

"License? *What* license?" The outlines of a frown encircled her childish face. "Let me see it!" No problem of such magnitude had ever confronted her before.

I took the document out of my seaman's wallet and gave it to her. The frown deepened. "A *master's* license," she gasped in dismay, *"Where did you get it!"*

"It says right on the face, Miss," I said carefully, as my annoyance began to match hers, "See? Port of Baltimore."

"Oh, yes!" For a moment she sat, hands folded, confronting this new and entirely unexpected problem and then said, "Well, you'll have to wait. The inspector is out for lunch. He won't be back for a few hours."

I sat down to wait, opened a magazine, and indeed, a "few hours later" the inspector returned. He took one glance at me, disappeared into his office and the secretary hurried in after him. Presently he emerged with my license in his hand, fortified to face this challenge to southern supremacy.

"Now what is it *exactly* that you want?" the inspector asked carefully.

"To get my license renewed."

"Yes. Well. Ah, where are you from?"

"We just got in from Bangor, Maine, with a load of potatoes."

"No, no, I don't mean that . . . I mean, where were you born?"

"Union Island, British West Indies. Why?"

"Oh, never mind." Turning to the girl the inspector said, "It's all right . . . he's not an *American* Negro, he's from the British West Indies. Give him his license."

I said no more. The girl gave me a slip directing me to the doctor for an examination and when I returned certified in good health, the inspector handed me my ticket.

Then he said, amazed at the fact himself, "I don't mind telling you that you're the first Negro in history to have his master's license renewed in the port of Tampa."

I returned to the ship somewhat uncertain whether my reaction to this bit of news should be triumph or despair.

The second incident took place that evening, making Tampa forever indelible in my memory. At about seven o'clock a dock hand rushed up the gangway to the bridge shouting, "There's a man down on the dock who's mighty sick . . . I think he's one of your men." I hurried down to discover one of our A.B.'s writhing in pain, and clutching his stomach. He was frothing, and almost passed out in the effort to tell me what was wrong with him. I finally understood that he had mixed almost equal proportions of watermelon and whiskey. In his agony he had tried to make it back to the ship and got as far as the dock before collapsing.

I called for an ambulance and minutes later the wagon of mercy screamed onto the pier and out on the apron. The driver leapt out and inspected the suffering man, a Puerto Rican of dark complexion. "Oh," he said, "he's a Negro, I can't take him. You'll have to call again and ask for the *colored* ambulance. I'm just for white people." With that he jumped back into his vehicle and sped off.

I made a second call, and we waited, waited . . . and waited. While the "white" ambulance had responded almost immediately it was two hours before the "Negro" vehicle reached the dock because, the driver explained, he had been so busy. This was not, I discovered, because so many colored people were getting sick, but because the ratio of white ambulances to colored, per capita, was in the nature of ten to one. We put the suffering sailor into the wagon, and he was carted off to have his stomach pumped. He returned to the ship the following morning as good as ever. Since then I have wondered if he had been seriously injured and bleeding to death would the "white ambulance" have left him to die?

After four trips on the *Dora Weems* my objective was accomplished. I had finally sailed as an officer in peacetime. When we returned to Baltimore I quit.

Of these years, dreary and difficult as they were, one experience stands out above all others – Zac Cullison's single-minded determination to win my promotion. I will never forget that short, stout, convivial soul inviting me to his cabin for a drink and a chat and the sound of his voice as he exclaimed, at almost every session we had together, "It's a damned shame, Hugh . . . a man like you with a master's license, unable to get a job! I'm going to see about it as soon as we get back to port."

See about it he did, many times through the years, and if he failed it was only because of the size of the job he tackled. For six years after his accident he remained at the helm of the *Delisle,* eventually falling victim to a ruptured gall bladder. Until the very end we kept in touch by mail, by phone, or an occasional visit. From time to time our paths crossed in Caribbean ports, union halls, or steamship company offices and we fell upon each other in mutual love and respect.

8

The years from 1922 to 1936 were the most miserable of my life. Though I was assured reasonably steady employment on the *Delisle,* and hence was luckier than those who had no jobs at all, I did not find $60 a month enough to keep four hungry little Mulzacs clothed, shod, and with full little bellies. Coupled with my family's immediate deprivation was a spiritual suffering – the fraying of my dream. It hardly seemed possible that I would ever sail on deck again, let alone in a licensed capacity. There was not a single colored officer in the entire U.S. merchant service, and though I continued to call at company offices throughout those years there was not a port captain or personnel manager who held out any hope for me. It was impossible to make ends meet; some months Marie and I had to borrow from more affluent friends to pay our bills and occasionally to appeal to charities for survival.

With an army of unemployed swarming around every dock, those of us still aboard the ships, despite ever worsening conditions, clung to our jobs more tightly than ever.

It is a law of society as of physics, however, that every action has a reaction. The increasingly intense exploitation we suffered from 1921 on, the ever downward wage spiral, the venality and corruption of the "crimps," the miserable, rotten food we were served aboard ships, and the always increasing threat to our jobs . . . all this coupled with the shipowners' refusal to consider any claim against the company, however just, the arrogance and cruelty of masters and mates, forced by the operators to further reduce costs . . . all these conditions constituted an increasingly desperate situation which had, eventually, to explode.

In the late '20's the bitterness of many sailors began to crystallize in a recognition of the necessity for action. "Seamen's Clubs" began to spring up almost spontaneously. The sinking of the *Vestris* in 1928, with its tragic loss of lives, dramatized our situation, at least among ourselves. The spread of the Marine Workers Industrial League "clubs" was speeded by the 1929 crash, and on April 27, 1930, delegates from many of them met to form the nucleus of a union. It issued a call to seamen and longshoremen to unite, and in the next four years succeeded in establishing branches of the Marine Workers Industrial Union in almost every port of the nation. In some, such as Baltimore, under the leadership of a young sailor, Al Lannon, we succeeded in establishing a central hiring hall, and in one two-month period struck fifty ships to enforce democratic hiring procedures.

Most important to me, the MWIU stood unequivocally against discrimination because of race, creed or color. As I had predicted back in the days of my school, one day white sailors would understand that the shipowners' prize weapon was playing black against white and white against black, and we would have white allies in our battle for equality on the ships. The MWIU was the first waterfront union to adopt such a policy, and contrary to time-honored arguments thousands of seamen flocked to its banner.

Of course I joined the MWIU immediately, and began to talk up the new union on the Bull Line ships, to which I had since returned. While not every seaman saw the light it was difficult for them to refute our arguments. It was clear to everyone that a change was in the making, especially when, following Franklin Delano Roosevelt's first inauguration, a fresh breath of hope blew over the land.

The first explosion came in a distant port, and not initially among seamen, but among the West Coast longshoremen. The 1934 West Coast longshoremen's strike is recognized by every sailor and dock worker as the real turnnig point in U.S. waterfront history.

Until 1934 longshoremen were hired by the "shape up." A dock worker would leave his home, say at five o'clock in the morning, take buses or street cars down to the piers and wait for the seven o'clock "call" when the pier boss would select his gangs. Often there would be two or three hundred men waiting for the thirty or forty jobs – and those who were called were usually those who had previously greased the boss's palm or agreed to "kick back" a good share of their wages. The rejected ones were idle that day – and every day until they "bought" their jobs.

Those who were hired were not much better off. Sling loads ranged up to five thousand pounds, dangerously heavy for worn nets, cables, and ancient equipment. The longshore casualty rate topped even that of the mining industry. There was no such thing as penalty cargo – obnoxious or dangerous freight – or extra pay for overtime work. Studies proved that before the 1934 strike the average longshoreman received less than $10 per week!

From the late '20's on, dissident members of the International Longshoremen's Association, whose national president, the notorious Joe Ryan, many years later was finally indicted for misuse of union funds, had been organizing and working closely with the MWIU and militant members of the old ISU. On May 9, 1934, they struck, and crew members of Pacific Coast vessels came charging off the ships in sympathy. The strike lasted eighty-two days, and has become a classic example of the workers' militancy and the brutality of the stevedoring and shipping companies, backed by the full power of police and state. Every time-honored technique to break the strike was utilized; venal newspapers raised the specter of revolution, police raided the union halls, and on June 16 the operators signed a phony agreement with Ryan, who tried to call the strikers back to work. They refused, and on July 5 finks, police, and the National Guard stormed the docks in the "Battle of Rincon Hill" to open up the sealed waterfront. Two ILA members were killed and 109 wounded on this day. "Bloody Thursday" has been commemorated by West Coast labor unions ever since.

Throughout this entire period the seamen and longshoremen under the leadership of Harry Bridges remained firm, and by July 11 the Teamsters joined the strike. Finally, the AFL Central Labor Council was forced to call out its 32,000 members in San Francisco in a general strike.

After nearly three months, during which few ships moved on the West Coast, employers and strikers agreed to submit the issues to arbitration. The strikers returned on July 31, and on October 12 the arbitrators handed down a ruling that provided for a jointly operated hiring hall, a sharp boost in wages, overtime rates, extra pay for penalty cargoes and, most precedent-shattering of all, a five-day, thirty-hour week! The foundation was thus established for the union, which two years later broke away from the ILA and became the International Longshoremen's and Warehousemen's Union, which to this day still paces the nation in wages, hours and working conditions.

Unfortunately, while the members of the MWIU and the more militant members of the ISU aggressively supported the West Coast strike we did not benefit from it directly. The rival marine unions – the MWIU and the ISU – were about equal in strength, and in the absence of either's power to conduct an effective strike the shipowners shrewdly withheld recognition from both.

The MWIU understood that this split could only perpetuate the intolerable conditions under which we were sailing.

Accordingly, a month after the arbitrators' decision was delivered, the MWIU addressed an appeal for a merger to the ISU leaders. Not only was our offer rejected, but to forestall any such turn of events the operators promptly signed a phony (no wage increases, no union hiring hall, etc.,) agreement with the discredited ISU!

This left the MWIU with only one avenue of action – a "merger from below." All MWIU members were urged to join the ISU and talk up the merger plan, raise demands for improved conditions and fight for the unity of all seamen. This we did, and on the *Margaret* and the *Delisle* many of us raised these questions incessantly. As this organization began to pay off and our strength grew we launched a program of harassing the shipowners and the ISU officialdom alike with "quickie" strikes – sudden sitdowns just as a vessel was to leave port. There was an abundant supply of issues – better food, white linen, overtime pay, an end to the two-pot system, or simply a sufficient supply of insecticide to help us stand off the overwhelming army of rats, cockroaches, and bedbugs on every ship. With such tactics even the most conservative seamen were gradually fired with union zeal, and our strength grew to the point where we were able to spread our message in our own paper, the ISU rank and file *Pilot*. From this point on events moved swiftly.

Not surprisingly, these events precipitated an anxious move on behalf of the shipowners by their Congressional colleagues. HR-8555, the "Copeland Act," was a bare-faced attempt to blacklist the militant MWIU members, an effort which requires some explanation.

At the beginning of every voyage seamen sign the ship's "articles," a contract covering the conditions of their employment for a coastwise or foreign voyage. At the conclusion of the trip, or in the old days when the period of service stipulated in the articles was terminated, each is paid off and given a Certificate of Discharge certifying that the conditions of his employment have been fulfilled. The certificate bears his name, "Z" number (a number on all seamen's papers), the name of the vessel, duration of the voyage, his rating, etc.

Unlike the single certificate used in the U.S. merchant service, Great Britain had long used the Continuous Discharge Book. This was a bound booklet in which all the above data was entered *plus space for the master's observations concerning the seaman's abilities, deportment, and character*. When the seaman went looking for a job he was required to show this identification and there spread out for the prospective master or company personnel director to examine, was his entire labor record! The Continuous Discharge Book thus served as an effective instrument to blacklist the best union members by revealing their past labor records to each prospective employer. HR-8555 provided for the adoption of the Continuous Discharge Book, soon labeled by the seamen the "Copeland Fink Book" after its sponsor (Senator Royal S. Copeland of New York), and was thus an obvious attempt to screen the more active MWIU members out of the merchant marine.

The threat of the "fink book" made already angry

seamen even angrier. It proved to be the straw that broke the camel's back. The number of quickie strikes was stepped up until finally the strike of the *California* set off a chain of events which was to culminate in the formation of the world's largest, most democratic and most militant waterfront union, the National Maritime Union.

During this period – late 1935 – I finally left the Bull Line and joined the *Virmar*, a six-thousand-ton vessel operated by the Calmar SS Company engaged in inter-coastal trade. After nearly ten years with the Bull Line I had lost touch with the ships of other companies, but discovered immediately that the rest of the industry was at least as backward as the Bull Line. There were no electric refrigerators aboard. The limited perishable stores were housed in iceboxes, and the few hundred pounds of ice were replenished in each port. There were canned and salt meat only, and an insufficient supply at that. As cook-steward I did what I could with the provisions the company put aboard, but now, twenty-six years later, I can admit that I could hardly eat my own cooking. The crew couldn't stomach it. Led by Joe Stack, later to become an NMU vice-president, we struck in San Pedro, Frisco, and every port on the West Coast, demanding fresh meat, fresh milk and vegetables. Enough was put aboard to get us to the next port – and there we struck again.

At one stop the port steward asked me, "How many men do you have on board?"

I replied, "Twenty-eight."

"I'll give you twenty bottles of milk and twenty-eight nipples!"

The crew refused the shipment, insisting on twenty gallons a day – and got it.

Meanwhile there was another East Coast vessel in Pedro – the *California,* a passenger ship operated by International Mercantile Marine (J. P. Morgan), which later became United States Lines. Antagonized by a wide range of grievances the crew, led by Bo'sun Joe Curran,

116

later NMU President, struck on March 3, 1936. Secretary of Labor Frances Perkins made a personal telephone call to Curran pledging her personal intercession on the crew's behalf if they would return the vessel to the East Coast. The crew agreed and brought her around, and upon their arrival sixty-four men were fired and black-listed. It is worth noting, as an aside, that steamship companies invariably promise *anything* when a vessel is in a distant port, and that just as invariably repudiate the promises the instant the ship reaches home port.

The *California* crew, however, refused to accommodate the shipowners and the government by quietly disbanding. They appealed to other crews for support, launching the so-called *"spring* strike" of 1936. By May 6, forty-five vessels, including the *Virmar,* had joined the strike.

During the *spring* strike I received an offer from the Calmar Line which showed its real attitude toward Negro seamen. The company was doing everything it could to sail its ships, including the recruitment of Nazi-orientated scabs from New York's notorious Yorkville section. When I arrived at the office to hand in my reports the marine superintendent advanced toward me cordially, hand outstretched, and after a brief conversation said, "See here, Mulzac, why don't you be a sensible fellow? The men aren't going to win the strike. Besides, you have a license, haven't you?"

"I have a license," I replied.

"Well," he replied expansively, "I'll tell you what I'm willing to do. We need a master on one of our ships in Baltimore, and I'm willing to send you right down."

"Cap," I replied, "for the past twelve years I have been registered as a master with Calmar. And now when there's a strike on you offer me a job! You understand why I must refuse, don't you?"

From the Calmar offices I went to 13 Union Street in Brooklyn, and registered for strike duty, and then to the Masters, Mates and Pilots Union on 11th Street to register for picket duty there, too. The hypocrisy at the MM&P office was almost as blatant as that at Calmar. While the mates would permit me to picket they had steadfastly refused to allow me to register to ship. This time however, the strike leaders promised they would register me if I did strike duty, and I was duly assigned to a daily two-hour watch, in addition to my watch with the rank and file seamen.

The *spring* strike never mounted full steam. It straggled on until May 28 when the members voted to accept the settlement terms proposed by the ISU Executive Board: a mediation committee would be set up to adjudicate the disputes, and no striker was to be blacklisted. While we did not win our major objective – a union hiring hall – we nevertheless succeeded in broadening our struggle for an honest union, and thus the *spring* strike was a necessary prelude to the *fall* strike.

Throughout the summer of 1936 we redoubled our efforts on the ships. The readership of the rank and file *Pilot* swelled to the point where its circulation was greater than that of the ISU paper, and it was obvious to everyone that a final showdown was brewing. Organizing drives were taking place throughout the nation – in the steel and automotive industries, among the electrical workers and in the coal mines. John L. Lewis was labor's hero of the hour, as more and more labor leaders began to realize that craft unionism left them powerless to organize big industry. How could ten steamfitters or twenty electricians effectively strike a plant employing thousands of workers?

We had good reason to understand this on the waterfront, too. In the ISU the engine, deck, and steward's departments were organized into separate, autonomous unions, and only the Marine Cooks & Stewards accepted colored members. On countless occasions a striking deck force would be unable to win the support of the other two unions, and the shipowners had merely to replace a dozen men to sail the ship instead of thirty. Among the

East Coast longshoremen it was, and remains still, the practice to organize the men into Irish gangs, Italian gangs, or colored gangs, each under a local chieftain and all bitterly competing with one another for control of the docks and jobs. Ryan's ILA, like England's empire, was divided into tightly-knit little nationalistic colonies which fought each other as vigorously as they fought the employers. So divided, the workers were easy prey for their racketeer leaders, and unable to make their collective strength felt. Thus, as far back as the MWIU days in the early '30's rank and file ISU sentiment had been firmly in support of one big union with equal rights for all members for all jobs.

Recognizing that the defeat of the *spring* strike was only a momentary setback and that the main battle was yet to be waged, the dissident ISU sailors did not disband their strike apparatus. Instead we elected a Seamen's Defense Committee to continue organizing and to spark the fight against the fink book. Joseph Curran was elected chairman, as we girded for the next battle. And again the waterfront employers, in their eagerness to destroy the incipient union, lit the fuse, this time again on the West Coast.

The West Coast operators were understandably outraged at the 1934 arbitrators' decision which had awarded such a totally unexpected victory to the longshoremen. By 1936 they had resolved to crush the new union once and for all. In just two short years the ILWU had demonstrated how intelligent and honest leadership could improve conditions.

No longer were workers forced to "shape up" on the docks; now they were dispatched from employer-union operated hiring halls by strict rotary shipping regulations. Further, by September of 1936 Harry Bridges was able to proclaim that unemployment on the docks was a thing of the past. "All are working, and the work is evenly distributed. And there are no longshoremen on relief."

As the contract expiration date approached, the Hearst press, the Republican Party, and the Liberty League let go a propaganda barrage against the union. Scabs and goons were recruited for a showdown battle, and arms were freely distributed to them by the police. The strike began on October 30, 1936. Three hundred ships were tied up. The federal government simultaneously instituted deportation proceedings against Bridges and appointed as hearing officer James M. Landis, then Dean of Harvard Law School. (This inquiry, like several subsequent attempts to find grounds for deporting the former Australian labor leader, ended in his complete exoneration from all charges, and he became a citizen in 1954.)

On the East Coast the Seamen's Defense Committee quickly called its own strike in support of the West Coast longshoremen and despite the frantic efforts of ISU leaders to restrain them the sailors left their ships *en masse*. The East Coast showdown came in a dramatic meeting at Cooper Union in New York on November 4 called by ISU to block the spread of the strike. The Cooper Union meeting lives in every old timer's memory as the turning point in the battle for honest trade unionism. Curran and other members of the Seamen's Defense Committee were barred from the meeting, though it was well attended by members of the police department and the press. But the ISU labor forces had finally bitten off more than they could chew; the rank and file, after a noisy demonstration, threw open the doors to Curran and other members of the Committee, and in a series of pointed questions, thunderously answered by the seamen, Curran exposed the ISU leaders before the press and police. The 1500 seamen voted to go on strike!

The *fall* strike of 1936–7 is one of the bitterest in seamen's memory. Young workers today, enjoying pension plans, three-week vacations with pay, health insurance, seniority promotions, overtime pay, air-conditioned fo'c'sles, excellent food, fresh milk and other benefits, really should learn how these conditions were won . . . . For *won they were,* not generously bestowed by suddenly philanthropical employers. As I write these words I have before me a recent issue of the NMU *Pilot* which reports a reserve (December 1962) of $45,506,339 in the union's pension and welfare plan! If anyone had suggested during the *fall* strike that twenty-six years after the Cooper Union meeting the union would be a thriving, multimillion dollar organization he'd have been carted off as insane.

Throughout those winter months U.S. Shipping Commissioners signed on scab crews with little or no concern for their qualifications, steamboat inspectors overlooked normal safety standards for the "duration." The Commissioner in the port of New York publicly promised to "sail the ships at all costs." One of the costs was the Grace Line's *Santa Elena,* which piled up on the rocks off Cartagena with a scab crew. Police in most ports provided escorts for scabs, and with this encouragement and cooperation thugs waylaid honest sailors on side streets, beat them with chains, and killed Wilbur Dickey, loyal union man, in Houston. A steady stream of defeatist literature streamed out of big "public relations" offices seeking to discredit us in the minds of the public, calling us Communists and riffraff, and in brochures addressed to seamen prophesied our inglorious defeat. This was, everyone understood, the showdown battle, and there were no lengths to which the shipping operators would not go in their effort to destroy the union before it was even formed.

Yet the worst enemy of all was not the police, scabherders, or propaganda; in the northern ports it was the deadly East Coast winter . . . . The Committee had no resources. Somehow we had to survive — to get food and clothing to hold out until our demands were won.

The SDC relief committees canvassed the neighborhoods and appealed to friendly merchants for supplies and money We begged churches, fraternal organizations and other unions for contributions. I was one of those designated as a speaker, and night after night tramped to gloomy halls in the snow to explain the issues of our strike and to plead for help. In that grim winter of 1936–7 there were still eight million Americans without jobs, and those who were working were not much better off. Yet night after night these poor workers emptied their pockets to help us eat. In every northern port men huddled together in bare lofts with newspapers for bedding, sharing their stew and coffee, and it was not uncommon for the best pair of shoes to see duty round the clock.

Despite these hardships the strike held solid. Throughout November and December the great majority of crew members piled off their ships as soon as they hit the dock. Scabs were harder to recruit, and the waterfront was shut down.

The Mulzacs held solid too, though. In 1935 I sold our little home in Baltimore and brought Marie and the children to New York. Now our family was on Welfare. The children took turns waiting on line once every other week for a miserable portion of prunes, flour, and lard. I could hear them quarreling:

"I won't go. I went last time," rebelled Joyce.

"No you didn't," replied Una.

"Did."

"Didn't."

They bickered endlessly, sometimes vehemently, sometimes halfheartedly. Knowing one would have to go, they sought to put off the moment of departure by their childish arguments. Marie shared their reluctance, but the food was needed. She hid the hated shopping bag under the coat of one of the sisters so that the neighbors wouldn't see and bundled her off. Pride bent before hunger. Twice monthly the little drama was enacted, and both mother and father, after everyone had gone to bed, tried to ignore the echoes of their children's humiliation.

After an eighty-six-day strike the shipowners on the West Coast finally capitulated, on January 24, 1937. The union hiring hall was formally recognized and signed into all agreements. A $10 wage increase was also won, and other conditions. On the East Coast the situation was muddier, since the designation of a bargaining agent was at issue, and the National Maritime Union existed in name only. The National Labor Relations Board began to hold elections on the vessels operated by the East Coast companies, and seamen voted for the new union by majorities often as great as nine to one. At an April meeting John Franklin, president of United States Lines – J. P. Morgan's old Merchants & Miners – finally agreed to recognize the union hiring hall; other big companies fell in line, one by one. In May the new union was formally set up, and held its first constitutional convention in July. The National Maritime Union was formally constituted with a membership of some 20,000, far and away the largest single union of maritime workers in the country; and almost immediately affiliated with the CIO.

There were several unique features of the new union. First, the independent, autonomous deck, engine, and steward's divisions were abolished in favor of one industrial union, ending craft jealousies and uncoordinated strikes. Second, the NMU was set up as a democratic union with conventions scheduled every other year and the election of officials to be held in the alternate years. Members were *required* to vote, and elections were supervised by the Honest Ballot Association. Attendance at union meetings was made compulsory to assure continuing rank and file control of the union.

Third, and most important for me, was the inclusion of a clause in the constitution providing that there should be *no discrimination against any union member because of his race, color, political creed, religion, or national origin.* This was a milestone in the history of the waterfront, and it is to the lasting honor of the NMU that, like the ILWU among shoreside workers, it was the first maritime union to establish this basic principle and to enforce it.

It wasn't easy, either, for the NMU had a large membership in Texas, Louisiana, Alabama, and other southern states, and many southern union halls. Seamen born and bred in the South came aboard ships with their fathers' prejudices, and in the early days refused to sleep in fo'c'sles or eat at the same mess table with colored seamen. The union's position was unequivocal: sail the ship or be brought up on charges in the union. Nor did the union members compromise with southern laws demanding segregated facilities; there was a single union hall in each of the port cities, serving colored and white equally.

The NMU's forthright position finally gave meaning to the struggle I and many others, both white and colored, had waged throughout the years. I believed then, as I believe today, that an aggressive attack on Jim Crow is the *only* way to solve the problem of race relations in America or, indeed, throughout the world. *Prejudice exists only to the extent that segregation is permitted to exist,* and not the other way around. Southern crew members, living with colored seamen, sharing the same fo'c'sles, the same messroom, playing poker together, working together, talking and arguing together, eventually start going ashore together, discover that their prejudice is artificial and socially contrived. *The destruction of the barriers that divide black from white in the neighborhoods, schools, factories, and offices of this nation is the main path to true freedom and democracy for all the citizens of the United States.*

9

Although the 1936–7 strike established the hiring hall for most unlicensed ratings once and for all, it left stewards in an ambiguous position – and me doubly so, since I never wanted to be a steward in the first place. Reversing their own timeworn arguments, the employers now insisted that stewards were *officers* who must be hired at the discretion of the company! The new union was just as insistent that they were not. A compromise was finally worked out: the union agreed to allow the companies to select their own stewards as long as they belonged to the union and shipped out of the hiring hall. Since the Bull Line was one of the few companies to remain with the old ISU, I could no longer ship on its vessels. Thus both necessity and the desire to exercise my strike-won prerogatives drove me to ship through the union hall as chief cook on the *Ormidale, Admiral Nulton,* and as well as other vessels.

It is difficult to describe the feeling of achievement we experienced as we were dispatched to our first ships. For thirty years – from 1907 until 1937 – I had had to haunt the waterfront and shipping company offices begging for jobs, paying *crimps,* following up every lead to find work. And now all I had to do was register in my own shipping hall and "throw in" for the job I wanted under the regulations of the rotary shipping system. Those who have never suffered the arrogance of employers, the insults of snobbish company clerks, and the airs of tyrannical mates and captains cannot understand what it meant to walk up a gangway with an absolute *right* to the job – and a right, furthermore, that was *enforceable* through the collective power of thousands of union brothers. No longer could a captain take my assignment slip and, noting that I was a shade or two darker than the man he expected, say with that air of injured innocence, "Well, for heaven's sake, I don't know why they sent *you* . . . we don't *need* a new man!"

The hiring hall, or closed shop, is the heart and soul of a trade union, a fact recognized by Mr. Taft and Mr. Hartley whose legislation has neatly sought to make it illegal. It insures that every man on the job is a member of the union and thereby subject to union discipline – the will of the majority. As an army weeds out the men unfit for combat and punishes deserters, so we had to guarantee that every man going aboard ship was a responsible union fighter who would not scab during a strike, carry tales topside, or weaken the agreement by working for sub-standard wages.

As far as the waterfront is concerned, the hiring hall made possible the rotary shipping system, guaranteeing every member of the union, black or white, Democrat or Republican, English or Spanish-speaking, equal access to the job.

The rotary shipping system works this way: When a seaman "pays off" a ship he comes to the union hall and registers for work at the registration window. He receives a shipping card with the date and time stamped on it by an electric clock. Union shipping rules, determined by the members according to the current demand for labor, permit him to stay ashore for thirty, sixty, or ninety days, or when shipping is extremely slow, even one hundred and twenty days, though of course he can ship the very next day if he can "compete" successfully for a job. If he remains ashore beyond the time limit, however, he goes back to the bottom of the shipping list.

All jobs are called into the union hall by the companies under contract (the union delegate aboard ship makes sure of that) and are posted on a giant shipping board for all members to examine.

This gives the name of the ship, the company, destination, time of departure, and the pier. There follows a list of ratings needed in the deck, engine, and steward's departments – for example, three able seamen, one ordinary, two oilers and an electrician, a second cook, messman or galleyman.

Jobs are called by the dispatcher at specified times throughout the day, at 10 p.m., 2 a.m., and 4 p.m.; with "pierhead jumps" – openings on vessels that are departing before the next call – announced as they are received.

Members of the union holding Coast Guard certification in the needed ratings "throw in" their shipping cards for the jobs they want, and the man with the oldest card, as stamped by the clock, wins the job. He can be a sixty-five-year old A.B. whose forefathers came over on the *Mayflower* or a nineteen-year old Chinese. *The only criterion for deciding who gets the job is the date stamped on his shipping card.* Furthermore, the applicant can be one who has helped "set down" (strike) a dozen Grace Line freighters in the past, but the company cannot reject him on these grounds — or rather, may do so only at the risk of having the entire crew refuse to sail the ship.

Such control of jobs on the part of the union may sound capricious, arbitrary, or a violation of the employers' rights to hire and fire as they please. After all, why should the employers not be allowed to pick the men they want? The answer, of course, is that for centuries employers *did,* and sailors were forced to work under the conditions previously described. Unorganized, we were at the operators' mercy; united, we evened up our strength and forced improvements in conditions. When employers chose the men they wanted, militant unionists and colored seamen did not get jobs. Under the union hiring hall men of every race, creed and color are assigned equally. Those who are so concerned with the "right to work" must also recognize its corollary — the right of men, united in defense of their conditions of labor, *not* to work. The hiring hall, by enabling workers collectively to withhold their labor, is in the last analysis the only power that enables them to improve their working conditions.

Curiously, the rotary shipping system worked against me when I tried to ship out following the strike, for after fifteen years of sailing as a steward I could not prove I was licensed as a chef for passenger vessels! Finally I found some old discharges and was sent to the *President Polk,* American President Line combination passenger freighter operated on a round-the-world schedule.

It was during these prewar years, the period from 1938 to 1941, that all the experiences of my life began to fall into place, and when, for the first time, I began to develop what can be called an international political outlook.

It will seem strange to many that it was not until the late '30's, at the age of fifty-two, that I began to develop a political philosophy. There are many reasons for this. There was my natural conservative "British" background, with all its emphasis upon "learning," manners and a deeply inbred loyalty to the crown. This was more intuitive than conscious. In actual fact, one could not be a seaman in the early years of this century without learning to despise British imperialism and its handiwork throughout the world. I saw the terrible effects of exploitation in most of the countries of the world, but did not understand economic and political relationships.

Another reason for my political naiveté was that throughout these years I had but one goal: to sail as master of an oceangoing ship. It did not take me long to understand that the principal difficulty was my color, but it took *decades* to learn that I could not wage this battle *individually*. For too long I regarded my goal as a personal crusade, not realizing that my fight was the fight not only of all the *colored* races, but of poor working people, black or white, and that it could be advanced only by the advance of all. For too long I fought my lonely battle for recognition with one arm tied behind my back.

This is not to say I never worked with others. I joined everything there was – the NAACP, social action groups in neighborhood churches, civic reform associations, fraternal organizations, and every trade union for which I was eligible from 1907 on. There was hardly an evening ashore when I did not go out for a committee meeting of one kind or another. But I was, throughout those years, driven by personal ambition and never understood my struggle in its wider *social* context.

The formation of the NMU changed all this. For the

first time I realized how it felt to be free to speak my piece at a union meeting without consciousness of color; free to compete for a job by throwing in my registration card against a white seaman; free to run for union office, if I chose. And most of all to walk aboard a ship with my shoulders thrown back in the clear, deep knowledge that no company official could reject me because I was not white.

This whole crystallization began to take place immediately prior to and during my service on the *Polk*, which accelerated these discoveries. Despite the fact that the President Lines had signed contracts with three different unions covering the deck, engine, and steward's departments* there was a healthy union attitude aboard ship. We didn't walk around with chips on our shoulders and challenge the officers to knock 'em off, but neither did we quietly accept the abuses that had prevailed before the strike. "Beefs" were settled with department heads or held in abeyance until the union patrolman could come aboard in a United States port. Union meetings were held frequently and attendance was compulsory, so that we worked as an organized body. The experience of working with a group of vigilant union men, determined to fight for their rights – and further, winning frequent victories – sparked my political development.

Work on the *Polk* was extremely hard. Even under the new contract, members of the steward's department could be worked nine hours in a spread of fifteen; that is, any nine hours between 6 a.m., for example, and 9 p.m., with six hours off in between. We carried 280 passengers and a crew of 95 – 375 people to be fed three times a day! Nor were the galleys the modern, gleaming salons of today; they were small, crowded and hot, and were devoid of

---

* Unlike the NMU on the East Coast, the West Coast unions – the Marine Cooks and Stewards, the Sailors Union of the Pacific and the Marine Firemen, Oilers and Watertenders – had not yet united into one union.

contemporary work-savers such as electric potato peelers, mixers, and ovens.

There were no days off. If you took a day off you were logged four for one. One trip in Havana, only two of my eighteen galley helpers showed up for the evening meal and three of us had to prepare dinner for the passengers. There was only one problem we didn't have – insufficient stores. Five large freezers were jammed to the bursting point with fresh meats and vegetables, and the steward, fully aware that the crew would steal whatever was not delivered to the table, allowed us to feed well. But nine hours a day in a crowded, steaming galley, seven days a week, month in, month out, is work indeed. I never fried an egg or flipped a pancake without wondering "What in hell am *I* doing *here?*" One can't work this way in a militant atmosphere without wondering about the meaning of work, exploitation, and the future – especially when one is fifty-two!

There were two other conditions on the *Polk* that aroused my political and social consciousness – the route we traveled and the character of the passengers. The *Polk* was on a round-the-world schedule, putting into twenty or more ports in more than a dozen countries, territories, and possessions. Usually the tourists, ashore only for the day, headed for the fanciest hotel or shopping district. At our first stop, Havana, they set a course straight for the *Nacional* or Sloppy Joe's, and spent most of the day in an air-conditioned bar, with, maybe, a daring sortie or two to buy a piece of lace, straw hat, or a bauble. The following day at sea they could be heard "analyzing" the problems of Cuba – the workers were lazy and filthy, the weather was too hot, prices too high, and Cuba was lucky America had taken such an interest in it – otherwise it would be even worse off! They learned *nothing* of this island's dictatorship which had been completely taken over by American sugar interests; its once rich, multicrop land converted into a one-crop estate which could employ the workers only a few months of the year. An Englishman could have formed equally valid views of America from a day in the Waldorf-Astoria bar!

From Cuba we headed for Panama, or more accurately the Canal Zone, except for another reckless excursion to Cristobal or Panama City it was as close to Panama as any of the passengers ever got. Here again, they knew nothing of Panama when they arrived and learned nothing while they were there. Of the whole domination by the United States from the time Teddy Roosevelt had organized the revolution to chip away this piece of Colombia, through the "gold and silver" discrimination against native workers, to our iniquitous treaty with Panama, they were entirely innocent – and disinterested.

Then we steamed up the coast to San Francisco, across to the Hawaiian Islands, and on to Yokohama.

In 1938 when I visited Japan for the first time on the *Polk,* some ninety-odd million Japanese were living on five islands whose total land area was less than that of the state of California – and only twelve percent of it arable. Japanese military and business circles were already well embarked on the program of expansion which was to erupt in the attacks on Pearl Harbor and the Philippine Islands just three years later.

Few of the *Polk* passengers gave any thought to the problems of war or peace. That Korea had been enslaved by the Japanese since 1905, that Japanese armies had already occupied large parts of China, that its military machine had moved into the islands of the South Pacific, almost none knew or cared – they were interested only in the "quaint charm" of Japan, a ricksha tour of the parks and gardens, a visit to the Ginza for bargains, and finally, for no trip would have been complete without it, a visit to Tokyo's *Yoshiwara* or Yokohama's *Homoku* sections, where numbered fifteen-year-old prostitutes were exhibited in store windows and could be "ordered" by number for four yen the whole night! This was "doing" Japan.

By contrast it is well to point out that by 1939 the seamen and West Coast longshoremen had already declared their own strict embargo against the shipment of scrap iron and oil to Japan, while the rest of the world was blithely trading with the aggressor. The bombs that rained over Pearl Harbor on December 7, 1941, were, in a very real way, our own steel chickens coming home to roost.

Steaming on, we reached Shanghai, the world's prime cesspool of imperialistic greed and international throat-cutting and intrigue. When Mao Tse-tung's armies liberated all of China in 1948–49 few seamen were as surprised as the diplomats. There was no country with such extremes of rich and poor. While wealthy *compradores* dallied with their mistresses in the elegant salons on Nanking Road the bodies of starved citizens were collected daily by the "street cleaning" trucks throughout the occupied section. Extraterritoriality prevailed – legal French, English, and American islands in the vast Chinese sea. Human beings were thick as lice and as easily deprived of life. I have seen taxis, rented on a monthly basis by a few United States Marines, go careening up Nanking Road, knock over a rickshaw and not even stop to determine whether anyone was hurt. No matter what the crime, Americans were tried in American courts and freed by American judges – for what was the life of a Chinese?

Coming up the Hwang Pu deck crews often broke out in the bitter song, to the tune of "Let Me Call You Sweetheart":

Meet me at the slop chute, on the old Whangpoo,
Bring along your dipnet, there's enough for two,
There'll be mashed potatoes and a good beef stew . . .
Meet me at the slop chute on the old Whangpoo.

The slop chute, of course, is the garbage scupper from the galley which empties into the sea. When we arrived in Shanghai I saw what happens to the sampan owners who gathered at the ship's side to catch the discharged garbage with their dip nets. Captain Hawkins, a master in the usual tradition of contempt for the poor, ordered the bos'un to turn the fire hoses on any of the frail little craft that approached the 20,000-ton *Polk,* and to sink them if necessary. One sampan containing a pretty Chinese girl and a man who we later learned was her husband nevertheless managed to cling to a dangling line. A Japanese patrol boat pulled up and a sentry killed the man with a single shot. Then the patrol boat overhauled the sampan and the sentry beat the girl into insensibility with his rifle butt. This sort of thing happened daily on the Shanghai waterfront. Vendors on Nanking Road sold pictures of Chinese revolutionaries caught by Chiang's troops before the Japanese invasion, their severed heads lying in the street where they were caught alongside their still kneeling bodies!

The tourists talked about these things of course – and in the next breath were chortling about the 14-course dinner they had at the Palace Hotel, complete with champagne, for only eight *mex* – about forty cents in "gold," with the yuan fluctuating from seventeen to twenty-two per dollar. Or the men, out of hearing of their wives, boasted about the beautiful White Russian girls they had met at the Casanova club, whose favors they had enjoyed for a quarter! No one missed the seventh floor of the Sincere Company, a large local department store where Chinese girls, parading with their *amahs,* could be bought by the day, week, or month for a few dollars – or sold into perpetual prostitution for so magnificent a sum as $100.

And so it went around the world – in Hongkong, Singapore, Calcutta, and Bombay; Port Said, Naples, Algiers, Gibraltar, and home. Ancient Rome could not have produced a more decadent, arrogant, and stupid class of patricians than those whom the *Polk* carried, trip after trip. They were absolutely impervious to the degradation and human misery around them. I once overheard a traveler in Madras exclaim, as she stepped over the bodies of suffering and dying Indians, "My! It's all so *colorful*!" It was as if India were a vast movie set and the Indians were dying to entertain her! The bored businessmen regarded the world as a vast plantation for the extraction of profits, while their wives supposed it was an elaborate bazaar held to tantalize them with bargains!

Wherever the *Polk* went conditions were much the same. The chronic starvation was greater or less; one or another type of epidemic periodically chopped down the poor. The oppressors were Americans, Englishmen, Germans, Belgians, French, or Dutch, but they were inevitably oppressors, and they were inevitably white. In every port the *Polk's* passengers blithely headed for the Cathay, Raffles, or Shepherds for political orientation over cocktails; searched relentlessly for souvenirs to dazzle the folks back home and complained about the "white man's burden."

I remained aboard the *Polk* for seven trips as chief cook while the world steadily disintegrated. Hitler's invasion of Austria, the Munich Pact and "peace in our time," the dismemberment of Czechoslovakia, and Franco's triumph in Spain, the beginning of the Japanese-Soviet War in Manchuria, and the invasion of Poland came as a horrible counterpoint to our endless entering and leaving of ports, union meetings protesting this or that, and the idiocies of the passengers. But even the tourists became a little grimmer as we left Port Said in the spring of 1940 bound for Italy. Suddenly "the hand that held the dagger plunged it into his neighbor's back" ... Mussolini declared war on France and we entered a Naples at war. Troop trains and fighting ships put in and out of the harbor daily. Throughout the city there were large posters of Hitler and Mussolini and at night bands of Italian workers crept along the dark streets splashing the posters with mud and gouging out the eyes of the painted heads of Hitler and Mussolini – a symbol of the fate that would befall both before the war was over. Jaunty fascist soldiers paraded through the streets. Years later, though I couldn't then have guessed under what circumstances, I was to have a renewed acquaintance with these soldiers when they were in a different mood.

1938, 1939, and 1940 were thus the crucial years in which, for me, the myriad forces of history began to stand out starkly and definably. Seven trips around the world on the *Polk*, slaving in a steaming galley with the tinkle of passengers' laughter filtering through the galley doors, my master's ticket still unused in my pocket, confronted in port after port with the misery and degradation of the world's poor, the fatuities of the rich, and the banal sophistries of capitalist diplomats for which the workers would sooner or later have to pay with their lives, crystallized suddenly in acute truths, sharp as a bayonet. I began to realize in a humble and powerful way that my allegiance did not lie with states, kings, or national boundaries *but with people!*

How stupid it was, I realized, even to owe one's loyalty to *one* people, a *particular* people, even Afro-Americans! Was not our fight for a decent life for ourselves inseparable from the struggle of Indonesians against the Dutch? The Congolese against the Belgians? The Algerians against the French? The Kenyans against the British? Or the Cubans against Batista and his American cohorts? Or the Haitians and Dominicans against their respective dictators? The essential thing to grasp seemed to me then, and seems to me still, that we are *one people* in *one world, and that our battles are inseparable.* The murder of Emmett Till injured a Kenyan, made *his* fight for freedom harder, as the jailing of Jomo Kenyatta was an insult to us all.

And now, in 1940, dictators fresh from triumphs in Spain and China were loosed upon the world again – and I was frying eggs for cafe society rich on a pleasure boat!

As these ideas took shape I resolved to quit the *Polk*

and fight once more to sail in my rating. When we returned to the United States in August the country's mobilization was well under way. Orders were flowing into the shipyards for new destroyers and dry cargo vessels, and again there were newspaper reports that licensed seamen would soon be needed. I couldn't help smiling at the irony of my position – like millions of others, the only time my country could really use me was when it was at war! In the years from 1918 to 1941 I could, for all anyone cared, go hang. But now I began to suspect that another opportunity to sail on deck was in the making and I resolved to be ready when the call came.

I wrote letters to the appropriate agencies and again made the rounds of the shipowners' offices, but the situation was not yet desperate enough to warrant hiring a colored mate or captain. After a month ashore I signed on the *President Taylor* for another round-the-world trip, and when we returned in January of 1941 made a twenty-day trip on the *President Jackson* and completed two short stints on the *Horace* and *Paul Luckenbach*. Then I resolved to concentrate once more on my goal.

10

By 1941 it had become apparent that sooner or later America must enter the war. My attitude toward this prospect was, like that of so many others, ambivalent, for America was a divided nation. On the extreme right Charles Lindbergh, William Dudley Pelley, and a wide range of fascist cohorts had hoisted the banner of "America First," arguing that we had rescued Europe just twenty years earlier at tremendous cost (and without commensurate "rewards"). On the left many unions and organizations were asserting that World War II was merely another imperialist attempt to divide up the world, and organized "the Yanks are not coming" campaign. Most Americans, while clearly sympathetic with England and France, were not yet ready to shoulder arms and uneasily awaited the turn of events.

I think it would be a fair generalization to say that the Afro-American population of the United States did not, prior to December 7, 1941, exhibit a great deal of enthusiasm for the war. Germany and Italy wanted to be colonial powers – to recover the territories lost in World War I – but Britain and France had been colonial powers for centuries. The world was aroused by the Nazi atrocities – committed against whites. Colored people did not condone them on that account, but they thought of their own suffering for centuries. After all, nearly as many lives were lost in a single state of Africa – the Belgian Congo – during seventy-five years of Belgian occupation as were lost by all the participants in World War II!

Somehow whites must be made to see that the terrors they understood for the first time in German fascism are those that Africans and many of African descent live with all their lives. Concentration camps, slave labor, police brutality, starvation, the wrenching of mothers from children, humiliation and insult – what could the Nazis teach the British, French, Belgians, Dutch, Portuguese, or Americans in these matters? (And such crimes are continuing almost two decades after the war has ended!)

So there was a strong feeling among colored Americans in 1941 that the colonial powers be allowed to destroy each other. As a former British subject I felt this keenly. And yet, early in 1941 it had become obvious that sooner or later we would join the Allies, and it seemed to me that under Roosevelt's leadership there was a strong chance that the war could really change the course of history. After June 22, as far as I was concerned, all doubt was removed; the Soviet Union's participation in the Allied cause, I considered, assured a democratic victory and changed the character of the war, and I could feel confident and enthusiastic about my own role in it.

But what was the role to be? By 1941 I had been a professional sailor for thirty-five years, and was still sailing as a cook or steward. Thirty-five years is a long apprenticeship; if a man is not equipped to do his job by the time he's fifty-five, when should he be?

Yet again, as I launched a renewed effort to sail on deck, I was almost alone in believing that I should be appointed master of an ocean vessel. I plunged into a series of daily conferences with prominent members of national Negro and liberal organizations, but while promises flew thick and fast little action was forthcoming.

First, naturally, I approached the National Association for the Advancement of Colored People. The answer was that while they naturally sympathized with my plight and would help me if they could, their principal concern was the advancement of civil liberties in the South. This was fine, it was as it should be, but wasn't there five minutes in the day of a third secretary to dictate a letter to Washington? Next I approached the Reverend Adam Clayton Powell, father of the present Congressman from Harlem. We met in his office in the Abyssinian Baptist Church and I laid my case before him. He was very sympathetic and said he would see what he could do. That was the last I ever heard from him. I called next on my good friend Ferdinand C. Smith of the National Maritime Union. A fine leader and hard worker, Ferd was not optimistic about my chances and did not play a decisive role in the final victory.

In all, I called on about thirty organizations that spring, talking to representatives of religious, philanthropic, fraternal, labor, and civic bodies – to anyone, indeed, who would give me a hearing and help press my case in Washington. Most thought there were easier places to break the color bar. There have been many bleak periods in my life, but in the spring of 1941 I very nearly lost hope.

Yet if I could not succeed in my own case there was much to do on behalf of my people. The Nazis were, by this time, in control of all of Western Europe. American factories were turning out the implements of war for our allies, workers were needed everywhere, and the time was ripe to win greater equality for colored workers. One afternoon I was asked to attend a meeting of the Brooklyn Chapter of the National Negro Congress. The subject was a program for improving conditions of the Brooklyn Negro workers.

Late in the evening discussion centered around the possibilities of securing more jobs for colored workers in the war industries. Steve Kingston, head of the Brooklyn chapter, had heard of my case and asked me to speak on it. Not entirely by accident I had with me the manuscript of an article I had prepared at the request of an editor of a local newspaper, detailing the story of discrimination against colored seamen, and minimum persuasion had to be exerted to get me to read it.

When I had finished one of the board members asked, "Do you really hold a master's ticket?"

"Of course I do!"

"Then yours is exactly the case we want."

It was decided that I should attend a city-wide meeting of the Congress that weekend and present my case to the delegates. That Saturday afternoon, following my report, the National Negro Congress unanimously decided to launch an aggressive effort to secure my appointment as master of a merchant vessel. In twenty years of earnest effort this was the first time that so large a group had agreed to help me, and that evening I was brimming with optimism.

The National Negro Congress was true to its word. Within a week letters had been dispatched to prominent civic leaders asking for their support, as well as appeals to shipowners and, of course, government officials. It is probably not necessary to report that most were never answered. Nevertheless, three replies were received. The first, from the Navy Department, said:

In connection with privately owned industries, you are advised that the Navy Department has no jurisdiction over such establishments and therefore can exercise no control over the employment of their personnel or their personnel policies.

The second, from the War Department, stated that "the character of employment desired by Captain Mulzac is not within the jurisdiction of the War Department."

The third letter was from the chairman of the United States Maritime Commission himself, Virginia-bred Admiral Emory S. Land. He wrote:

The Maritime Commission is not now engaged in the operation of merchant vessels. Those vessels it formerly operated have been transferred to private operators either through sale or charter. The present owners and operators assume sole jurisdiction over the employment, assignment and promotion of their entire seagoing personnel. The Commission does not now, nor does it intend in the future, to dictate to or interfere with the established methods of private steamship owners and operators in the selection of officers.

We are unable, therefore, to be of any assistance to Mr. Mulzac.

Throughout the thirty-five years that I went to sea I was always dependent upon white men for jobs. All of the steamship operators with the exception of Marcus Garvey, were white. All of the key personnel in their employ were white. The U.S. shipping commissioners were, without exception, white, the police and guards on the dock were invariably white, the doctors who came aboard at quarantine were white. Even the shipping crimps, back in the old days, were white. The waterfront has always been and is a white man's world, and colored people have been its servants. Because I was dependent upon white men for jobs I avoided, throughout the years, provocative formulations and concentrated in my public utterances upon those issues and undertakings which could *unite* black and white and not further divide them.

But at this writing I am seventy-six years old and it is unlikely that I will ever walk a bridge as master again. It is incumbent, I think, that Admiral Land's letter be answered.

It is a matter of public record that in 1941 President Roosevelt was seeking to prepare the country for a much greater role in the war, demanding the fullest mobilization of our manpower and material and spiritual resources. While our national effort was still directed toward enabling England and France to withstand the Nazi onslaught, this was a full year after Dunkirk, seven months after Pearl Harbor, and barely a month before the Wehrmacht was to storm across the Soviet frontier. There could be some excuse for the man-in-the-street's not understanding the gravity of the situation, but could there be any uncertainty on the part of a high administration official that there was an *urgency* to our mobilization that took precedence over "traditional" ways of doing things?

Nor was this all. It is also a matter of public record that the United States government, through taxpayers' dollars, was contributing *hundreds of millions* of dollars a year to the so-called "private" shipping industry. This support from the public till took the form of construction, operating and mail subsidies, most of which wound up in "private" pockets. If, therefore, Admiral Land was in a position to be so generous to the shipping operators, could he not have distributed some of this *largesse* among the people – specifically among those taxpayers who manned the ships, and *particularly* among those sailors of color to whom these same "private" interests refused equal employment opportunities?

In 1941 *there was not a single colored officer in the*

141

entire American merchant marine! This was no accident or "oversight"; *dozens were qualified.* Those who had "sole jurisdiction" over employment, as Admiral Land affirmed, *refused to hire them!*

What then, was the responsibility of the people's servant? To "dictate" or "interfere?" *Of course!* If the shipping operators refused to offer equal employment opportunities to colored citizens, especially in times of public crisis, *who should make them, if not the "servants" of the people?* I could not make them, the NMU could not make them, the National Negro Congress could not make them – none of the individuals and organizations which had taken up the battle over the years could make them. Who *could* make them? *The Maritime Commission,* which was paying them with the people's tax dollars!

But even these arguments are extraneous to the central one – the fact of a United States Constitution guaranteeing equal rights, and the commitment of Presidential appointees to uphold the Constitution. Would it have been a violation of his oath of office for Admiral Land to suggest to the operators that it might be a good idea, in view of their annual assaults upon the public till, to pay some tiny homage to the Constitution by hiring a colored officer, especially when the officers were certified as qualified by the government's own Department of Commerce? *On the contrary, it would have been to act in the highest traditions of public office!*

Outrage and frustration for us all were the only results of our 1941 campaign. After these and other rebuffs even those who were trying to help me began to lose heart. Eventually a lawyer for the Congress said, "Man, they're not going to give you a ship . . . it's too big a job for a colored man." Breakthroughs were easier on other fronts. However set I was on my course I could not fail to understand that the National Negro Congress had other battles to fight.

Time ran out . . . money ran out . . . there was no alternative but to return to sea, this time aboard the S.S. *Montanan,* an American-Hawaiian ship bound for Suez via the Cape of Good Hope. Carrying flour and ammunition for the British Army we left New York late in May and arrived in Capetown on a significant date – June 22, 1941, the day the Wehrmacht stormed across the Soviet frontier. I was leaning against the rail talking to a longshoreman when a dockworker shouted up the news. "Well, that's it," the longshoreman said, "after Hitler takes Russia he'll have all the grain and oil he needs. It's a bad day for England and the rest of us."

"Don't you believe it," I said firmly, "he'll never make it. No one has ever attacked Russia and gotten away with it. It's too big."

"He'll be in Moscow in two months," the South African said.

"You are wrong. Hitler will be finished before Russia is." Later I learned that many in positions of power in the United States thought that Hitler would cut through Russia like a knife through butter. But the lowliest ordinary seaman on the *Montanan* knew the Germans were in for a different kind of fight, that Soviet citizens would defend their homeland to the last cellar.

We took on stores in Capetown and proceeded through the Mozambique Channel, though German and Nazi U-boats were already reported lurking there, and reached Aden safely. There we took on bunkers and steamed through the Red Sea where, in July, the temperature reached 140 degrees on deck. At Suez we dropped anchor alongside a White Star Line transport troopship, the *Georgic.* Early in the evening a patrol boat pulled up alongside and ordered us to move to another anchorage, one of those fortuitous wartime contingencies by which our lives may have been saved.

For that evening our baptism of fire began. Just before 9 p.m. the alarm went out and we heard the bombers droning down from the Mediterranean. The shore guns, *bofors*, and forty millimeter's opened up – every ship in the harbor was ablaze except us, for technically we were not at war. The sky was laced with tracer bullets, and as the bombs began to fall I heard what was to become for the next four years a familiar sound – the heavy c-r-u-n-c-h of bombs. Suddenly there was a tremendous explosion off our starboard side: the *Georgic* had caught a 500-pounder right down her stack and erupted in one incredible, brilliant, terrifying explosion. Minutes later hundreds, perhaps thousands, of men were in the water, desperately clinging to wreckage or striking out for the nearest vessel. Patrol boats scurried about hauling them in. The explosion broke every light bulb and mirror on the *Montanan*, but we were not otherwise damaged. Five other ships were sunk that night in Port Suez.

In the morning we moved to the docks, and in the following five days, while we discharged cargo and repaired the damage, there were no further attacks. We were glad when our orders came; we were to proceed through the Red Sea to Karachi. There we picked up several thousand tons of iron ore and hoisted anchor once more for Soerabaja, Java, and another outstanding example of "enlightened" Western administration of an eastern country.

It is popularly believed that the Dutch were efficient colonial administrators – and so they were as far as the harvesting of profits was concerned. Not even Belgians could have exploited Indonesia's riches more thoroughly. But the people – one thousand to the square mile in Java, one of the most densely populated areas on earth – lived like vermin. In the evening I often walked down to the riverhead and watched thousands of natives taking baths, washing clothes and going to the toilet in the same stream – and then carrying home buckets of drinking water! The dock workers loaded the *Montanan* with bales of rubber so huge that they had to be deposited on the carrier's shoulders by four men. Then the wizened worker would stagger up the gangway and heave it down the hatch. How many billions of dollars worth of rubber, oil, tin, manganese, copper, nickel, gold, and silver were carried on the shoulders of the Indonesians for a few cents a day?

The date was December 7, 1941. We had passed through the Makassar Straits, Borneo to port, Celebes to starboard, and were heading for the broad stretches of the Pacific when the news arrived. We headed South at once, and the following day – December 9th by our calendar – fresh orders arrived: we were to make for the Cape of Good Hope and proceed to Baltimore via the Atlantic Ocean. Twenty-three days later we stood off Cape Henry, and a destroyer signaled us to remain outside until morning – submarine nets were being strung across the entrance to Chesapeake Bay. We steamed in circles that evening, and toward midnight the sky suddenly lit up near the shore. Seconds later the reverberations from the explosion rolled over the water and no one needed to ask the cause – just below the lighthouse millions of gallons of burning oil illuminated the night sky. At dawn we watched the bow of an inbound tanker finally settle into the sea. There were no survivors.

I I

America was at war. We had been away seven months and I was stunned at the change that had taken place in the country. The savage attack on Pearl Harbor, while Saburo Kurusu and Admiral Nomura were negotiating with Cordell Hull a "peaceful settlement" of United States-Japanese problems, had shocked the nation out of its apathy. Thousands of young Americans had volunteered for military service following the declaration of war, and factories which only weeks earlier had been turning out watches, automobiles, and silk nightgowns were already concentrating on fuses, tanks and parachutes.

It was time, I thought, for a concerted, all-out drive to win the fullest participation of the nation's colored "ten percent" in the war effort. I paid off the *Montanan* in Baltimore and caught the first train to New York. I kissed Marie, gave the children the gifts I'd brought from Capetown, Egypt, India, and Soerabaja, and called Steve Kingston. He told me later that he was dismayed to hear my voice, realizing that he was only going to be asked to go through the whole effort over again, but, nevertheless, he asked me to drop right over. The following day we called upon Malcolm Martin, who also agreed to return to the battle. Again the National Negro Congress machinery began to hum; new publicity releases went out to the press, letters were dispatched to Washington, and public figures were again invited to join the campaign to win war jobs for colored citizens equivalent to their training.

Again I began to make my daily round of steamship company offices, patiently filling out application forms. I wrote once more to the Army Transport Service, which operated a fleet of vessels with merchant crewmen, to the Navy, the War Manpower Commission, and the United States Maritime Commission, still headed by the infamous Admiral Land. In each instance I received a reply advising me to get in touch with the appropriate local office. For example, at the suggestion of Captain Edward McCauley, Deputy Director of the War Shipping Administration, I again sought out Captain Charles Zearfoss, WSA's New York chief at 45 Broadway. "Ummm, yours is a very difficult case," Captain Zearfoss replied, "I'll have to refer it back to Washington."

The port captain of the Isthmian Steamship Corporation, wholly-owned subsidiary of United States Steel, was more direct. "I don't think you have enough experience," he told me.

"How can you possibly know that?" I asked.

"Besides," he went on, "you're fifty-six ... that's too old for us."

"You have many skippers over fifty-six on your ships at this very moment," I said.

"Well, I'll file your application," he replied, and then after a moment added, "but it won't do you any good."

Officers of the Marine Cooks & Stewards Union, which had reciprocal shipping privileges with the NMU, appealed to the War Shipping Administration and other government bodies. No answer. Naturally I could not expect any assistance from the Masters, Mates and Pilots Union, but it was a disappointment that the NMU did not fight my case harder than it did. Ferdinand Smith, Negro secretary of the union, while completely sympathetic with my ambition, believed it was a hopeless cause and that the union should concentrate on issues affecting all of its membership.

Yet all was not lost. A final, urgent appeal to Captain Edward McCauley, Deputy Director of the War Shipping Administration early in September, gave us a glimmer of hope. He would, wrote Captain McCauley, be pleased to meet with me on the morning of September 19.

On September 19 in Washington I sought out the WSA offices. The secretary ushered me into Captain McCauley's office after a short wait, and the director, a large, handsome, graying man, advanced cordially with outstretched hand. "Well, Captain Mulzac, how are you? What can I do for you today?"

I don't suppose Captain McCauley ever realized how ironic this greeting was. It had taken me twenty years to reach such an office, and he asked what he could do for me "today." "The same thing others could have done twenty years ago, ten years ago, or last year," I was almost tempted to say. But Captain McCauley was obviously a very warm and sincere man, and I really couldn't take offense.

In the preceding months the Recruiting and Manning Organization, a division of WSA, had conducted an extensive advertising campaign throughout the country appealing for recruits to the Merchant Marine. Experienced sailors in all ratings were desperately needed, the ads read, and indeed, this was true. Nazi U-boats were waging an aggressive and costly war in the Atlantic as Hitler, having lost the battle of Moscow the previous winter and now beginning to suspect that the Allies were not going to be as easy to conquer as he had supposed, had struck with relentless fury at Allied shipping lines. By the fall of 1942 Liberty ships were already being routed through the Panama Canal and the Straits of Magellan to Capetown and the Middle East to avoid the dangerous South Atlantic. As for the North Atlantic route, no seaman who made the summer run of 1942 to Murmansk will ever forget it. Some 100-ship convoys were almost completely destroyed as they steamed off the Norwegian Coast, day after day under unremitting Nazi attacks. Some 5,000 merchant seamen were lost that first year of the war, most of them skilled veterans whose services were badly needed.

I had collected several newspaper ads and bound them into a large portfolio, which I now spread before Captain McCauley. "I came to answer these ads in person," I said. "I am a United States citizen, and have held a master's license since 1918. In the past twenty-four years I have never been able to sail on it." I put my license on the desk. "Here is my license. Here are two diplomas in ocean navigation," putting them alongside the license, "and a certificate in wireless, a certificate for the Sperry gyroscope, and here are my discharges as a chief mate during World War I. The country needs skilled ratings, the ads say, so here I am."

Captain McCauley barely looked at the mound of clippings, ads, licenses, and certificates in front of him, and stopped me with a gesture. Finally he said slowly, "This is rank discrimination on the part of the government. I will attempt to take care of it. Excuse me a moment." He picked up the portfolio and licenses and left the room.

I sat alone in Captain McCauley's big office wondering what would happen. If Captain McCauley failed me there were only two appeals left – to Admiral Land and President Roosevelt himself. It was doubtful, of course, that I could reach either, and thus for all practical purposes my career was now in Captain McCauley's hands. Looking out the window over Washington it seemed impossible that my lifelong dream should not come true. And, paradoxically, just as unlikely that it should.

While I was hoping against hope that Captain McCauley's next words would be favorable, thirty-five years of rebuffs had prepared me for disappointment. Sailing as a steward, I began to rationalize, after all was not so bad, not nearly as hard, for example, as being a skipper. The only work, really, was supervising the members of the department, doling out soap, matches and linens, making up store lists and arguing with the skipper about the cost-per-day ratio. And with the government paying all the bills there would be precious few arguments!

Anyway, I knew the struggle would go on. If my efforts proved to be mere skirmishes on the road to equal opportunity, some other sailor some other morning would be sitting in an office like this, and would be luckier. Who was to say whether the time was really "ripe" or not? Perhaps my ambition was, as so many had said, "premature?" How could I be so sure that my determination to sail on deck was not just a childish dream that I'd cherished all these years? Where would I be next month, I wondered, master of my own vessel or steward on another old rustpot? All the nights of study, all the hard work on the old *Wolf*, and the *Sound of Jura,* and the *Waken,* and the *Beatrice,* and all the other ships. All the special courses, all the efforts and hopes of others ... old Cap Cullison, and Steve Kingston and so many others who had helped me fight through the years. The trouble was, I thought, that no matter how well one prepares oneself for life the future is always in other hands!

As it turned out all my elaborate rationalizations were not needed. Half an hour later Captain McCauley strode back into the room with the look of one who has accomplished his mission. "Captain Mulzac," he said firmly, "it has been decided to name a ship, now in a California shipyard, the *Booker T. Washington*. We are asking Miss Marian Anderson to christen her. And Captain, we think you would fit in just perfectly as master of the *Booker T.*"

Captain McCauley raised his eyes to mine and his face fell as he saw the look of confused joy and dismay that must have been reflected in my features. How could I explain the bitter and cruel irony of his offer! The American Revolution had been fought in 1776, and a Constitution written guaranteeing equality for all. A Civil War had been fought eighty-three years earlier over the same issue of freedom for colored citizens. And here we were in 1942, engaged in the greatest war in history, in which one of the major issues was the ruthless extermination of a minority people, and demanding the fullest mobilization of the nation's manpower. If there was ever a moment when the real meaning of democracy *could* and *had to be* demonstrated to the peoples of the world, the moment was *now!* What was America's answer in this hour of need? *A jim-crow ship! Named* for a Negro, *christened* by a Negro, *captained* by a Negro, and no doubt *manned* by Negroes! Captain McCauley's next words came as no surprise. "Captain," he said, "we were wondering, do you think you could get an all-colored crew to sail with you?"

In my very limited subsequent relations with Captain McCauley and other WSA officials I had few difficulties. They were all, I am convinced, sincere men, devoted to their country, and doing everything they could to win the war. Captain McCauley seemed to have understood that the full and effective participation of the nation's 14 million colored people was not only essential to a military victory, but a political demonstration to the world of the real meaning of democracy.

The problem was that with all their goodwill and honest intentions these men were incapable of understanding the Negro drive for full freedom. Except for a few tiny pockets of Negro nationalists the colored citizens of America are *not* fighting for the right to have their "own" banks, insurance companies, restaurants, or ships; we are fighting for our legitimate right to the share of the nation's wealth to which our labors entitle us, an equal share of its culture, opportunities, and rights on an equal basis with everyone else.

How could I explain to Captain McCauley that, for possibly the noblest of reasons, he was preparing to launch a jim-crow ship in the very name of democracy? There isn't a colored citizen anywhere in the world who would fail to recognize such an act as *prima facie* evidence of discrimination in America.

I didn't want to offend Captain McCauley, especially since I understood clearly enough that there was a way of transforming his plan into a legitimate symbol of democracy. I finally said, "Captain, I appreciate your goodwill and your offer. And let me say that I can get enough colored sailors to man one ship, five ships, or ten ships. But it would, in my opinion, be wrong, for they would be *jim-crow ships.* That's what we're fighting *against,* and for me to lend my name to such a project would be wrong."

"I don't understand," Captain McCauley said, "you said you wanted a ship and now I'm offering one to you and you turn it down. What do you want us to do? Do you expect that white men will sail under you?"

"Captain McCauley, I can get an entire crew of white sailors, too, if need be, but that would be just as wrong. I think we should get crew members without any regard to their color. Do you ask white captains to get all-white crews? Of course not! The union would forbid it. What we should do is put in a call to the union hall for a crew, white or black. I cannot accept the appointment on the terms you are offering me. Give me an appointment the same as you would any other man."

"Well, think it over, Captain," Captain McCauley said, "I will call you when the *Booker T.* is ready." The interview was over. We shook hands and I left.

I reported our conversation in full to Malcolm Martin and Steve Kingston, and none of us was sure what to think. Actually, nothing had been decided. After several days a letter arrived, reading as follows:

My dear Captain Mulzac:

In connection with our recent conversation concerning the naming one of our Liberty ships the Booker T. Washington, *I have just been informed that the vessel will be ready for delivery about October 20th. Will you please furnish me immediately full particulars concerning the crew recommended and what their union affiliations are?*

Yours very truly,
(Signed) Edward McCauley
Captain, U.S. Navy
Retired Commissioner

I telephoned Steve Kingston at once and the committee met jubilantly. Naturally we interpreted the letter as confirmation of my appointment. In the next few days newspapers got hold of the story, and since there were garbled versions the National Negro Congress thought it expedient to issue a formal news release, which was reprinted widely. The WSA however, and I must say correctly, considered the publicity premature. In all justice, since I was the first colored citizen in the nation's history to be appointed the master of an ocean vessel, the announcement should have come from Washington. Accordingly, a few days later Captain *McCauley wrote again:*

My dear Captain Mulzac:

There has been considerable publicity directed toward your appointment as master of the Booker T. Washington.

So that there may be no misunderstanding as to the commitments which were made I wish to recapitulate my understanding of our conversation. It was agreed that you were to suggest a crew to Mr. Dimock, Director of the Recruiting and Manning Organization, to man the vessel. Such a crew to be mixed, consisting of colored and white officers and seamen. It was agreed that you were to be appointed master of the vessel, provided you could meet the standard qualifications of the War Shipping Administration. It was agreed that you were to submit your credentials as master mariner, and an outline of your experience immediately to the Division of Operations of the War Shipping Administration in order to facilitate the assignment. It is my utmost desire to promote a fair and equitable treatment of all men employed in the American Merchant Marine regardless of race, color or creed. Therefore, you may be assured that you will be given fair and equitable consideration.

> *With all good wishes,*
> > *Sincerely,*
> > > *(Signed) Edward McCauley*
> > > *Deputy War Shipping Administrator*

Captain McCauley's second letter took us back a bit, since nothing had really been settled. A few days later, however, "orders" arrived assigning me to Fort Trumbull, Connecticut, for a refresher course for all masters who had not had a command for "two years." It seemed at last that my appointment was official, but remembering "there's many a slip . . ." I still did not feel like celebrating.

At the same time I received a call from the RMO – the Recruiting and Manning division of War Shipping Administration – urging me to notify them of the officers selected to man the *Booker T.* Since Captain McCauley had doubted that white men would sail under me I had decided to make the point clear by enlisting *all* Negro officers to the bridge. The chief mate I had already decided on – Adolphus Folks, one of the graduates of my Nautical Academy back in 1922.

Adolphus had been sailing as A.B. and bo'sun throughout these long years, from time to time, like myself, quitting the sea in discouragement to work ashore. He was working ashore when I went to his house one night. He had seen the press announcement of my appointment and when he saw me he clapped me on the shoulder and said "Man, I see you got yourself a big job! Congratulations!"

And I slapped him right back and said, "And man, *you* got *your*self a big job too – you're the new chief mate of the *Booker T!*" And we stood grinning, our arms wrapped around each other's shoulder, for five minutes.

"Well, you always said some day we'd make it," Adolphus said over and over again, "you always said someday we'd make it . . ."

Finding a second mate was almost as easy. I went to the NMU hall on 17th Street and asked some friends if they knew any colored sailors with mate's tickets.

"Why there's a fellow working on tugboats right here in the harbor," replied one, "his name is Clifton Lastic."

I had lost touch with Cliff during the years, but was delighted to hear he was still around. I got his address, and went around to his apartment one night. I wasn't sure he had heard about the *Booker T.* and decided to have some fun with him. After we'd settled down with a couple of bottles of beer, I talked about inconsequential things for quite a while, and Cliff grew more and more fidgety. Finally he could stand it no longer. "When you gonna ask me?" he burst out, *"when you gonna ask me?"* And I had my second mate.

A few days later I dutifully reported at Fort Trumbull, where I was greeted cordially by Lt. Commander William C. Ash, and put through a two-day course dealing principally with convoy procedure and a new signalling system. I remained at Trumbull for nine days, when a wire arrived ordering me to Los Angeles.

En route, I stopped in New York and with Marie and the children enjoyed a quiet *pre*-celebration . . . for even at this point I was not confident that nothing could go wrong. The following morning, the 12th of October, I departed on an American Airlines flagship for L.A. with Adolphus, Clifton, Jessie Brooks, third officer, and Cecil Blackman, wireless operator.

The *Booker T.* had already been christened, but missing this event was a minor disappointment more than compensated for by my new command.

From the moment the American Airlines plane discharged us at Los Angeles Airport to the moment we left the dock eleven days later my life was not my own. There were, first of all, official obligations. For reasons I never understood the WSA had wired Commander E. W. Hollis, director of Merchant Marine officers on the West Coast, that I had not completed my Fort Trumbull assignments and needed further refreshing. Commander Hollis, puzzled as I was, invited me to a "banquet" aboard his training ship, and I use the word carefully, for the steward had prepared a dinner fit for the President himself. During dinner Commander Hollis and I had a friendly chat. He "felt me out" regarding my fitness for a command and I gave him the answers he wanted. The following day he wired the WSA that I was capable of assuming command. The Luckenbach Steamship Corporation, to which the *Booker T.* had been consigned, was advised of my readiness and my formal, official, signed and sealed appointment was delivered a few days later.

There really are no words to express how I felt that evening when the final "i" was dotted, the final "t" crossed, and I was master of my own vessel. Everything I ever was, stood for, fought for, dreamed of, came into focus that day. The concrete evidence of the achievement gives one's strivings legitimacy, proves that the ambitions were valid, the struggle worthwhile. Being prevented for those twenty-four years from doing the work for which

I was trained had robbed life of its most essential meaning. Now at last I could use my training and capabilities fully. It was like being born anew.

There was not too much opportunity to enjoy the triumph, however. There was too much to do. First I had to get a crew. Luckenbach had an agreement with the National Maritime Union; the assignment of the *Booker T.* to an NMU contract company was, I presume, more than a fortuitous contingency. The NMU's policy on racial questions was known throughout the world, and it would have been inappropriate, to say the least, to have assigned the vessel to a company having agreements with the West Coast Sailors Union of the Pacific which could offer only a few Hawaiians as evidence of their stand on racial integrity.

Nevertheless, the NMU membership's reaction to the call, when I went down to the San Pedro union hall to get the crew, was interesting. A member called a meeting and moved to suspend shipping rules on the grounds that it was a signal honor to crew up the *Booker T.* and the union should provide the most experienced men available! The motion was passed unanimously, an interesting commentary on Captain McCauley's earlier query, "Do you think white men will sail under you?" Not only were they willing, but competed eagerly for the honor, with the result that we became a kind of miniature United Nations. Two Danes, a Turk, five Filipinos, a British Guianan, a Honduran, two British West Indians, a Norwegian, a Belgian, and sailors from thirteen states of the union constituted the *Booker T.'s* complement.

Finally, of course, there were social commitments, especially after my appointment became offcial. The significance of the *Booker T.* had not been lost on the militant California trade unions. Invitations to speak and congratulations poured in from all over the state, and indeed the nation. The California State CIO tendered a banquet for the crew and officers on October 15, a gala affair.

Another day I spent at the Metro-Goldwyn-Mayer studios meeting many film stars. There was a party almost every night of our stay.

The greatest moment came when I met the *Booker T.* herself . . . . She was lying in an outfitting basin, her fat, ugly hull splashed with red lead, when I boarded her the first time on the afternoon of October 17. It had become popular, early in the war, to disparage the virtues of the Liberty. She was the "Ford" of the shipping industry, simply built for mass production, and without the more luxurious accommodations and elaborate equipment that marked bigger, more permanent vessels. But as the war progressed the Liberties became real heroes, and the sailors' respect for these "ugly ducklings" increased.

Like all other Liberties, the *Booker T.* was a flush-deck ship of 10,572 deadweight tons, 441.06 feet in length, a 56.10-foot beam, and a cruising radius of 16,000 miles. The wide beam was disproportionate to her length, giving her a squat appearance, and fully loaded, as Liberties almost always were, they rode low in the water, almost like a barge. Liberties were fat because they were designed to carry an immense amount of cargo, slow because they had to be expendable, and ugly because they could not be designed for speed or beauty. They were good, solid ships nevertheless, and greater men than I have declared they won the war. Some may have preferred the lithe, speedy C-1's, others the haughty Victories, and still others the C-2's, C-3's, or tankers. For me, no doubt because it is the only vessel I ever commanded, the Liberty was the Queen of the merchant fleet.

And the *Booker T.* was one of the finer specimens. When I first boarded her I could not believe she would be ready in three days. Electricians were still wiring the fo'c'sles, the decks were strewn with air hoses, cables, and equipment, and crates of machinery and supplies destined for the engine room were still on the dock. The shipyard foreman insisted she would be ready for her trials on the 20th, however, though I claimed it would be a miracle if she were ready by Christmas.

One of the high points of my visit was meeting Peter B. Ross, the Negro shipyard worker who was literally "father" of the *Booker T.* It was Peter who had the idea of naming several Liberty ships after famous colored citizens and organized a gang of welders to join him in writing a letter to President Roosevelt. Several days later they received a reply : the President thought it was a wonderful idea and would pass it on to the Maritime Commission. Thus it was to Peter Ross that I really owed my job, and I thanked him effusively.

On the 18th I returned to the yard to meet the Captain who was to conduct the vessel on her trial run. When we were introduced I learned that his name was Granderson, and a faint bell rang in my memory. As we talked he learned I was from St. Vincent. "A lovely island," Captain Granderson remarked, "I've put in there." Suddenly I recalled how I knew the name. "What a coincidence," I said, "that *two* Captain Grandersons should have visited St. Vincent. Back in 1907 I sailed under a Leif Granderson from Kraagerow, Norway. He was master of a barque, the *Aeolus.*"

Captain Granderson's face lit up. "What a coincidence *indeed!*" he exclaimed, wringing my hand, "Leif Granderson was my father!" He invited me to have dinner with him that evening and I showed him my discharge, signed by his father, and he showed me pictures of his father and the *Aeolus.*

The shipyard foreman's estimate turned out to be correct. When we boarded the *Booker T.* the morning of the 20th the splotches of red lead had disappeared behind a coat of battleship gray, the decks were cleared of debris, her rigging was in place and the most welcome sight of all, fumes were rising from her stack. Captain Granderson was in command as we let go the lines, and riding high and proud we steamed out of Pedro on our trial run.

A few miles at sea he began to put her through her paces – hard right, hard left, full ahead and full astern, crash stops. She was a lively ship, eager to go, in perfect operating condition. We returned that afternoon, and I knew the report would be favorable. That evening we moved to a dock in Wilmington and I was advised by the WSA that we were to load for Panama and the East Coast. Being sent around to the Atlantic meant that the *Booker T.* would probably operate in the European theater with New York as our home port, welcome news for me since I would be able to see my family.

The longshoremen began to load the ship that night and worked around the clock for three days. Nor did they pause when the holds were filled and the pontoons and hatch covers were in place ... *still* the cargo came aboard, more than 3,000 tons of it, lashed to the deck, up to the level of the bridge. Simultaneously we took on bunkers, stores, and supplies. The crew members began to plaster pictures of scantily-clad girls on the bulkheads, taunt the gun crew, and the night before departure, when I found several of them playing poker in the crew mess I knew the ship had really been "christened" at last.

On the afternoon of the 23rd of October, 1942, the longshoremen lashed down the last crate of deck cargo and began to clear the ship. There were to be no formal festivities, of course, since our departure was "secret." Well-wishers nevertheless came down to Wilmington Harbor from Los Angeles and a steady stream of telegrams arrived throughout the afternoon. Company representatives, War Shipping officials, Coast Guard personnel, harbor employees were all over the ship at one minute ... and the next they were gone. When the last guest disappeared down the gangway, the A.B.'s heaved it up and lashed it into place. The eight to twelve watch stood by on the fo'c'sle head, the twelve to four on the stern, and for the first time in my life I had the privilege of standing out on the wing and shouting, "Let go your spring!" I watched the A.B.'s fix the stoppers, as I had fixed them on so many previous occasions, heard the windlass whine as the spring line was hauled in and coiled just forward of number one hatch. Then the headlines, breast, and stern lines . . . the gap of water between the hull and dock widened and the tugs began to swing us around and point us toward the open sea. "Slow astern . . . stop the engines . . . slow ahead" . . . I felt self-conscious giving the commands, as if I should be following the orders instead of issuing them.

The *Booker T.* responded quickly to the telegraph and to the wheel; the bow came 'round, the tug lines fell away . . . "Half ahead" . . . and the big, triple-expansion reciprocating engine slowly began to mount to that rhythmical pounding I was to live with for so many hundreds of thousands of miles during the next six years. We dropped the pilot with a last "Good luck," and I rang down full speed ahead. The harbor began to fall away behind us, and with it the insults of hundreds of company clerks and sneering port captains, the memory of every savage racial slur. At last I was master of my own ship, with forty-two fine sailors under me, 10,000 tons of cargo entrusted to my command and a friendly port ten days over the horizon. What sweeter triumph could a man wish for himself, his race, and his country?

12

As luck would have it, we cleared Wilmington Harbor to run straight into a heavy fog. I remained on the bridge all night and though I am a congenital optimist I couldn't help visualizing the headlines if the *Booker T.* hit another ship in its first few hours at sea! Fog is the sailor's worst enemy; far more ships fall victim to it than to high seas, even with radar; then too new an instrument to grace the *Booker T.'s* bridge. All we could do was to keep our whistle going, alert the lookouts and keep a sharp ear for another ship. I didn't have a second's peace until noon the next day when we broke into a bright sea and I was able to work out our position. As soon as our course was plotted and everything topside was shipshape I sent for the ship's delegate, Harry Alexander, and notified him we would hold a meeting of the crew on number four hatch at two o'clock.

During the war thousands of unlicensed sailors sat for their tickets and subsequently sailed as masters, mates or engineers. This led to some interesting situations, for here were men who, like myself, had been founders of the union back in the '30's and were now "company representatives" aboard ships. Several were even former officials of the union. At the same time, however, most of those sailing below were raw recruits fresh out of high school, without any idea what conditions on the waterfront had been just seven years before. Thus, the traditional roles of officers and sailors were often reversed. The officers, who might very well be sailing below decks again when the war was over, were often most interested in preserving and improving the union's contract, while many of the sailors, "in" only for the "duration," had no vested interest in union conditions. Consequently, it was not uncommon for captains, mates, and engineers to hold shipboard educational meetings for the crew members and even, when necessary, prefer charges against them in their own union!

While I may not have been the first master to call a union meeting aboard ship no one ever called one *faster* or took a greater *delight* in doing so. The crew knew as well as I did that the eyes of millions of friends and enemies, many in high stations, were upon the ship – not only Americans, but eyes of dark-skinned and under-privileged people throughout the world. Our detractors, including some in Congress, were eagerly awaiting an "incident" to prove that the "experiment" could not work. I reminded the men that we must avoid provocations, for even the most trivial event might make the front pages back home, especially – particularly in Atlanta, Memphis, and Mobile.

The sailors knew, of course, that I was a charter member of the NMU, and that my door would always be open to their elected delegates. At the same time I explained that there were special obligations that devolved upon me which they must appreciate; while we might not always see eye to eye we must all try to be fair. I promised to be as liberal as I could insofar as port watches, time off ashore, draws, etc., were concerned, and they should establish their own union discipline to handle malingerers and gas hounds.

Harry Alexander, the chunky deck engineer and union delegate, responded on behalf of the crew and promised its full cooperation. Our meeting was one of the shortest and most amiable on record. Virtually from that moment on the *Booker T. Washington,* due to the extraordinary unity and cooperation between licensed and unlicensed personnel, became one of the most smoothly operating vessels afloat.

Our run down to Panama was uneventful save for one incident which indicated that the WSA still had some misgivings about my capacities as master. Admiral Land or one of his colleagues, apparently finding it impossible to believe that a colored skipper could find his way into so tiny a port as Balboa unassisted, sent out an "escort" to guide us. Six days out of Wilmington we noted a big four-engine plane gliding over us, circling, and finally heading off toward Mexico. In Panama we learned that it had been dispatched to determine whether we were on our course and if not to guide us to our destination!

What an unexpected surprise to find a cheering throng of Panamanians gathered at the dock gates when we tied up. It was a demonstration that reminded me of the reception accorded the *Yarmouth* back in 1920. Newspapermen, government officials, and dignitaries flocked aboard, and that evening, at a reception arranged for the crew, a local editor, Mr. G. W. Westerman, gave us a thick packet of fan mail from local well-wishers. It turned out that the population had been looking forward to our arrival from the time we left Los Angeles, and that the local press had run almost daily articles about us – all this when the movement of war vessels was supposed to be a guarded secret!

Anxious as we were to avoid incidents, our first took place in Panama City with men of the United States Navy.

While almost all old-time sailors frowned upon the use of uniforms, considering it a symbol of military control, wearing one was a matter of individual conscience. Many of the younger seamen preferred them, and Jessie Brooks, our young third officer, had outfitted himself in a resplendent white outfit appropriate to his rank. Returning from the city one night he was accosted by several Navy men, who remarked, "Where did *you* become an ensign, *nigger?*" Jessie was rough and quick-tempered and a few taunts were all he needed to set him off. A lot of punches were thrown before the police intervened; a few reports were exchanged and that was that.

We discharged cargo in Balboa, and had the ship "depermed," her steel hull demagnetized to ward off mines, and on December 4th anchored in the harbor. At a brief conference that afternoon I learned we were to proceed to Guantanamo Bay, Cuba, in convoy. We sailed in the evening with five other vessels and an escort of three destroyers, for German submarines were very active in the Caribbean at the time.

Guantanamo proved to be merely a staging area; our destination was Antilla on the northern coast for a cargo of sugar for New York. There had been speculation that we would pick up cargo in Guantanamo for the European theater or the Persian Gulf, and of course no tears were shed when it was learned that whatever our ultimate destination we would have a few weeks ashore – including Christmas – first. The trip around the eastern tip of Cuba was not difficult, but when we learned that five other vessels had been sunk in the previous seven days we took all possible precautions as our escort had left us at Guantanamo and we had to sail alone. I ordered a fire and boat drill before we left the Bay, and hugged the shoreline closely all the way with lights out, portholes sealed, and a vigilant watch. We put in at Antilla at 12:48 the following day – December 7, 1942. I had no time to note the significance of the date until Cuban officials had left the ship, and we were secure alongside the dock.

Antilla was a Cuban port of about 15,000 inhabitants, more than 60 per cent of whom were employed on the big sugar estates. The largest single employer was United Fruit Company, which owned not only several plantations but also its own mills, and ran Antilla very much like a feudal fief. Most of the village houses were owned by United Fruit, which rented them to the workers for $15 per month. This seemed reasonable enough, until you learned that the workers were paid $15 per week and worked only six months a year. Their rent was thus about one-half their annual income. Most of the balance was spent at company-owned commissaries, and usually all a worker had to show for his six months' wages was a clean slate at the commissary, entitling him to credit so he would not starve until the next crop came in. The workers were mostly colored people who had migrated to Cuba from Haiti and Jamaica.

It was in Antilla, at the United Fruit Company's commissary bar, that our second "incident" took place. The first evening ashore Bill Shepard, an A.B.; Ted Young and Louis Albi, cadets; and William Barker, our purser; wound up a gay evening at the commissary. Albi and Young were white and the other two colored. They sat down at a table, ordered *cerveza* and were engaged in the seamen's favorite topic when a well-dressed, semi-intoxicated American approached. Standing behind Albi's chair he looked directly at Young and said, "Say, young fellow, aren't you ashamed to be sitting at this table drinking with niggers?"

Young was startled and weighed my injunction to avoid fights. He rose to his feet and was saying, "Say that again," while Barker was exclaiming "I resent that!" But Shepard, a former professional fighter and not one for conversation, moved in swiftly, with one punch knocked the heckler to the deck, where he lay unconscious, blood streaming from his mouth. In the turmoil that followed the boys slipped out of the bar and returned to the ship. Later we learned that the man's nose and jaw were broken.

Next day the news was all over Antilla that the vice-president of United Fruit had been found unconscious in the street near the commissary. The official story was that he had been kicked by a horse. The whole affair was hushed up, and nothing more was heard of it.

When we finished loading on the afternoon of the 15th I went to the United Fruit office, for the company was also agent for the vessel, to arrange our departure. After our business was cleared away my host asked if I would like to meet the other executives of the company, and of course I said yes. We set out on a tour of the offices and I was finally introduced to a young man with a terribly swollen head, swathed in bandages. He had, I was told, been "kicked by a horse." The young vice-president extended his hand and averted his eyes. "I am very sorry to hear of your accident," I told him, "were you unkind to the horse?"

We left Antilla at 9:15 that evening and steamed through Crooked Island Passage, again observing maximum security precautions. Portholes were dogged down tight, lifeboats were swung out on the davits, and radio silence was unbroken. Except for a brisk northwester the third day out, which slowed us to five knots, the trip was uneventful and the morning of the 23rd we stood off Ambrose Lightship waiting to take on a pilot. As he came into the wheelhouse he extended his hand and it was the first inkling we had of the reception awaiting us in New York. "Congratulations, captain," he said, "all the New York papers are writing about you today."

"Well, that's fine, thank you," I replied, "what're they saying?"

"Most of 'em are saying how good it is that America finally has a colored ship."

"*What?*"

"Well, you know," he said uneasily, "I mean the fact that you have an all-colored crew . . ."

"But we *don't* have an all-colored crew," I told him. "Look around you . . . look at the wheelsman . . . look at the cadets. We have eighteen different nationalities aboard, and men from thirteen different states. This is a mixed crew like every other crew."

Of course the most casual glance around convinced him I was right. "Well, to read the papers anybody'd think it was an all-colored ship. Anyway, I know it'll be a great success."

When we reached quarantine the doctors and immigration officers were also very friendly, but the real surprise came when we moved into our berth at the foot of 39th Street, Brooklyn. Hundreds of enthusiastic well-wishers had come from all over New York to welcome the ship, shouting and waving little American flags as we tied up. Luckenbach officials were out in full force, and had brought along nearly the whole office staff. Even the longshoremen from "Tough Tony" Anastasia's local were cordial – many came to the bridge to tell me how pleased they were that I'd finally received a command. The New York papers carried lengthy stories about our arrival, and for once union men were praised rather than condemned. All in all I felt like the skipper of the *Queen Mary.*

The next thirteen days, while we discharged and loaded cargo, were among the busiest of my lifetime. Nearly every evening was taken up with receptions, banquets, and parties. It seemed impossible for us to refuse any of these invitations, for almost every one was a "command" affair sponsored by various government agencies, the shipping industry, the union, or close personal friends, including Steve Kingston and Malcolm Martin who had played such important roles in winning my assignment. The festivities, indeed, began the night of our arrival. I had expected to spend a quiet evening with my family, but when I arrived at our apartment at about 9 p.m. every room was jammed with guests and more were arriving by the minute. Jubilant friends were still dancing and singing at four o'clock in the morning. Finally the last one left, and Marie advised me it was time to begin making the pudding for Christmas dinner!

Of course I sought to pull rank. "Do you think, now that I'm a captain, I should still have to prepare the Christmas pudding?" I said sternly. "Do you suppose Eleanor makes Franklin D. prepare plum pudding for Christmas every year?"

"When you become the first colored *President*," was the answer, "we'll reconsider. Now get in the kitchen!"

The biggest affair of our stay in New York was a banquet sponsored by the Greater New York Industrial Council, representing all the CIO unions, held at the Hotel Commodore. More than 1,200 people attended, including representatives from the government, the shipping industry and the unions. Administration leaders included Rep. Joseph Clark Baldwin, Elmer Henderson, Secretary of Labor Anna Rosenberg, Craig Vincent of the WSA, and others. Port Captain Francis V. Lowden and Luckenbach's general manager, Mr. H. M. Singleton, represented the company. Frank J. Taylor appeared on behalf of the American Merchant Marine Institute, trade association for the shipping companies. Joseph Curran, Ferdinand Smith, and dozens of other officials and members came from the NMU, Allen Haywood and Saul Mills from the CIO, Mike Quill, Joe Selly, and other presidents of unions from their respective associations. Paul Robeson, Langston Hughes, and Congressman Adam Clayton Powell gave brief and touching testimonials to the symbolism of the *Booker T.*, Chief Engineer Smith and Harry Alexander accepted the tribute of the guests on behalf of the crew, and Hazel Scott sang. President Roosevelt sent a message declaring that it was the firm policy of the United States government to encourage full participation of the entire citizenry in the defense program, regardless of race, creed or color.

Finally, of course, I was introduced and on behalf of the whole crew thanked the audience for its warm reception and pledged that we would realize the trust placed in us by the government and the people. Only a year earlier I had been pounding on locked doors, crying to deaf ears about the plight of colored seamen, trying to get a deck officer's job; and now here I was, the master of a Liberty ship and the CIO Council's guest of honor before 1,200 guests at one of New York's finest hotels!

After the banquet I went home and rose at five for a 6 a.m. meeting at the Luckenbach offices, and then to other meetings with the Coast Guard, WSA and the Navy. That afternoon I returned to sign on the crew and leave for another meeting at 17 Battery Place for a naval briefing attended by all masters, commodores, gunnery, and convoy officers who were to guide us on our journey. The conference lasted until 11:30 p.m., when we were suddenly advised that the convoy would leave at 1:30 a.m., just two hours later! A radio signal would be sent out, I was told, and the instant the operator received it we should prepare to let go lines. The meeting ended on a happy note, however, for a friend showed me a copy of the WSA inspector's report on the *Booker T.* when he had come aboard at the conclusion of Voyage Number 1. "The crew" read the report, "behaved excellently. There was no overstaying of shore leave, no missed watches, no fights or disputes, no complaints or 'beefs.' Each member donated a pint of blood for the war effort, pooled and divided his overtime equally, and said he intended to stay aboard as long as he was able." A good omen for Voyage No. 2 indeed!

There was no time to rush home to bid the family goodbye – a hurried phone call had to suffice, and I hopped into a cab for Brooklyn. But when I got out and walked through the cargo shed to the *Booker T.* my heart fell. In the time I had been away the longshoremen had loaded deck cargo almost to the level of the wheelhouse! I checked the draft fore and aft and searched for the Plimsoll mark* amidships – it was nowhere to be seen! The load line for winter in the North Atlantic was at least a foot under water, a condition dangerously affecting the stability of the ship.

I rushed aboard and called Adolphus. "What the devil have you let them do?" I charged. "Our load line is a full foot under water!" And this was a winter crossing of the North Atlantic! Adolphus, as I might have guessed, replied that there was nothing he had been able to do – when he had protested, the Army insisted it was in charge, and loaded the ship as heavily as it pleased.

In peacetime there would have been no question of what to do; I would have refused to sail the ship, and so would the crew, until a sufficient amount of deck cargo had been removed to bring up our mark. But under conditions of war, even though the *Booker T.* was technically assigned to Luckenbach, there was no question that the WSA was the real operator, and was responsible, ultimately, to the Army.

Before I could get in touch with the Army, however,

---

* Show symbol – The depth to which a vessel can be safely loaded for various seas at different times of the year.

our signal for departure came. The pilot was aboard, the booms were topped, the crew was standing by; there was nothing to do but let go lines, make an emphatic note in the log, and slip quietly out of the harbor for our rendezvous off Scotland Light. As we dropped the pilot we could see the rest of the ships maneuvering for position, and found our place in the convoy without trouble. Sometime after 3 a.m. the order arrived that was to set this mass into motion, and the 100 ships began to move on their predetermined course and speed, a ghostly fleet in the night, laden with the materials of war for our allies.

With the CIO banquet, the activities of the preceding day and now our late departure I had had only a few hours rest in the past fifty hours. As soon as our position in the convoy was established and we were moving smoothly I told the third mate I was going to lie down for a few hours and to call me at once if anything seemed amiss. Then I went to my cabin and sprawled fully clothed across my bunk, dead to the world in seconds.

I woke to a gray and misty morning, with the vessels on the outer fringes of the convoy obscured by fog. The sea was light, our course almost due east. Every few hours the Commodore flashed a change in course or to accelerate a knot, and it was clear that we were going to dogleg our way across the Atlantic. I hoped the fog would not get worse as we approached the Gulf stream, for I had had only four hours sleep. And though it held off in the forenoon, around 1 p.m. it began to close in, and I spent the rest of the day on the bridge. By midnight it had lifted enough for me to feel safe in leaving when the third mate, Mr. DuPort, came on watch. I headed below for the first full night's rest I had had since we arrived in New York.

At 6:30 a.m. I was awakened to the familiar "Rise and shine," and there was the steward with a steaming cup of coffee. As I pulled on my bathrobe I went to the porthole, opened the "dogs," and rubbed my eyes in disbelief — though it was a clear morning there wasn't a ship in sight!

"Where the devil is the convoy?" I asked the steward, but before he could answer I rushed up the ladder to the bridge, where Clifton was on watch. "Where the devil is the convoy?" I shouted at him.

"What convoy?" he replied. "There wasn't any convoy when I relieved the third mate." I sent for Mr. Du-Port, the third officer, and he gave us a clue: the rest of the convoy, he reported, had just picked up and sailed out of sight! Sparks had not received any signal and so the *Booker T.* had just poked along. It was obvious what had happened, a speculation later confirmed in London. Somehow we had missed the Commodore's signal to increase speed and were now off course and a few hours behind the other ships. The rest of the convoy was now over the horizon. It was an embarrassing situation as well as dangerous. Here I had fought twenty-four years for a command and had lost my first convoy in just twenty-four hours!

The sun came out at 8:30 and we established our position. We were 41° 30′ N. and 67° 10′ W., just off George's Shoal, 240 miles from Halifax. I analyzed the courses open to us. First, we could "open her up" and try to catch the convoy which, since it would be doglegging, would be no easy matter. Second, we could take the "straggler's route" which would be given in my sealed orders, and sail directly to our destination; or third, we could head for Halifax and join a later convoy. The third course was undoubtedly the safest, and we set a course for this major staging point, arriving there the following afternoon. There I reported our plight to the American Consulate and the British Admiralty, and received instructions to stand by for three days to join the next convoy.

Halifax is one of the world's most unattractive ports in the middle of January. During the day the temperature climbs to fifteen or twenty degrees, and at night plummets to ten below zero. Water brakers in the life boats froze and split open, the runners and guy lines were coated with ice, and it was hazardous even to walk out on deck. We had to idle the winches day and night to keep them from freezing solid. It was so cold none of the crew members even wanted to go ashore.

Four other ships had also lost the convoy and, like us, had sought the safety of Halifax. On the fifth day we were called to a naval conference and early in the afternoon steamed out of port under escort to join a 120-vessel convoy twenty-two miles out. It was the largest flotilla I had ever seen in my life, stretching literally from horizon to horizon. Our position was at the end of line fourteen, toward the center of the fleet, and we examined our neighbors with pleasure to starboard and to port with dismay. Off our starboard side was the hospital ship, the *St. Ives,* carrying a sizable complement of doctors, nurses, and plenty of drugs and life saving equipment. Her job, depending upon the circumstances, would be to pick up survivors in case of a torpedoing and we felt a little safer with her so near. But to port was a large tanker, probably loaded with high octane gasoline for the fighters over London . . . if *she* caught a "fish" she would disappear in seconds.

Our course was East-North-East true – 67°, our speed nine knots. The sea was moderate, the wind westerly at six miles an hour and the barometer steady at 30.01. It looked like an uneventful night, and after supper we sat around the saloon talking, as seamen do. But along about 8 p.m. the ship began to roll, and I went to the bridge. The wind had swung around to the northeast and increased in velocity, the barometer had fallen to 29.35, and we began to suspect we were in for some rough weather.

A normally rough sea is no problem for a modern steamship. You can always reduce speed and if necessary change course to run with the sea, reducing the hazard. But sailing in convoy during the war was a different matter. First, we were heavily overloaded; second we could not reduce speed without permission from the Commodore, and third we obviously could not, except under the most extreme circumstances, depart from the convoy to run with the storm.

By midnight the barometer had fallen to 29.01, and the *Booker T.* began to wallow heavily. Nine knots was clearly too much for the overloaded ship, and I cursed the fates that had put us in such an impossible position. Hour after hour we battled the ever-increasing waves, wondering how long the huge crates on deck, exposed to the storm, could take such punishment. Then, at about 3:30 a.m. a heavy beam wave smashed us; we rolled heavily to starboard and back to port, and several of the big crates snapped their lashing and slipped to the port gunwales. The ship would not come back, and we carried, from that moment on, a six-degree list, with the port side regularly awash.

Dawn finally broke, and at 7:30 I flashed the Commodore an urgent request, explaining our difficulty and asking him to reduce the convoy speed two knots. He could not comply, he answered; we were being trailed by submarines and any ship that fell behind was likely to be sunk.

The reply was like a death sentence, but we determined to do the best we could. The important thing was the deck cargo. All lashings were already loosened by the rolling and pitching of the ship. We strung lifelines fore and aft, and throughout the day the deck force crept among the crates, tightening turnbuckles and shoring in here and there. All booms were topped and there could be no thought, in such weather, of trying to shift the bigger crates. The North Atlantic was becoming more tumultuous by the hour, and I found myself hoping that Pete Ross and his colleagues back in Wilmington had done a conscientious job. We could barely maintain our position in the convoy; the port gunwales were often underwater, and the wheelsmen had difficulty holding the ship on course.

Darkness fell swiftly, early in the afternoon. By 5 p.m. we could no longer see the vessels in the adjacent columns. The wind increased to forty-five miles per hour and, combined with the savage thunder of the sea smashing the deck cargo, forced us to shout to be heard in the wheelhouse. Then suddenly the *Booker T.*, wallowing helplessly, was struck by a gigantic sea. A huge crate, covering nearly all of Number 3 hatch just forward of the deckhouse, slipped heavily to port, snapping the lashings and shearing the bolts that had secured it to the deck! The ship lurched heavily, two port lifeboats tore away, the port storm door was smashed and ripped from its sockets, and water poured through the portside of the vessel flooding the fo'c'sles and plunging into the engine room!

There was no question now of keeping up with the convoy — we couldn't if we tried; the main problem was to keep afloat. Frantically we threw up a makeshift storm door to keep the water, boiling over the gunwales with each roll to port, out of the deckhouse and the engine room. Hour after hour the storm grew in intensity, and as the deck cargo kept sliding the danger of our capsizing became imminent.

By midnight I was convinced that moving as we were there was little chance of surviving till morning, and finally gave the command everyone had been awaiting for hours. "Put her hard a-starboard, Mr. Lastic." The A.B. on watch put the wheel over swiftly, and for what seemed like an hour, we waited for the *Booker T.* to respond. Gradually her helm began to swing around, carrying us away from the gale. We had no radar, and of course could not see another vessel, and I had no way of knowing whether we were still in the convoy or had already fallen behind. In any case we slipped away toward the southeast, steadying on a course toward the Azores.

The storm continued throughout the night and the following day, but now, riding away from it, the vessel pitched rather than rolled, with the sea off the stern, and the deck cargo rode more easily. We reduced speed to seven knots, taking the sea as it came, and by dawn of the second day, though the sea was still rough and the sky overcast we knew we were sailing into clear water. At 8 a.m. I broke out the entire deck gang and for the next several days we sought to straighten out the mess on deck. The huge crates, many weighing several tons, had all shifted and jammed against each other. We broke out the jumbo boom, hauled them into place, and lashed them securely once more. The carpenter, Joe Ring, with plenty of time now, made new, secure storm doors. There was nothing we could do to replace the lifeboats which had been washed away, but the two on the starboard side, plus the rafts, were more than enough if trouble came.

We steamed southeast for three days and finally, 300 miles from the Azores, at latitude 41° 20′ N and 34° 20′ W longitude, dawn broke one morning bright and clear, over a calm sea. I opened our sealed orders to discover that our destination was Liverpool. Shortly before noon I called Mr. Smith, the chief engineer, and told him to get ready to give her all she had, that we were going to run northeast as fast as we could. We stationed lookouts fore and aft, on the bridge and in the crow's nest, to keep a sharp eye for telltale periscopes, and at noon swung around and headed for the North Irish Channel.

From that point on our voyage was completely uneventful. Despite our heavy cargo we made as much as thirteen knots in the smooth sea, making 1,370 miles in five days, though of course the ship was lightened by our oil and water consumption. Eleven days out of Halifax we entered the channel, and I broke radio silence to wire for orders. Three hours later we came within sight of Liverpool light vessel and London replied, ordering us to Belfast. We were already far past Belfast Lough Grey Point, so we had to put back.

Our first intimation that we had done very well indeed came from the small guard boat at the entrance to Belfast

Harbor, which hailed us as we steamed in. "What ship?" We supplied the information, and then were asked, "What convoy?" We replied again and explained that we had lost our convoy. "You're all right," came the reply, "proceed . . . your convoy is behind you." Our pilot later confirmed this intelligence; our convoy had had trouble all the way across. Several ships had been lost and the others had had to steam several hundred miles off course to evade submarines.

There were many times during the war, as every sailor or GI knows, when you were so busy just staying alive that you lost any awareness of the significance of your actions. When we reached Belfast we were so happy to be safe in port that we couldn't have cared less about the cargo we were carrying – we'd fought the sea to save our ship and lives, not the crates on deck. But we felt a little guilty for cursing the Army for overloading us so dangerously when we discovered that we had delivered seventy-five fighter planes to the British. Bombs were, at this time, raining on London nightly, and the Royal Air Force was desperately short of planes and ammunition to stem the attack – so short indeed that a runway had been set up near the Belfast docks and the planes were assembled and flown away a few days after they were discharged. It was possible to imagine that some of the planes we delivered were in the air and shooting down Messerschmitts forty-eight hours later.

On our third day in Belfast orders came to proceed to Cardiff, South Wales, to discharge our general cargo, and at 10 a.m. in the morning, sailing out the bay, we met part of our convoy coming up! Passing the Commodore I signaled, "Glad to see you!" He replied, "We thought you were sunk." I answered, "Not yet" and received a parting "Good luck." Later we learned that the hospital ship *St. Ives* had been lost, as had the gasoline-laden tanker on our port side. The *Booker T.*, had we remained in convoy, would have been in the thick of the attack and, crippled as we were might have been lost right there. A Canadian corvette had also been torpedoed, and our side claimed two submarines.

January of 1943 was the turning point of the war. The relentless blows of the Red Army had smashed the German lines in the Ukraine and von Paulus, with some 300,000 troops, surrendered on the 31st. The Allied build-up in North Africa was proceeding apace, and though the second front was still some seventeen months away, the invasion of Italy was clearly on the agenda. The British people, long suffering and fighting virtually alone for so long, had begun to sense victory, and were wildly appreciative of all aid. Even under these circumstances we were unprepared for the welcome accorded us at Cardiff. Our arrival must have been one of the worst kept secrets of the war. As we pulled into the dock we heard happy cries, "Welcome *Booker T. Washington!* Welcome to England, Captain Mulzac!" Waiting for us were forty or more colored Red Cross girls from London, Bristol, Liverpool, and Southampton, plus a squad of reporters, photographers, and Admiralty dignitaries. Everyone was invited aboard for a party that rocked the waterfront.

The following day there were page-one stories and complete photographic coverage in all the Cardiff papers, and the dock workers and townspeople seemed to have no other topic than our arrival.

The high point of the reception was a visit the second day from the Lord Mayor of Cardiff and four Admirals of the British Navy. I conducted them on a tour of the ship, showing them the damage sustained in the storm, and later we had lunch in the saloon. It was interesting that the Britishers considered me a *landsman,* and questioned me about Union Island and my earlier trips to the British Isles. We had a warm and friendly visit, which compensated for our disappointment in the fact that not a single American representative, except the Red Cross girls, ever made an appearance.

Notwithstanding the cordiality of the Admirals I received a rude shock the following day when I was notified that there was to be a formal inquiry into my reasons for having left the convoy. For several hours I was subjected to a most intense cross-examination. "What were the exact conditions of the ship and of the sea at the moment I had decided to change course? Did I know that the *St. Ives* and the tanker on my left had been sunk? How did I justify slipping away when the Commodore had specifically ordered me not to?"

I explained my position as fully as I could, declaring that the alternative had been, in my opinion, to founder with an overloaded ship. Finally the inquiry was ended, and the Admirals said, "We congratulate you on your judgment in leaving the convoy and bringing your vessel safely into port three days ahead of the convoy." What was unstated, but was equally acknowledged by all I'm sure, was that we had also been extremely lucky. If many ships had dispersed we would all have been sitting ducks for the U-boats. Proceeding alone, with the subs concentrating on the convoy, the *Booker T.* had been able to sail for ten days without detection.

A few days after our arrival someone noticed that several Cardiff theaters were advertising a newsreel on the *Booker T.* and several of us decided to go. We chose a theater on Beaut Road and arrived well ahead of time only to find a long queue stretching from the box office, around a corner and down a full half block. Naturally we took positions at the end of the line, but had overlooked one thing: we were in uniform. The first to identify us was a little six-year-old boy, who, pointing at me, said to his mother, *"Isn't that him? Isn't that him?"* Those near us turned and before long the line had broken and a throng had gathered around. The news must have passed up the line, for within a few moments the manager of the theater appeared and said, "Sir, you don't have to stand in line! And you don't have to pay, either. Come with me!"

Come we did, and were escorted through the foyer to the best seats in the house. Throughout the show there were more eyes on us than on the screen, though the films were excellent. There were scenes of the crew eating in the messroom, the cooks in the galley, and a lifeboat drill which we had staged for the occasion. There were fine closeups of the Lord Mayor and myself in the saloon and with the Admiralty visitors on the bridge. The films were widely shown throughout the Commonwealth. Wherever I went in later years people would exclaim, "Oh yes, I saw you in the newsreels years ago."

Our weeks in Cardiff while we discharged and loaded were one of those welcome respites from the war that, because they are so rare, are especially memorable. I suppose this is particularly true because of our battle with the North Atlantic on the way over. Many soldiers enjoying brief furloughs from the front have commented that life never seemed more beautiful. Their senses are sharpened by the horror they've seen, the noise and turmoil of battle and the constant fear that the next shell might have your name on it.

Our feeling was similar, although less acute. We were never worn down by the daily grind to which GI's were subjected – sloughing through snow and mud to capture a point, constant exposure to bombing and mortar fire, inadequate rations and sleep and rigorous discipline. After all, however difficult our battles, once they were over you could take a hot shower, eat a good meal and enjoy a sunbath on deck. The snow never looked lovelier, the firesides of the townspeople, to whose homes we were invited, were never mellower, or human companionship so dear.

There were, of course, a few "incidents," continuing the pattern of Panama and Cuba. Like the Panamanians and Cubans, the British were effusively friendly and grateful, but there is no warmth too great for a Southern American to chill. The occasion arrived with an invitation to speak at an American Red Cross luncheon. Of course I accepted, and at the appointed time presented myself at the head-quarters. "I beg your pardon," said a voice at my side, "but where are you going?"

I turned to see a rather pretty but agitated girl in uniform hovering between me and the doorway to the lounge as if one more step would bring catastrophe upon us all. I explained that I had been invited to a luncheon, and was simply wondering where the room was. "Oh, well," said the little Southerner with obvious relief, "*you* must want *Miss Ward's* section. That's down the street. This is the white section . . . you understand."

I understood . . . and understood too well her nervous skittering about, agitated expression and excessive politeness. I thanked her and turned to go, but at the door turned around and said "I am on a ship that has just brought seventy-five fighter planes for the defense of England. No one cared about our color when they asked us to bring these planes over, but the Red Cross cares about color when it comes to a luncheon, doesn't it?"

"I'm sorry, sir . . . it's the policy."

"It's the policy." What wrongs such glib phrases conceal! It's a way of saying, "I let others do my thinking for me and they've thought up a policy." Some people, I'm sure, live through their entire lives following "policies" without the experience of one refreshing, independent thought! Does it ever occur to them that some policies are *good* and others *bad*, that the good should be supported, the bad changed?

The gulf between the pretty little Southerner and me could not be bridged by a protest, and I left. But at the luncheon at the jim-crow club of the Red Cross I made the subject my topic and the audience, mostly colored, understood very well.

Discharged at last we were ordered to Barry Docks across the Bay to load cargo. Two tugs helped us shift, for the Cardiff current is notoriously strong, and we breasted into a pier lined with the little narrow-gauge British railroad cars laden with freight. We were light and high out of the water, and looking down on our freight, I had a feeling that the crates were suspiciously familiar. I called Mr. Folks, the chief officer, and we went down to investigate. There was no question about it. This was the cargo we had just discharged across the Bay, right down to crew member's initials and a big *"Booker T. Washington"* carved on several crates. Such *snafus* of course, are not uncommon in a war.

Nor was this the only surprise: a message awaited me at the dock advising us to prepare to carry twenty-seven officers of an Army Engineering Battalion to our North Africa destination. Few orders startle a skipper more than the announcement that he is to carry extra passengers. Where were they to sleep and eat? I raised these questions with the appropriate authorities and a detail was assigned to build twenty-seven bunks in the 'tween decks. The new men were all colored radar experts who were being sent to man a new installation near Oran, and the first troops carried by the *Booker T.* In view of the fact that we were later to be asked to carry as many as 700 troops, this request turned out to be mild indeed.

We left Cardiff March 17, 1943, in a small convoy of twenty-five ships in weather that was beautifully cooperative. The enemy, however, was still there, and if we could escape his surveillance in the vast stretches of the Atlantic we could not as we drove down the Bay of Biscay to round the Spanish Peninsula. From the second we entered the Bay of Biscay until we reached Oran we were under surveillance: Nazi observation planes hovered in the distance daily, and their radio broadcasts described our progress, destination, and even the names of ships in the convoy. We girded for the attack, and three days out of Cardiff the first alarm was sounded.

The *Booker T.*, like all Liberty ships at this stage of the war, was equipped with eight 20 mm. anti-aircraft guns, one 5" 50 astern, in the middle of a huge "gun tub" built above the poop, and a three and one-half inch gun on the fo'c'sle head. The gun crew of twenty men, under the command of Lieutenant Curley, was supplemented by the entire merchant crew off watch. From the time we had left Wilmington we had had gun drills at least twice a week until the merchant crewmen were nearly as proficient at manning the guns as the armed guard.

Thus when the dozen bombers appeared out of the southeast – the direction of the Spanish mainland – we were well prepared and blazed away with everything we had. The bombers, however, sailed high above our curtain of flak – only the big guns could reach them, and we saw a British destroyer score a hit. The plane dove in a long, smoking spiral and the entire crew cheered as it smashed into the water and exploded, sending up a gigantic geyser. Almost immediately, however, one of the small British freighters in the convoy began to smoke too. A destroyer stayed with her as we sailed on and we learned later she was lost. Twenty minutes after the attack had begun the bombers headed back toward the southeast, and our only casualty was the tire of a truck on deck, torn away by a large piece of shrapnel. This was our only action of the trip, though observation planes kept us in sight daily.

Oran, our destination, was one of the largest French naval bases on the North African coast. In March of 1943 it had become a huge supply depot for the North African campaign and later, for the leap across the Mediterranean and the invasion of Italy. We put in on March 26th, my birthday, to find the harbor so jammed with ships that we had to lie in the stream for two days before a berth could be found for our muchhandled cargo. Yet there seemed to be two ships on the bottom for every one afloat. Charred wrecks poked above the water on every side, stark reminders of earlier battles. Many had been sunk during the Vichy reign by Allied bombers, and now Allied vessels were being sunk by the Fascists. Looking at the blackened skeletons, resting on the bottom in complete anonymity, all one could think of was the horror of war for *both* sides. Allied and Nazi bodies alike were decaying in the hulls, waiting for some grim accountant, years later, to pronounce them dead.

One of the vessels whose ensign was still flying high as we put into the harbor was the great British battleship H.M.S. *Nelson,* the 35,000-ton flagship of the British home fleet, nicknamed the "Cherry Tree" class because she had been "cut down by Washington." The allusion was to the 1931 London Treaty which had restricted her size to 35,000 tons when she had been designed as a 48,000-ton vessel. She was still a mighty ship to behold, with three 16-inch turrets forward and a massive deck structure of fire control and navigating platforms.

Shortly after we dropped anchor we were surprised to see a small boat put out from the *Nelson* and head in our direction. When it reached our gangway a voice sang out, "May I come aboard?" We welcomed the visitor, Mr. Desmond Tighe, Reuters special correspondent, who had been sent by the *Nelson's* Admiral, Commander George Blandell, to interview me. He presented me with a handsome portfolio of British warships and a friendly note from the Admiral. It was a gracious gesture, and Mr. Tighe and I spent an hour together.

Nor was Mr. Tighe our only visitor. Shortly after he left another launch put alongside. It contained a delegation from the Red Cross – colored, of course – including Evelyn Vaughan of New York, Geneivra Howard of Washington, D.C., and Raymond Miller and Roy Credelle of Chicago. All were familiar with the *Booker T.'s* story and welcomed me and the entire crew to the port and to the use of their facilities.

March 29th we were ordered to a berth and began discharging. Day and night Oran was a beehive of activity. Ships were discharged around the clock, trucks and railroad cars moving the mountains of cargo out to supply depots, building up the vast store of weapons, ammunition and supplies that were needed to support the imminent invasion. *How* imminent, of course, we didn't know, though it was broadly hinted that midsummer would see Allied troops in Italy. Liberties, Victories, tankers, and rusty freighters poured into the harbor daily for the massive buildup. The *Booker T.* was but a tiny part of the vast military machine that was throwing hundreds of thousands of men, millions of tons of material, into the gigantic maw of war.

Evenings we went ashore, to an Army movie, the native markets, and on weekends embarked on sightseeing expeditions. We usually wound up our shoreside excursions at the "jim-crow" Red Cross facilities on the edge of town where, it was no secret, the best food and jazz were provided. It gave us satisfaction that while we were not admitted to the "white" club white GI's were welcomed at the jim-crow club, and there were many evenings when there were as many white GI's as colored present, singing, dancing, and talking in perfect harmony.

On April 9 our stay came to an end. Early in the morning I was summoned to the Port Commandant's office and advised that the *Booker T.* was being returned to the United States for more supplies. The crew, keyed for battle, was disappointed, but after all, who could object to being sent home? We left the same day in a small convoy, to a signal honor: the *Nelson* had learned that we were leaving port and as we drew abreast saluted us with a salvo of rockets and small arms fire! It was a fine tribute for so magnificent a battleship to pay a little Liberty, and we acknowledged it the only way we could – with ten parting blasts of our whistle.

The convoy was gathering as we got outside, deploying in the sparkling sunlight on an unimaginably blue sea, and I wondered if 2,000 years earlier some Roman admiral had not stood on the bridge of his galleon, deploying for an attack upon Carthage, just a few hundred miles East, or some North African city-state. War, war, *war!* Would mankind never learn to solve its antagonisms peacefully? It seemed such a contradiction that thousands of ships and millions of men could be ordered into vast attacks, but that we could not mobilize the same resources for peace, or even mobilize all of society's resources in the fight against such patently absurd and obsolete customs as racial discrimination!

The convoy gradually gathered and at a radio signal I ordered "half speed ahead." The *Booker T.* responded, and we moved slowly ahead, setting our pace to that of the ships around us, toward the Strait. We passed Gibraltar, that monolithic symbol of Allied power, during the night and reached the sea. The following day the convoy divided, half breaking off to the North for another load of supplies from Liverpool, Cardiff, and Southampton, the rest of us pointing our bows into the great circle route for home. On April 20th we stood off Newport News safe and sound, our second mission completed.

13

By May of '43 the Allied attack on the "soft underbelly" of Europe was almost ready. Enemy troops had been cleared from North Africa on the 15th, and the massive buildup of Allied power had been proceeding for months. The Russians had reconsolidated following the great Stalingrad victory and were preparing the gigantic offensive which was to sweep them across Europe to the banks of the Oder by February of 1945. It was widely supposed that the Allied offensive from the South would begin at about the same time, and enemy troops would then be engaged from Leningrad to Sicily, with British-based bombers attacking the Nazi heartland nightly.

The *Booker T.'s* role in this vast plan was a tiny one, but many such small efforts merged into the big thrust. We slipped out of Newport News on May 9th for an uneventful run to Casablanca. Uneventful, that is, except for a shipboard tragedy that depressed everyone – the sudden collapse at sea of our steward, William Bradshaw. For two days we had signaled his symptoms to the nearest escort vessel, begging for medical advice, always receiving the same reply: "Administer sedatives. Absolute bedrest."

But neither sedatives nor rest could save Bill. A life of militant trade union and anti-fascist activity demanded payment. Bill was one of the NMU'ers who was having his second go at Hitler. For two years he had served on a Loyalist blockade runner delivering ammunition to the embattled citizens of Barcelona; on one occasion he helped carry out the bodies of 500 children killed in a school that was hit by a fascist bomb. When the call for merchant seamen went out early in the war he closed his Harlem restaurant, and was torpedoed on the Murmansk run. This was his first trip on the *Booker T.*, and his last. Late one afternoon he leapt out of his bunk in a spasm of intolerable pain and collapsed. The escort vessel came alongside after he was dead, and the young Navy doctor's verdict was swift: "acute coronary thrombosis." We were only a few days out of Casablanca, and buried him there in a wooden box made by Chips, the ship's carpenter, covered with an American flag. The Army provided two trucks to drive us all out to the cemetery. "At least," one of the crewmen observed, standing on African soil, "he's home."

Casablanca was bustling with rumors. The invasion was expected at any moment. And so it was, but again there was no cargo for the *Booker T*. We were sent home again, and were barely at sea when news came of the capture of Pantalleria on June 11.

Gradually the ship settled into a "milk run" from the east coast of the United States to Algeria, Casablanca, and Oran. Shipboard life drifted into a routine, voyages began to merge one into another, and Oran became our second home. We returned in July when the invasion of Sicily was fully under way. Mussolini was driven from power on the 25th, escaping north to join his Nazi partner. Again we hoped we would be assigned to the trouble zones, but again we were thwarted. The *Booker T.* was just a number on the long assignment sheets, and we were ticked off for a return trip. We were back in New York when the invasion began.

If in its first trips the *Booker T. Washington* was not distinguished by any heroic engagements or unusual assignments, our missions were satisfying for quite a different reason — the activities we had begun to adopt on board and the exceptional competence of our crews in their work, talents, and political acuity.

It is understandable that for the first few trips I was not without certain apprehensions. However much one may *think* he knows, the real test of knowledge comes in the *performance* of a job and not in achieving a mere technical mastery of it. Though I had won my master's license many years earlier, and for two decades of sailing as cook or steward had always considered myself a captain, the fact remained that I had yet to serve as one. Therefore, while I approached my new job with considerable confidence, I was subject to certain pressures that a white skipper didn't have. Suppose some reactionary sailor took a job on the ship just to get material for the kind of "exposé" that columnists like Victor Riesel or Westbrook Pegler like to print? Suppose, as occasionally happens (even to white captains) we were driven on the rocks in a gale? The slightest incident would be magnified many times over, and I had to be especially sharp and cautious.

Gradually these apprehensions proved groundless. All the books and experience I had absorbed over the years were at my command. I could get a ship into or away from the dock in a swift stream, or without tugs, as well as any man and better than most of those, certainly, who also received their first commands during the war. I could take all the necessary steps to secure the vessel, its cargo and crew under perilous conditions, protect the owners' inter-

187

ests in shoreside dealings, and navigate with the best. But even beyond all these essential abilities of a master I discovered one advantage most of the others lacked. Because I had sailed for so long as a member of the unlicensed personnel I shared the crew's point of view, and was able to command their respect and cooperation.

This is no mean feat, for despite their occasional joint ventures – particularly when their contracts with the shipowners expire – the antagonism between the licensed and unlicensed personnel is traditional. Like foremen in shoreside plants licensed officers invariably get in trouble with crews. Every old-timer, while he may be understandably reluctant to discuss such matters publicly, learned long ago how to deal with such men. Back in the old days we'd pull a slow down . . . it was amazing how little work could be performed by a united crew! On other occasions just before the ship was to sail we would "sit her down" for fresh milk, white linen, or artichokes. Sometimes the battle would continue at sea . . . every single tool aboard ship, for example, would magically "disappear" (over the side) during the night, or the firemen or oilers could turn on the steam in a hold loaded with perishable cargo. Sometimes the treatment was frivolous – a snake, lizard, or good rank flying fish would be found in the hated officer's bunk. Sometimes it was more severe – log books are full of entries recording that the chief mate or second assistant engineer "failed to return from shore" and a replacement was signed on. It was also the easiest thing in the world for a cook to doctor a dish and give a victim several uncomfortable days – and a lesson in crew relations.

During many years of sailing as cook or A. B. I had served under many a cruel and tyrannical master; therefore next to my basic responsibility to guarantee the safety of the ship, cargo and crew, my deepest concern was to run a "smooth" ship. And that's one aspect of the *Booker T.'s* operation which constitutes a proud page in maritime annals. To accomplish this it was essential that men understand as fully as possible the significance of their actions, that they be allowed to participate as fully as possible in decision-making, and that they always be treated fairly.

There was always a solid corps of veterans aboard to teach the younger men not only the rudiments of work in the various departments, but to explain the character of the war as well. Many of the old-timers understood Fascism from direct experience. Not only had we put into many fascist ports before the war, but hundreds of NMU members had fought with the Loyalist armies in Spain just a few years earlier. We were familiar with Soviet Russia's aid to the Spanish Republic contrasted with the Allied boycott, and had longed for the day when England, France, the United States, and Russia would join in an all-out effort to smash the Fascists once and for all. If in the last analysis morale is a function of understanding, our morale was high because of our deep understanding of Fascism and our total dedication to victory. As part of this purpose we were united to smash Jim Crow.

There are those today, as there were during the war, who do not understand the coincidence of these purposes, who supposed the war could be won by minor concessions to colored people to win their allegiance. We had a different victory in mind on the *Booker T*. We saw each step toward full integration uniting broader and broader strata of the people, not only toward victory over Hitler but toward a victorious peace as well. We understood that only a *just peace* that gave freedom to the oppressed of the world could make the war fully meaningful.

Today, seventeen years after the war has ended, there can be little doubt that this is the victory that was won. In 1945, when the founding meeting of the United Nations was held in San Francisco only fifty-one countries were admitted to membership. Today the roster is one hundred and ten, a large number of the late members sovereign countries which were colonies at the end of the war. Nearly one and one-half *billion* people have won their independence since 1945, and fewer than 150 million, barely six percent of the world's population, still live in colonial bondage! *This* is the victory for which we were fighting on the *Booker T.* That's why Jim Crow has never been as thoroughly vanquished as he was on the *Booker T. Washington!* Throughout the war we were a proud, floating bastion of racial amity – at least at sea. In port we found "Jim" happily going about his business and though we lost many a battle with him it can be said we never ducked a struggle.

While our understanding of the nature of the war and dedication to defeat fascism and Jim Crow constituted the morale basis of the *Booker T.,* there was also the indispensable element: a concrete program.

We understood that a people's war demanded the overcoming of those artificial barriers that divide mankind, and that the first of these barriers is racial discrimination. Thus we set out to train the untrained, educate the cynical and weak, win over the bigots, and consciously to weld sailors of diverse backgrounds into a united crew. I think it can be said, and I hope truthfully, that there was no seaman so meager in his intellectual resources, so stripped of confidence and hope, so responsive only to his own private ambitions, that he was not to some degree uplifted by his experience aboard our ship.

How, specifically, was this accomplished?

I had long ago decided that if I ever received command of a merchant vessel the first thing I would do would be to establish an upgrading program for the men on the ship. True, there were schools ashore – Sheepshead Bay for raw recruits and the officer's training school at Kings Point, both near New York. But most merchant crewmen were beyond the former and unable to qualify for the latter.

The lowest ratings on a ship are wipers in the engine department, ordinary seamen on deck, and messmen, scullions, and bedroom stewards in the steward's department.

Wipers, when they have enough sea time, can take their examinations as firemen-watertenders or oilers, and then as junior engineers, deck engineers, electricians, refrigeration engineers, third, second, first assistants and chief engineers. Ordinary seamen can, after three years of sailing time (six months during the war) qualify as able seamen, and then sail as bo'suns, carpenters, and quartermasters until they have enough sea time to take their third mate's examinations. In the steward's department the promotions are to the galley – third cook, second, and chief until an examination as steward is taken.

During the war it was a common practice to waive endorsements and simply promote a wiper to oiler when none was available. On some ships, for example, the entire deck force could be composed of ordinary seamen, and I have heard of ships being taken out when not a single member of the deck force had ever been to sea before! The New Orleans longshoremen had to top her booms, and the Britishers lower them on the other side.

There was no opportunity on Voyage No. 1 from Pedro to New York, to put our upgrading program into effect, nor, of course, during the hectic Atlantic crossing and subsequent stay in Cardiff. But in Oran, where we were temporarily restricted to the ship, we finally devoted a ship's meeting to the subject and discussed the pros and cons. Seven subjects, it was finally decided, would be taught: mathematics, by myself; radio, by "Sparks"; cooking and baking by the steward (though it was difficult for him to refuse to allow me to show off from time to time); engineering by members of the engine room staff; hygiene and first aid by the purser; seamanship, by the deck officers; and finally, "upgrading" in a somewhat different sense, a course in trade unionism and world events by the deck engineer and ship's delegate, Harry Alexander.

"Chips" Reed had the honor of constructing our "classroom" in the 'tween decks, a handsome little private school complete with blackboards, benches, and desks folding down from the bulkheads. We decorated the room with banners, posters, and maps, built shelves to accommodate the ship's library, and gave the whole place a very serious and learned air. Every night from six to eight, beginning in Oran but continuing in dozens of ports on four continents over the next several years, in fair weather and foul, the *Booker T.'s* "professors" held forth before their eager students. In the succeeding years it became impossible for me to keep track of our alumni, but I have run into dozens of mates and engineers who told me that they got their start at old *"Booker T. 'U.'"* There we would sit, in the dim light, life jackets at our sides, studying and learning, though any second a torpedo might tear through the plates below and we would be taking our next instructions from St. Peter. But the courses paid for themselves over and over again, not only in higher wages commanded by those who won their promotions, but as a step toward alleviating the manpower problems of the industry and our own personnel requirements as well. It became commonplace on our ship to promote men to higher ratings, for we were never without sailors with the proper credentials at a time when the union halls were sorely pressed to provide skilled replacements.

The formal classes were only the beginning of educational activity aboard the *Booker T.* As any good teacher knows, once you start students thinking in a new way it is impossible to stop them. Discussions and arguments raged throughout the ship on fine points of deck work, engineering or politics, and contests sprang up among many of the lower ratings to see who would get his endorsement first!

With this kind of spirit developing it was inevitable that we should have a ship's newspaper, and *General Alarm,* "the paper that wakes you up," appeared shortly thereafter. Witty, informative, and salty, it buoyed our spirits in many a trying period, especially after we began carrying troops. We were rarely without an artist aboard, and *General Alarm* was illustrated with many "signed originals," none likely ever to grace the walls of the Museum of Modern Art.

As might be supposed the *Booker T.* was also a hotbed of political action. There was hardly a moment when half a dozen crew members were not raising funds for their favorite causes, from the French Red Cross to Yugoslavian War Relief. Of course I solicited contributions for the National Negro Congress. Some evenings were designated as letter writing nights, and it was not unusual for us to pepper our Congressmen with letters from every member of the crew on pending legislation like the seamen's bill, which was calculated to give members of the merchant marine benefits equivalent to the GI "Bill of Rights."

At about the same time our gunnery officer, Navy Lieutenant (j.g.) Charles Elliott, wrote an article for *General Alarm.* He said:

> *How fortunate are you men of the* Booker T. Washington *for your splendid attitude. Each man aboard this ship seems so well to recognize his responsibility. You are, each of you, obviously determined to win this war. You are engaged in a hazardous task with a bold, aggressive attitude. You make evident to others the fact that harmony is necessary to success. Do not the petty differences, permitted on board some ships to become violent disputes, really act as an aid to our enemies? ...*
>
> *You who have been long aboard this ship do not realize how well you are accomplishing a splendid purpose. For your attitude of cooperation with naval personnel aboard it is my desire to say 'Thank you.'*

In addition to these activities we had the routine ship's committees – a Food Committee, Library Committee, and Safety Committee. There were so few "beefs" about the food, however, that the Committee disbanded after the first few trips. The Library Committee kept us well supplied with books, newspapers and magazines, so well in fact that we frequently donated cartons of precious reading matter to friends and troops overseas. The Safety Committee kept a sharp eye out for dangerous working conditions aboard – deck cleats which had been fixed to carry deck cargo and needed to be removed, slack chain rails, faulty gear, or careless working habits on the part of younger crew members. The Committee was so diligent that we suffered only one shipboard casualty among the crew after five years – a cook who cut his finger in the meat slicing machine.

There were other unique facets of life on the *Booker T.* Where else, for example, would you find murals on the boiler faces? They were the work of fireman-watertender Walter ("Red") Herrick. Herrick and his wiper buddy, Freeman Kincaid, decided one day that the ship's engine room should be the most beautiful afloat, and got the idea for a series of murals. Former head of the California Artists Union, Herrick did eight powerful drawings depicting the rise of Afro-Americans from the slaveridden past to the moment – still in the future – of full freedom and equality. You can imagine the expressions on our visitors' faces when they were conducted on a tour of the ship and saw these powerful drawings standing out in the eerie light of the engine room.

Another unusual aspect of life on the *Booker T.* that contributed greatly to the morale of both the crew and, in later days, our troops, was the almost continuous entertainment. Some evenings there would be eight or ten boxing matches covering every class from flylight to heavyweight. Of course we insisted on 16-ounce gloves and no one ever got hurt. Many crew members and GI's had been amateur or professional boxers before the war and there were some thrilling encounters on number four hatch. Other evenings there were full programs of original skits lampooning Army life or the typical shoreside adventures of merchant seamen. Quite often it was possible for us to get together a "combo" for a concert. Jazz never sounded better than on the deck of that gently rolling ship on a quiet sea at sundown

Life at sea on the *Booker T.* was so busy there was seldom time for any of us to engage in those three principal activities of seamen on most ships – reading, playing poker, and bragging about sexual accomplishments. And when we reached shore it was not much different. There were meetings ashore with trade union leaders, representatives of international relief organizations, parties, and dances; many in our honor, and I was frequently invited by the Army or the Navy to address colored battalions at army camps or other ships' crews in port.

Others besides ourselves thought highly of our shipboard life and program. There was hardly a trip which did not bring appreciation from the Transport Commander, armed guard lieutenant, convoy commodore, or letters circulated and signed by the troops aboard. Nearly every one called attention to the excellent relations between colored and white crew members, as well as between the crew members and both colored and white troops, the high morale aboard, exciting program of ship's activities.

Most of the programs I have mentioned were the ideas – and the work – of others. All I had to do was say "go ahead." We received the publicity that we did because a colored captain walked the bridge, but the *Booker T.* would have made a lesser impact upon the nation's consciousness had not the men who sailed her given such life and meaning to the symbol she represented.

Who were these men? In the ship's five and a half year career there were several hundred, of course, and space forbids mention of very many. But following voyage number one when the Wilmington membership meeting of the NMU adopted special shipping rules to provide an experienced crew, our crews were characteristic of the membership as a whole.

One such seaman was Antonio Plaza Blanco. The ship's

articles carried the bare statistics: he was five feet eight inches tall, twenty-four years of age, an oiler, and born in Spain. War was not a new experience for Antonio. He had fought through the Spanish Civil War at Almeria, Malaga, Teruel, Valencia, and Madrid, where he was finally wounded by a Nazi bomb and captured. Imprisoned in a concentration camp at Seville he bided his time and one day, working along the Guadalquivir river, he resolved to be free or dead, and dove for the river. With bullets zinging all around he reached the other side. Hidden by day by friends and sympathizers he stole through the fields at night until he reached La Linea, where he masqueraded as a fisherman, hired a boat and rowed to Gibraltar. Ultimately he came to America – and to the *Booker T*.

Fred "Chips" Reed, the carpenter who built our schoolroom, had a career too chequered to summarize in a paragraph. He had been torpedoed seven times, three times during World War I and four times by the time he joined us, in World War II. He'd been hit twice on the Murmansk run a year earlier, within a few hours. Chips' other adventures included knocking out a United States Shipping Commissioner's teeth (and thus losing his mate's license), tossing a Seattle cop over a balustrade into the street twenty feet below, and calling members of a Congressional witchhunting committee "sons-of-bitches" for daring to inquire into his political associations. His first wife had died in childbirth, his second was killed with three of his four children driving a steam automobile at a high speed on the Boston Post Road, a brother was killed racing on a French track, his father and another brother were killed in a "blow" while helping to build the Holland Tunnel in New York. His son was killed in a Japanese attack in the Pacific. Death stalked Fred wherever he went, always capturing someone but never Fred. Yet there was no more competent or gentle soul on the ship, or one more beloved by his shipmates.

John Beecher, our clerk-typist, or purser, was the descendant of a John Beecher who came from England in 1637, the great-great-grandson of Lyman Beecher, founder of Lane Theological Seminary in Cincinnati, seedbed of the abolitionist movement, great-grandson of Edward Beecher, first president of the first college in Illinois, and with Elijah Lovejoy cofounder of the Illinois anti-slavery society in 1837. His great-grandfather's sister was Harriet Beecher Stowe, author of *Uncle Tom's Cabin,* and another member of the family was Henry Ward Beecher, anti-slavery preacher. From such an illustrious tradition it was not surprising that our John was a firm New Dealer who had served as southern representative on President Roosevelt's Fair Employment Practices Committee before joining the *Booker T.* On his last voyage with us John, who had taken copious notes, wrote a fine book on our wartime adventures, *All Brave Sailors.*

There were so many more – men like our first assistant engineer, Leroy King, a bible-reading, ex-Wobbly, ex-union organizer and, at the time he returned to sea at the beginning of the war, chief engineer in a large Massachusetts paper mill and one of the most popular men on the ship. Little Joe Williams who had been born in Annapolis and did not understand for years that the caste system made it impossible for him to go to the Naval Academy. He had switched to the Merchant Marine Officer's Academy at Kings Point, becoming, after a rough struggle, its first colored graduate. There was Alex Treskin, with Harry Alexander the "fireball" of the *Booker T.,* aflame with ideas and unlike most idea men always willing to act. And so many more – affable Irving Smith, our chief engineer, and Bernie Kasbohm who succeeded him; Clifton Lastic and Adolphus Folks, both students of my "nautical academy" in the '20's, now both dead. And so many more . . .

These were the men who made the *Booker T. Washington* what it was throughout the war, a floating bastion representing America's finest traditions of democracy, integrity and working class ingenuity. Sailing with such men made the years from 1942 to 1948 the happiest years of my life. It does not come to many men, much less to many members of the colored races, to realize fully their true function. It is difficult enough, indeed, to discover what our function is, let alone achieve it. Thanks to such men and to the programs they were instrumental in developing, I discovered what it was to *experience* democracy for the first time in my life, and to realize my own fulfillment in a way that would otherwise have been impossible. Whether individually we all *became* better men for our work together is impossible to know. But we all *felt* we had and that, in a short life, is satisfaction enough.

14

Voyage number 5 began auspiciously: We were ordered to Maryland Drydocks in Baltimore to be converted into a troop carrier Five hundred bunks were built into the upper holds and 'tween decks, and the minimum facilities provided to keep a shipload of GI's healthy, if not happy, for weeks at sea. Speculation was rife regarding the significance of the changeover; most of the crew was convinced that we were heading for the second front. The job was completed late in September and we were ordered to Newport News to pick up an engineering battalion of 500 men. The weekend before departure I headed for New York to spend the last few days with my family, and Sunday afternoon – we were to sail at 6 a.m. Monday – I joined purser John Beecher for the long train ride back to Richmond and the bus to Newport News and the ship. John and I not only shared the same seat on the ride down from New York, but were engaged in a vigorous debate about Wendell Willkie when we reached Richmond.

As we continued our argument in the bus station – I had been reading Willkie's *One World* and was trying to persuade John that Willkie, like Roosevelt, was one of those businessmen who, despite his business prejudices, had a realistic vision of the future – we gradually became aware that people were staring at us. At first I supposed that those around me had not seen a colored man in a Captain's uniform before and were wondering who I might be. John, an old Southerner, admitted later that he understood the reason immediately but decided to say nothing. As we went on arguing the whole waiting room turned into one great, silent stare.

Suddenly a policeman burst through a side door, and one of the station personnel motioned in our direction. The cop strode over to us and bent down toward John. "Isn't he colored?" he whispered, jerking his thumb toward me.

"He's American," John replied crisply.

"But isn't he *colored?*" the cop persisted.

"He's the Captain of an American Liberty ship with one of the finest records in the war," John retorted. "You can check the facts with Washington. What's his color got to do with anything?"

"This is Virginia," the cop exclaimed, "don't care who he is, can't no colored man sit in the white folks' waitin' room in this state."

"He's taken thousands of tons of cargo across the ocean to our allies – and to a lot of soldiers from Virginia," John replied. "He's good enough to do *that* but *not* good enough to sit here?"

"Can't help it . . . I got my orders to put him out."

"Then you'll have to put me out too," John fired back.

"I can't help it," the cop muttered, "I got to do my job."

It was one o'clock in the morning; the bus wasn't due for half an hour, so we decided to walk around outside. We stalked defiantly through the waiting room and the white faces turned away as we passed. Outside another small crowd had gathered, but this time a friendly one –

the news had got around the neighborhood that I was in town and some of Richmond's colored people had come down to shake hands. We talked with them until the bus came, and then both got aboard and walked together to the rear and sat down in the "Colored Section." The sullen cop said a few words to the driver and there were angry glances but no one said a word. We moved through the night along the James River, past Jamestown where, in 1619, the first Dutch ship had arrived with twenty Negro slaves aboard. Now, 324 years later their countrymen were still segregated in a bus station. That's what they mean in the South by "going slow."

At 6:30 a.m. the *Booker T.* cast off and steamed down the bay to join sixty-three other ships making up outside. The 500 Army Engineers aboard were a fine group of American youngsters. Heading for their first wartime service they were in high spirits and we got to know many of them well. Relations between the merchant crew and the Army were so cordial, as a matter of fact, that we voted them a share of our rations, and brought twenty-five into the messroom each meal. It was on this voyage that the bakers volunteered, as a special answer to the Richmond police force, to cook pie once a week for the 500 troops – and that's an awful lot of pie!

The GI's expressed their gratitude in *General Alarm*: "As long as there are soldiers to talk and pass on their experiences the *Booker T. Washington* will live. These simple acts of yours will reach well around the world, told and retold as an example of the spirit of true brotherhood. Please accept our thanks . . . we will not forget."

The medical officer attached to the battalion was a Dr. Cohen, a most warm and gracious man. We struck up a close friendship and spent many hours in my stateroom discussing the war, race relations, and other matters.

Whatever ambitions we had had of joining the second front were smashed as we passed the Azores and received orders to break away from the convoy and head for the

Mediterranean. But perhaps we were to strike from the South? At Gibraltar however, new orders were signaled – we were to proceed to Oran again! On the morning of the 12th day at sea we pulled into Oran harbor and tied up alongside a British transport where we learned that our 500 passengers were to be transferred for India and the Far East. Troops and the merchant crew alike were disheartened at the news – we had wanted to sail into battle together. There were many moving farewells and good wishes as the troops began disembarking at 4:30 that afternoon. Dr. Cohen and I exchanged addresses and said we would meet again. A new load of troops streamed aboard and three hours later we were at sea once more, this time bound for a second destination.

That night we received a warning that Nazi submarines were beginning a savage offensive in the Mediterranean. The *Booker T.* was the leading ship in our five vessel convoy, and I set a crazy zigzag course for two days into one of my favorite ports of call on the old *President Polk*, for our secret destination turned out to be Naples, liberated only a few weeks earlier.

Pre-war visitors will remember Naples as I did – a tree-filled city, sheltered by hills studded with lovely houses, narrow, winding streets, and great treasure-laden churches. But it was a far different Naples that confronted us now. As John described it in *All Brave Sailors*, "blasted ships careened at the docksides, stacks and masts sticking out of the water, smashed docks and warehouses, smoke-less factories, broken concrete, twisted cranes and bridges, mile upon mile of many-storied workers' tenements, grim enough formerly, now utterly tenantless, blackened stone shells with beds and chairs spilling down from collapsed floor to floor. Far off in the heart of the city the stark ribs of what once had been a big dome thrust toward the sky."

In addition to natural military targets such as the power plant, the viaduct bringing in water from the North, and big hotels into which the invaders might move, the Nazis had destroyed sanitariums, hospitals, and homes for the poor. A huge delayed action mine had been planted in the post office, and though the building had been searched thoroughly the mine went off killing almost everyone in the block. The beaches on which I had more than once sunned myself were a tangled mass of barbed wire and military stores. Ragged, dirty children everywhere begged *mangiare,* food, or shouted the merits of their sixteen-year-old "sisters," whose favors we could enjoy for thirty-five lire – thirty-five cents at the current exchange!

There were few docks left. We tied up to a sunken hull alongside a bombed jetty, and as soon as the gangway was in place I went ashore to seek out the American consul and enter the ship. As he registered the *Booker T.* he glanced up and said, "Terrible news, the English vessel, wasn't it?"

"What English vessel?"

He mentioned the name. She had been sunk the night before with all hands lost. I stood there dumbfounded – this was the ship to which we had transferred our engineering battalion in Oran only two days earlier! She had suffered a direct hit, the story went, and had gone down so fast that no one had been able to escape.

The crew was shocked when I reported the news, but we were suddenly too busy saving our own skins to worry very long. The Nazis, only thirty miles away, were paying nightly visits, and before we could discharge our troops or a stick of cargo a fighter plane streaked in from the north, dropping flares to light the way for bombers behind, and the Naples night sky turned bright as noon. The massive c-r-r-u-n-c-h of exploding bombs provided a resounding base to the staccato chatter of the poms-poms and our own 40-millimeter guns; tracer bullets streaked through the sky and acrid smoke began to roll out to us from the shattered city. Two docks away a bomb sent up a shower of rubble; then a bomber exploded in the air and fell in a fiery, shrieking parabola across the sky, ending in a tremendous explosion as it smashed into a city. Luck was still with us, confirming that mysterious feeling to which everyone on the ship was privy – nothing could happen to *us* – the *Booker T.* was a magic ship.

The following day we moved to one of the few remaining docks to discharge our explosives, and for two hours I wandered through the city looking for familiar landmarks. A bare, rubble-strewn lot between two shattered buildings marked the site of a *trattoria* – cafe I used to frequent. A church with walls still intact stood open to the sky; a few old women were kneeling among the marble columns, but there was no sign of life behind the altar.

The contrast between the rich and poor sections was interesting. Up on the heights the modern villas, occupied by the type of people we used to carry on our round-the-world President Line voyages, were virtually untouched. The women, with the Nazis only weeks gone, were dressed in furs and silk stockings, stared coldly at us as we passed, and I could imagine them complaining to their husbands about the shortage of perfume. The proclamations of the Nazi governor were still in place on the walls, undefiled by any nationalistic passion.

Down in the rubble-strewn workers' section, where the streets wound between piles of rock and the nauseous stench of corpses still came from the bombed-out-tenements, the poor shouted *"Vive gli Alleati"* (Long Live the Allies). Nazi posters had been torn down as the hated Germans retreated through the city. Scrounging for food, begging you to buy a trinket, or pleading with you for a few lire, the poor still had time to say they were happy that you had come.

After three days in Naples we were ordered to Palermo, Sicily, for a shipment of used and useless Army equipment – old trucks and tires, obsolete plane parts and other materials the invaders had left behind. We picked our way carefully through the harbor, dodging sunken hulls and marker buoys, and tied up at one of the few remaining docks. As the last line was made fast I heard a familiar voice hailing me from the dock ... "Captain Mulzac ... Captain Mulzac ..." And I looked down in the haggard features of Dr. Cohen!

He came aboard as soon as the gangway was in place. It was a happy reunion, for I naturally supposed he had been lost. He confirmed the Consul's report. The transport had left four hours after us; Dr. Cohen was in his bunk when the ship had been hit by three torpedoes. She had gone down so fast that the suction had taken everyone with her, including himself. Luckily he had come up near some dunnage – scrap lumber used in shoring cargo – and had hung on for two hours until a destroyer picked him up. The escort vessels had combed the area for survivors but, as far as he knew, he was the only one saved.

But we found them a few days later, after we had taken on our cargo and steaming home passed the spot where the troopship had been hit. The sea was surrendering its grisly booty. Our friends were floating on the placid Mediterranean, clinging together in clusters of three and four in death. As far as our eyes could see the bodies floated face down, suspended by life belts. It was a tragic sight. We turned from the scene sick, for there was nothing we could do but plow through the sea of corpses toward home and another cargo.

In the following months the *Booker T.* made two more trips to Oran and other North African ports – Algiers, Sfax, Tunis, and Casablanca, often shuttling between them and Naples supporting General Mark Clark's drive North. Throughout these months, as the hardened Fifth Army veterans captured villages along the old Roman roads, we were never far behind, frequently discharging cargo a few miles from the German lines. It was a rare night when a bomber did not appear over the harbor, and it was almost a relief to get back to sea where only an occasional submarine could threaten us.

Often we carried Italian prisoners of war from North African internment camps to Italy and German prisoners in the other direction. The war was not over for the Italians; they were being sent to the front to fight their former allies. What more poignant commentary could there be on the senselessness of war than that these helpless humans, who only months earlier had been aiming their rifles at Americans and Englishmen, were now asked to turn around and shoot Germans?

Several of our Italian-speaking crew members were able to talk with the prisoners, and learned that while most were willing to return to the front to fight the hated Nazis they would refuse to fight under the *"signorine"* – their equally despised Italian officers. The *"signorine,"* they maintained stoutly, had either deserted the battles in North Africa by surrendering to the Allies or fled to the protection of the Germans. We too learned to treat the *"signorine"* with contempt. They sat by themselves on the hatch covers during the day, treated their troops abusively, and even insisted upon having breakfast served to them in the hold . . . until I found out about it. When we asked the soldiers how they expected to avoid serving under such officers one smiled connivingly, flexed his trigger finger and jerked forward, shoulders out, simulating a man shot in the back.

On one of our trips we had the only accident, luckily without a man or ounce of cargo lost, that we suffered during the war. We were approaching Bizerte late one afternoon in January of 1944. Storm warnings had been flying all day, and as evening approached the convoy commander suddenly signalled that a hurricane was due to strike and every ship was on her own. We were loaded with troops and valuable cargo, and I decided to put into the harbor overnight instead of striking out for our Italian beachhead or circling outside until the convoy could reassemble. We dropped anchor inside the harbor, battened everything down tight and waited for the storm to strike; we were confident that we could ride it out without incident.

Shortly after 9 p.m. the winds began to rise and the storm swept over the harbor with all the fury it had gathered over the endless West African wastes. We were reasonably light in the water, however, and I thought there was no real cause for concern.

Just before midnight Chief Mate Lionel O'Neill, who was replacing Mr. Lastic on that voyage, called me to the bridge. A Norwegian freighter, which had been a good half mile off our starboard bow when we dropped anchor, was now only a few hundred yards away ... heavily loaded, she was obviously dragging her anchor in the gale. At once I called all hands on deck to shift the vessel to another part of the harbor, but as we began to take in the hook the hurricane struck with full force. We put the wheel hard over as the Norwegian bore down on us and almost got away – but not quite. Her stern struck us amidships, tearing away our starboard lifeboats and puncturing the hull. We crept away, and the engine crew sought to determine the extent of the damage. We'd been hit opposite the starboard settler tanks just below the water line, but the tanks were holding and the only water we were shipping came through a jagged gash above the water line as large waves struck or the ship rolled. We dropped anchor again and sweated out the night.

In the morning we radioed our plight to the shore authorities and were ordered to come in and discharge; our troops and cargo would be taken by other ships. We picked our way through the harbor, clogged with sunken hulls and with the hurricane's havoc now added to war's destruction. Two ships had capsized during the night and three LST's had been driven on the beach. We discharged in a few days and were ordered up the river to a dry dock at Ferryville. Enroute we saw one of the most amazing sights of the war – Algerian soldiers digging irrigation ditches along the river under *German* guards! The French, colonialists to the end, knew they could trust the captured Nazis more than their own Algerian troops!

Provoked by this and other examples of French "democracy" in Tunisia the crew resolved to show the Ferryville population where *we* stood. We asked the United States Army Special Services personnel for help in renting a hall to have a little party, and quietly passed the word to representatives to the Tunisian trade unions. There had been, we were told, no more gala turnout in the city's history – more than 2,000 people jammed the big hall and another thousand were locked out by frightened United States Army officers who expected a "riot." It is indicative of the attitude of the United States Army as well as of the French Army that when the workers of different countries got together they could only expect a riot! They got a riot of sorts, too, though not the kind they expected, for we had taken up a "tarpaulin muster" on the ship, and when at the midnight ceremonies I announced the contribution of 5,000 francs to the Algerian Resistance Movement the place became a riotous bedlam of good fellowship. The United States officers stiffly informed us later they would never have helped us get the hall if they'd known what we were up to.

All along the North African coast, trip after trip, we battled Jim Crow at the Red Cross Canteens. The paradoxes of racial discrimination are often complex and staggering. In Oran, as I have pointed out, the Red Cross maintained segregated facilities early in the war, but as the front passed to Italy and North Africa became only a staging area, the two clubs were combined into one. But segregation remained. The white troops enjoyed the club's facilities on Mondays, Wednesdays, Fridays, and Sundays, while the colored troops occupied the premises on the other days. Since there were no local Algerian girls, however, the same French girls served as hostesses to both groups. The girls were absolutely free of any prejudice toward us. As a matter of fact many told us that the colored sailors and GI's were more *"gentil"* than their white patrons. But Arabs – that was a different matter! I happened to be present one evening when the French mothers and chaperones gathered in high dudgeon and threatened to boycott the club because one of the colored GI's had brought an Arab girl to the dance! It was perfectly all right the *mesdames* felt, for their white charges to jitterbug the night away with colored Americans but *never* in the company of "white" Arabs! Either the girl had to leave, they insisted, or they would never come back.

Our major altercation with the Red Cross came on another trip, our Christmas visit in 1943. Chiquita Lonewolf, a colored Red Cross worker, had arranged a party in our honor. Significantly, though her name indicated that she came from stock long antedating the Puritans, she had been assigned to the colored staff, and naturally the party was scheduled on a "colored night." During the afternoon several of us drove out into the hills around Oran to collect a few fir trees, and returned to decorate the quarters with popcorn, tinsel, and a few gifts.

At the appointed hour the crew began to appear at the club and an MP on guard barred their way! "Sorry," he said, "Colored only, no whites allowed."

"But *we're* from the *Booker T. Washington*," the crew members protested, as if this should make a difference. "The party is being given for *all* of us!"

"Can't help it . . . orders is orders."

"Whose orders?" the crew wanted to know.

"The Army's . . . we don't want any trouble."

I arrived in a cab as these exchanges were taking place, and the crew explained the problem. There was no point in debating with the MP and I asked to see the club director. In a moment he appeared and confirmed what the MP had said. "We don't want any trouble over the girls," he explained. "If we had colored and white breaking in on the same girls there'd certainly be trouble."

We were not prepared to separate, with colored members remaining to enjoy the party while our white union brothers stayed outside. Such issues have to be fought out on the spot, and fight it out we did. I intimated to the director that I was on close personal terms with everyone from President Roosevelt to the head of the International Red Cross, and that if my crew was denied access to the club that evening we would raise a holler that would reverberate around the world. In the face of such threats the club director finally capitulated and we all went in together. It goes without saying that we had a fine time, and later in the evening when colored GI's joined the party, black and white cut in on the same girls without incident.

15

The moment mankind had been awaiting for so long came on June 6, 1944 – the opening of the "second front." Military historians have chronicled the events of those momentous days much better than I can or, indeed, have any right to, since the *Booker T.* was 1,500 miles from the scene, homeward bound out of Naples. As soon as Sparks rushed to me with the news I made the announcement over the public address system, and the crew staged an impromptu celebration. In the old sailing ship days the master would have broken out an extra ration of grog, a tradition I thought should be respected; I sent down bottles of bourbon to the crew and officers' mess.

Unfortunately, all we could do on the *Booker T.* was celebrate the event. The war passed us by in these final stages and though we were on essential assignments we considered them secondary and felt humiliated that we were not in on the great engagements.

As it turned out, however, there was another assignment for me. Those who live ashore and receive their mail piece by piece, day by day, are likely to regard it as one of life's normal experiences like telephones, automobiles, and TV. Not so the sailor. Whatever stamps they bear, however far in advance they are mailed, most letters rest in company mailrooms until the vessel returns to port. This was especially true during the war when even the WSA didn't know where a vessel might be and when so much mail never reached its destination at all.

During the war when the *Booker T.* returned to home port there would be as many as fifty or sixty letters for me. There was the usual quota of announcements from the Coast Guard, the Navy, and Luckenbach. Then there were personal letters from friends and relatives which I tucked away to be answered at sea the following trip. There were also the letters from unknown well-wishers or organizations asking me to speak or appear at a public event. Most welcome of all were letters from children, especially those from the Walden School on West 88th Street in New York City. Early in the war the Walden children had *"adopted"* us and we had adopted them. We corresponded regularly, and when we were in port crew members often visited the school or the children the ship.

When we tied up in August of 1944 at the end of Voyage No. 7 there was in important-looking envelope bearing a special delivery stamp and the return address of the National Citizens Political Action Committee. I opened it to read a warm and urgent request from the chairman, Sidney Hillman, to get in touch with him.

A few days later I sat in his office and heard his message: would I consider leaving the *Booker T. Washington* the next trip to campaign throughout the country on behalf of Franklin Delano Roosevelt? With the war now entering its decisive phase the President would be unable to campaign for his fourth term and well known Democrats were being asked to tour on his behalf. The extraordinary publicity the *Booker T.* had received, Mr. Hillman said, my war experience and popularity in labor and colored circles would make me a good campaigner.

After two years of service without relief I had earned a vacation, and while this was not exactly the kind I had had in mind what could I do? F.D.R. had, for many of us, become so inextricably entwined with the whole conduct and meaning of the war that it was disturbing to think of *anyone* else in the White House.

Arrangements with the WSA and the Luckenbach Line were completed swiftly, and a week after returning to port I found myself bound for Chicago with Ferdinand C. Smith, Secretary of the NMU. We were met at the station by many union officials, conducted on a tour of the city, and that evening addressed a large meeting at Du-Sable Center on the South Side, headquarters of the United Packinghouse Workers and other CIO unions.

My theme at these meetings was on the meaning of the war and the necessity of continuing the leadership of F.D.R. to secure the peace. It was under his leadership, I pointed out, that working men and women had first won the right to form unions and to bargain with their employers under the Wagner Act. It was under his presidency that social security laws had been enacted. It was under F.D.R. that Afro-Americans had finally got Executive Order 8802 which established a Fair Employment Practices Committee.

And it was President Roosevelt, I reminded them, who with the British prime minister, had proclaimed the doctrine of the "Four Freedoms" with all the rich promise this contained for the end of colonialism in Africa.

It is ironic to look back upon these sentiments today, for history has proved that not only could the Republicans not be trusted to live up to these promises but neither could the Democrats. For just eight months later F.D.R. was dead and Harry Truman, the "little man from Missouri" who succeeded him, promptly repudiated everything he had stood for.

Finally I told our audiences about some of our experiences abroad and of life on the *Booker T. Washington,* the only piece of America I knew which was entirely free of racial prejudice. Wherever we sailed, I explained, we were welcomed by men of good will and heralded as a symbol of prejudice-free relations that one day would prevail throughout the world. This too, I argued, had come under the President's leadership, and since my appointment two other members of our race had won commands. To extend our gains even further, to build the kind of society in which *no* citizen would be denied the job to which his talents entitled him, it was imperative that we return F.D.R. to office.

From Chicago we left for Pittsburgh and another cordial reception from the steelworkers and the United Electrical Worker's Union, and spoke at civic gatherings as well as trade union functions. Then on to Detroit, Akron, Cincinnati, San Francisco, Seattle, Los Angeles, St. Louis, Louisville, Milwaukee, Boston, and Philadelphia, with many other stops between. Wherever we went we were greeted by large and enthusiastic turnouts, and there were times when both Ferd and I got the feeling that we were candidates ourselves! It was an inspiring tour, and one that symbolizes to my mind the highest form of popular political action.

Toward the end, however, I began to tire and to look forward to rejoining the *Booker T.* On October 30th we returned to New York, two days after she had come in from another trip to North Africa and the crew welcomed me with a special shipboard meeting to hear all about the campaign. Before we left Norfolk we had a chance to vote and it gave every one of us a feeling of satisfaction to know that individually and collectively we had helped the Commander-in-Chief achieve another resounding victory.

Early in November we were back at sea again, this time bound for Marseilles. The war had not, of course, slowed down to accommodate the American political campaign. Paris had fallen, southern France had been invaded, the Russians were driving on Berlin and Mark

Clark's Fifth Army was pressing hard at Milan. The nightly bombing of Germany had, if anything, grown in intensity now that adequate fighter protection could be provided from French bases.

Like Naples, Marseilles was, for me, a familiar port, but it was no longer a familiar Marseilles that greeted us. Before the war it had been the second largest city of France and its second most charming. Gay, lively cafes had lined the boulevards, and in the center of the city, along the old harbor, boatmen used to beg the visitor to ride out to the Chateau *d'If*, legendary site of Dumas' famous tale, *The Count of Monte Cristo*. Lovely restaurants beckoned, each with its special bouillabaisse, and near the city was an open-air amphitheater where on soft summer evenings it was possible to sit on a rock promenade and listen to some of the finest opera stars in Europe.

But now Marseilles was a shattered port. One crew member counted fifty-seven hulls resting on the harbor bottom as we threaded our way to the dock. The port had been captured by Allied troops only a few months before and evidence of the battles and bombings were fresh in the pock-marked buildings, shattered quays and patches of rubble. Yet the city was already trying to recapture its pre-war gaiety; flower vendors were again selling their delicate blossoms, a few ancient but spritely French taxis sped along the boulevards, and the restaurants were desperately trying to convert their meager commodities into the epicurean delights that had once made the city famous and would again. Only the blackout and the occasional whine of the air raid sirens reminded us that we were still in a land of war.

However, all this changed abruptly on December 16. At dawn that day the Nazis struck with all their fury in one last, desperate offensive in the North, driving the First Army out of Germany and laying siege to Bastogne. This six-week battle was to take 40,000 Allied lives. Until then we had enjoyed our stay. Some of the crew members had taken the train to Nice on weekends, while others stopped off in the little villages along the Riviera which the war seemed barely to have touched. The sudden onslaught shocked us out of our playmaking and once again the *Booker T.* became a hotbed of political energy, with crew members vying with one another on behalf of their favorite shoreside causes. It got so bad that we finally had to have the appeals centralized through the ship's committee.

A few days before Christmas we were ordered to Oran. No one likes to be away from home during the winter holidays, but of all the places to spend Christmas Oran is the least likely. Yet as we were all figuratively and literally in the same boat I decided to surprise everyone Christmas day by preparing dinner myself without the help of a cook in the galley. I sent out a few invitations to Red Cross representatives and a few other friends in port and Christmas morning got up at 4 a.m. to prepare the turkeys and all the Christmas trimmings. The mate got into the act by breaking out the signal flags and flying them from stem to stern, and it was a gala day, with many surprise gifts, singing, and camaraderie. Inevitably news got around that the *Booker T.* was flinging a party and by late afternoon almost every sailor in port had joined us. The turkey gave out but there was plenty of powerful Algerian wine (which was 18 per cent alcohol) and the celebration lasted well into the night.

Two days later we were dispatched to Naples for a load of war prisoners, and a tattered, raggedy bunch this vaunted *Wehrmacht* was. Our accommodations for them were really not adequate; many had to sleep on the steel decks in the hold with dunnage for pillows, but when one complained a crew member retorted, "Look Fritz, it's better than Dachau!"

Everything went well until we approached Gibraltar, when the convoy commander suddenly signaled us to keep all prisoners below decks – some were diving over the side in an attempt to swim to Spanish Morocco! The destroyer escort wheeled around to pick them up, but a few escaped. Fortunately I had not yet opened the holds and my charges were confined below decks. Not until we got a hundred miles at sea did I finally let them out, and none of the Nazi supermen seemed willing to risk the swim. We might very well have let them try it!

Half-starved, sick and beaten as they were it was impossible for me then, as it is now, to be "fair" about the Germans. Sympathetic as I tried to be about the social and political forces which drove them to be what they were, I could not sympathize with them in person. Even in defeat they were arrogant, especially the officers. Most of those we carried were convinced they would be welcomed with open arms in America. One, a typical Prussian named Kurt, argued that it was a ghastly mistake that we were fighting each other – we should be fighting *together,* he kept insisting, against the Bolsheviks and the "yellow races." We had voted to translate *General Alarm* into German so our prisoners could follow the war, but we were almost back in Newport News before we could find an English-speaking German reliable enough to do the job. Each tried to work in sly remarks against the Jewish people, and to twist the news stories to make it appear that Germany was winning the war!

There was little fraternization between the prisoners and crew members. The enemy was divided into three groups, and each was allowed above decks four hours a day – none before dawn or after sunset. A full complement of MP's, tommy guns at the ready, stood guard over them throughout the day, and they behaved well as long as they were kept busy at routine tasks – chipping, painting, working in the galley, and keeping the vessel shipshape. Once in a while a crew member would engage a group in conversation and try to explain the causes of the war, and its progress. None of the Germans knew about the conditions underlying the Nazi attacks on Czechoslovakia, Poland, the Western countries or the U.S.S.R. They professed not to know about the gas ovens in the extermination camps, or the atrocities. They did not show any signs of regret, remorse, or even great interest.

Or so we thought, until the final night at sea. That evening, just before sunset, one of the prisoners sent a message through John Beecher that a group of them would like to talk to me on deck. I went down and about twenty of the Germans were gathered around an interpreter. He began haltingly, trying to make it clear that he was speaking for the whole group, but gained confidence as he went on, and his words, as John has recorded them, were as follows. "Our leaders told us democracy in America was a fraud. They told us that you were hypocritical when you claimed that all men were free and equal. They told us the colored people were no better than slaves in America. But what we have seen on this ship, the happiness, the comradeship among you, your fairness to us when we had been told we would be abused and beaten, all this has made us think. At night, down in the hold, when the lights go out, we talk about it, all of us, and we wanted you to know."

That's all. No more, no less. We had not won them over, but we had made them think.

What an ironic position to be in. For the next morning we were to dock at Newport News, Virginia, where the colored population was suffering from bitter discrimination!

Voyage No. 10 finally broke the monotony of our relentless runs to the Mediterranean – we were ordered to Cherbourg March 7th, the day the 9th Armored Division under General Bradley finally crossed the bridge at Remagen. Our convoy of 124 ships was the largest we'd been in since the beginning of the war. Everything was fine until we were four days from port. Then dense fog closed in. Fog is bad enough when you are running alone, but in a convoy of 124 ships it's extremely dangerous, especially without radar. There are natural and inevitable lags in carrying out the course changes signaled by the commodore, with the result that after a few hours ships began crashing into one another. In the melee some lost the convoy altogether, and others simply dispersed. I posted the entire deck force on lookout. We had a few close scrapes but with everyone on the alert we had the capacity to maneuver instantly. Eight other vessels, however, were reported to have been lost.

On the last fog-bound day we had a different scare. As we were approaching Cherbourg Chief Engineer Bernie Kasbohm and I were talking in my cabin when a terrific explosion shook the vessel. We rushed to the wheelhouse and I rang the general alarm, ordered the carpenter to sound the bilges to see where we were hit, and the chief mate to survey the damage. Kasbohm rushed to the engine room to stand by. Minutes passed . . . finally the chief officer returned to say that he could find no damage and Chips reported that the bilges were absolutely dry . . . just as another explosion shook the vessel! Again we tried to ascertain where we'd been hit. The crew stood by boat stations wondering what was up, but again the answer was the same, there was no discernible damage. The ship was holding steadily to her course, turning a rhythmic 68 r.p.m. How could she get hit by two torpedoes, I wondered, without giving any sign that she was hurt?

The mystery was cleared up twenty minutes later: a British destroyer slipped alongside and when she was about 100 feet away a voice hailed us from the bridge. "Captain! Did you feel anything?"

"We sure did!" I shouted back, "we thought we were hit. What happened?"

"We sank a Jerry right under you," the Englishman replied. "He was trying to get through the breakwater with you. We got him with two depth charges." We felt relieved, and a little bit abashed to discover that we were as sound as ever.

All except me, that is. Four days and nights on the

bridge under the tension of guiding the vessel through the fog had exhausted me. As soon as we'd tied up I discovered I could hardly stand. I went to bed and awoke a few hours later to discover that I *couldn't* stand – my legs were swollen and black. I rang for the steward who sent for the doctor. After a preliminary examination he ordered me to the hospital. I refused to go, and the French doctor resignedly wrapped my legs, ordered me to bed, and rigged up a sling to suspend my legs from the overhead. And there I lay until we were fully discharged and ordered back to the United States.

April, 1945. The Red Army was crashing toward Berlin from the East while British and American troops were storming through Germany from the West. In the Pacific the Navy had gathered 1,000 vessels of all descriptions for the assault upon Okinawa. And in the Atlantic, four days from Cherbourg, with 500 troops aboard, the *Booker T. Washington* was sailing in clear, beautiful weather. In neat rows on both sides of us, three rows of five ships each, were fifteen war-weary Liberties and Victories shepherded by five destroyers. The atmosphere aboard was jovial – the troops, all veterans of many campaigns, were joyous at quitting the war, and the crew was happy that the bitter North Atlantic winter was over. The prospects were for an uneventful crossing.

I was standing on the port wing lazily inspecting the other ships through my binoculars to see if they were as clean and well-maintained as we were. My binoculars swung around to a destroyer . . . someone was tampering with her flag. Down the flag came, then stopped at half mast. I turned the glasses to a British destroyer and there, too, the Union Jack was fluttering . . . down, down, hesitating and then dropping at half mast.

Chief Engineer Kasbohm, who was on the bridge with me, located the signalman and he flashed our question to the commodore. In a minute the reply came back: "The President of the United States is dead."

For the next hour or so a pall settled over the ship. Men went off by themselves, standing at the gunwales, staring off at the horizon, some in prayer, others shocked into stupor, still others silently weeping. The card games on the hatch covers ceased; the GI's picked up their quarters and dollar bills and drifted away, gathering into little knots of men for a moment, then breaking up in bewilderment. No command had to be given the A.B. on watch . . . he went back and lowered the flag, and every eye on the ship watched as it fluttered to half mast, symbolically representing the collapse of the President.

I summoned the ship's officers, the armed guard lieutenant and the troop commander to my stateroom and we decided to observe the solemn moments of the burial. A few days later, when the President was interred at Hyde Park, the entire merchant crew and half of the troops gathered on the port side, and the armed guard and the other half of our passengers on the starboard side in separate services. The ceremonies were brief. I explained as best I could what F.D.R. had meant to me and to the nation, from the dark days of 1933 when he had said that we had "nothing to fear but fear itself," to his most recent insistence upon unconditional surrender. Then I read a few appropriate passages from the Bible and we disbanded.

It was a black day for the men of the *Booker T.* and for all mankind.

16

By April of 1945 the *Booker T. Washington* had been in almost continuous service for two and a half years. She was ready for an overhaul and, I discovered at the Marine Hospital in New York, so was I. The Staten Island doctors gave me a thorough examination when I reported upon our return, and found that while the rest of me was hardy enough, my legs were fifty-nine years old. An operation for varicose veins was scheduled, and the *Booker T.* and I went to our respective drydocks simultaneously.

Engineers and doctors know their business and I am grateful to them for their services to our respective rusty pipes. But it has always seemed to me a bit humiliating that after six years of war duty, counting the years prior to America's entry, I should have been flat on my back at the conflict's glorious triumph. During those three and one-half months that the *Booker T.* and I were laid up some of the most momentous events in history took place. Mussolini was captured near Dongo by the Italian partisans, executed and dragged through the streets; Hitler committed suicide the next day. Soviet troops stormed into Berlin and the German armies sued for surrender. The United Nations was founded in June, Churchill was voted out of office by a grateful but resolved British people who had begun to understand how they had been ushered into war in the first place. Clement Attlee unexpectedly joined an equally unexpected Harry Truman at the Potsdam conference, the first atomic bomb exploded over Alamogordo in July and the second over Hiroshima August 6th. World War II came to a dramatic end, with millions of men hurled into the final battles. And where was I? *In bed!*

During these months, trading stories with other old salts at the hospital, I found myself fighting against the hope that the war would last long enough for the *Booker T.* to engage in one last battle or at least to help in the mop-up of some by-passed island. But it was not to be. I was pronounced fit early in August and rushed to Newport News where my reconditioned friend was lying low and lovely in the water, as eager to be off on a new voyage as I. We left for Bari, Italy, on a postwar voyage, and the elaborate program for the Greater East Asia Co-Prosperity Sphere collapsed the same day.

The war in Europe had been over three months when we put to sea on Voyage No. 11, and the formal surrender of the Japanese was just two weeks away. For the first time in its career the *Booker T. Washington* enjoyed the luxury of sailing free of convoy, escorts, and an undersea menace. Our eleven-day voyage was without disturbance of any kind and I must say that I enjoyed it to the hilt.

Bari, on the east coast of the Italian "heel" had been badly damaged during the Eighth Army's advance, and was jammed with homeless people. Shortly after the invasion, through some *snafu*, German bombers one night found the harbor lighted and ships packed close together. They had hit an ammunition ship which blew up and set fire to another, which also blew up, and when the evening was over seventeen ships were resting on the bottom of Bari Harbor.

As usual we discovered a "charity" – a Yugoslav partisan group. The crew elected to buy out the entire "slop chest" and give all the clothing, cigarettes, candy, etc., to the partisans. We contributed food, money, musical instruments, and practically everything that wasn't nailed down.

An amusing incident took place on the way home. We were carrying 500 Nisei troops, members of the famed 442nd Hawaiian Battalion, and it was agreed that crew and troops each would put on a skit. Chief mate Ralph Tucker and several crew members got together and turned out a very funny comedy dealing with the adventures of a GI wife while her husband was overseas, but I thought this was not quite the thing to do before the veterans, many of whom had been away for several years, and asked them to write another one. The laugh was on me, for at our theater evening the Nisei troops staged their own show – almost line for line the one I'd rejected in the interest of their morale!

There was an interesting story to the play we put on, too. The young crew member chosen to play the female lead in our presentation was a young Georgian who had been noticeably "correct" in his relations with the colored members of the crew. His "husband" in the play however, was colored, and there were several "love scenes" in the script. Art is stranger than life; at the end of the performance, which followed two or three rehearsals, the Southerner's prejudice had been noticeably modified, and no one was more amazed than he himself. Once thereafter I overheard him lecturing another crew member on the evils of racial discrimination.

Voyage No. 12 will live long in my memory for three unexpected events that serve to demonstrate the kind of fix that a sea captain can occasionally get into.

We left Norfolk late in October, bound for Marseilles. Winter was approaching, food supplies were short, internment camps were still jammed with Nazi prisoners and the displacement camps full of refugees. French troops were being discharged and flung on the labor market, but there were few job opportunities. The battlefields of Europe had not yet been converted to fields of grain, and the black market was flourishing everywhere, especially in the port cities – and Marseilles was the number one port of France. Practically the only way to survive was by stealing, trading and otherwise living by your wits.

Under these conditions the Allied military authorities were taking every precaution to guard the docks. Guards were on twenty-four-hour-a-day duty at the gates, and MP's were assigned to every ship. One morning at about 6:30 I was awakened by the unmistakable sound of a rifle shot. I rushed out on deck to see a cluster of longshoremen already gathered down on the apron. An MP on duty had spied an eight-year-old boy breaking into a carton of canned goods on the dock and fired. The little fellow fell over dead, still clutching the can of evaporated milk.

"What in the devil have you done?" I shouted at the MP, "Why didn't you go down and chase him away instead of shooting him?"

"I don't take orders from you," he replied, "I take

orders from my commanding officer, and my orders are to shoot."

If it had been within my power I would have locked up the MP and had him court martialed. But there was nothing I could do. The longshoremen, however, who were Communists to a man, held a meeting on the spot and struck the ship at once. Two days of delicate negotiations followed, and they finally agreed to return to work the third day. The crew took up a collection for the little boy's family, and lost no chance to express its sympathy with the longshoremen.

The second incident was not so easily resolved. After discharging we shifted to another dock to take on several hundred troops, and the afternoon before departure I had an appointment with the Coast Guard Commander. In the corridor of the Coast Guard building I was approached by a very pretty girl who asked, in fluent English and in a rather authoritative way, "To what ship do you belong, and when are you leaving?" Assuming she was someone's secretary, I replied, "The *Booker T. Washington*. We have no departure date, but I expect it will be tomorrow."

She asked a few more questions before I began to wonder whether she had any business reason for wanting this information. "Why do you ask?"

"I am married to an American soldier who has been sent back to the United States, and want to join him there."

"Well, young lady, we are a troopship and your problem is no concern of mine. You must see his commanding officer." I left her in the corridor, made my report, went to town to see the American Consul, and returned to the vessel at 4:30 that afternoon.

At 6:30 an Army Colonel came aboard to inspect the troop quarters, for we were to leave the following day. The third engineer, Arthur Coco, was assigned to lead the Colonel on an inspection tour. About half an hour later they returned, and I will never be able to understand what was in Coco's mind, for he was a wonderful engineer and a solid union man. Nevertheless he sidled up to me mysteriously and whispered, *"She's beautiful,* Cap. Don't worry, I locked her up below."

"What the devil are you talking about?" I asked.

"The girl, *the girl,"* Coco insisted embarrassed at talking in front of the Colonel. The Colonel, quickly realizing I didn't have any idea what they were referring to, then said that they had seen a girl in the troop quarters. She had run away from them and they had locked her in a room.

I demanded that Coco bring her to me at once. It was the same girl who had accosted me earlier at the Coast Guard office.

"How did you get aboard?" I asked her. No answer. "Did one of the crew members help you? One of the Army personnel?" She would not reply to a single question. "Well, there's nothing to do but put you ashore," I said at last, and put her in charge of the Colonel to turn over to the shore authorities.

The Coast Guard learned of the incident when the Army Colonel turned in the girl and the following day I was served with a summons demanding my appearance before the Commandant. There I was charged with having conspired to enter an enemy alien into the United States, for the girl turned out to be a German national. The ship was put under port arrest, and as soon as the troops were aboard we were ordered into the stream to await trial.

Two days later the Coast Guard Commandant and his aides came out to the *Booker T.* for the hearing, bringing the girl with them.

A word of explanation may be in order. At the beginning of the war responsibility for discipline of the merchant marine was transferred from the Department of Commerce to the Navy and by the Navy to the Coast Guard. Thus, for the first time in American history, the traditionally "free" civilian merchant marine was removed from civilian control and brought under the authority of men with military training and concepts. Throughout the war merchant seamen, acting in the traditions of the merchant marine, often found themselves violating *military* regulations and being tried by Navy and Coast Guard officers. In some areas these personnel were intelligent men who tempered their authority with an understanding of the customs of the merchant service. In others, however, they worked in the high-handed manner of a military aristocracy, guided solely by the articles of war, and considering no evidence or circumstances not allowed by the regulations.

I established quickly enough that I knew nothing about the girl. It was, moreover, the Coast Guard's and Army's joint responsibility to keep enemy aliens off the Marseilles docks and ships. I proved that the Army maintained a gangway watch at all times, that the French Customs had a man at the gate, and it was therefore not my responsibility if someone sneaked aboard. Second, how had the girl got into the Coast Guard office, where I had met her in the corridor? Not even Americans were allowed in the area without a pass. She must have got aboard under the same false credentials or ruse which she had used to get into the Coast Guard building.

The girl steadfastly refused to reveal how she had got aboard or under whose auspices. Under direct questioning, however, in reply to the query, "Did Captain Mulzac bring you aboard?" she replied, "No." I have often wondered, suppose she had said, "Yes?" Is there any doubt that the Coast Guard might then have found me guilty and removed me from the ship, wrecking my whole career on the word of an enemy alien? Suppose the girl had been a devout Nazi who had been taught to hate "inferior" Jews and Negroes, and through some twisted logic supposed she was supporting the Aryan cause by implicating me? Or suppose some malevolent anti-Negro Coast Guard officer bribed her into incriminating me? By such narrow threads does more than one fate hang.

The charges could not stick, however, and the case was dismissed. I demanded and received a written statement of my release, the vessel was removed from port arrest and we were allowed to sail.

Our departure led to the third incident of Voyage No. 12. Our 600 troops were all colored, under three white and six colored officers. Throughout their overseas duty the troops had learned to despise one of their white officers, a southern "gentleman." A few days after we got to sea I was alone in my cabin on a fine afternoon when suddenly the door burst open and the white officer rushed in shrieking, "Captain, Captain, there's a nigger after me!"

"Who's after you?" I asked.

"That nigger out there . . . he's trying to kill me."

"Well, I didn't know we had any niggers on this ship," I replied, "but if we *do* have I'd rather he got you out on deck than in my stateroom." It was a real temptation to order him out, but I could see the troops congregating angrily on the foredeck. I called one of the officers to disperse them, but they were thoroughly aroused; they refused to return to the hold, and something had to be done.

I ordered the chief mate to lock the southern "gentleman" in his own stateroom while I went down on deck.

"We are going to have a meeting in the troops' quarters," I announced, "everybody below decks." Everyone immediately headed for the ladders and a few minutes later the troop quarters below were solidly jammed. I stood up on the table and reminded them, first of all, that the *Booker T.* had made quite a record during the war and that it was *not* going to be spoiled now if I could help it. The *Booker T. Washington* had become a worldwide symbol of good race relations, I argued, and while I appreciated their grievance it had to be taken up through different channels: the *Booker T.* was not the proper place for a race riot.

The soldier who had threatened the southern lieutenant stood up and asked to speak. "Captain Mulzac, we know about this ship and we respect it. We know of its record, and we will defend it. But do you realize what it's like to be at the front with bombs exploding all around and have to suffer this man's insults and abuse? We think that now we've got the Nazis cleaned up it's time to start on our own Fascists — and this lieutenant is *one*. By God, we're going to have some peace on this homeward voyage if we have to throw that son-of-a-bitch overboard!"

"While you were talking," I said to the young colored sergeant, "I have been thinking back to my own beginnings. You ask me if I can understand how it feels to be in the middle of an attack with bombs dropping all around, snipers trying to blow your head off, and *in addition* have to take the insults of this Southerner. *Of course I know* . . . I've been taking these insults since I first came to America in 1907! Life itself, for all our people, is such a battle . . . war is just a more violent form. But we can't throw everyone overboard who insults us! What do you suppose would be the consequences of such an action in Atlanta? In Birmingham? In Detroit? You could inflame the whole country at the very time we're trying to establish a just peace and friendship among nations!

"I can tell you this," I went on, "if this Southerner were a member of the crew of the *Booker T.* we would know how to handle him. We wouldn't dump him overboard — we'd order him to come to classes every night in the history of the Negro people. He'd have to defend his views every night in the messroom, and if he used the word 'nigger' he could be brought up on charges and expelled from the union. Through our work and patience we must win the majority of the American people to the same view."

There was some muttering of disagreement, but most of the troops accepted my view. Throughout the trip you could hear them arguing at the gunwales day and night about discrimination and how to cope with it. Frequently a member of the crew would join in the discussion, and it gave me a real sense of accomplishment to see how well-equipped the crew members were at providing leadership in such discussions.

After a week at sea the denouement came regarding the mystery of the German girl. I was out on deck one day when one of the crew members came alongside and said, "Cap, I've got something to tell you. The German girl was brought aboard by the chief butcher."

"What? How do you know? Why didn't you tell me before?"

"I just found out. But I'm telling you now. As soon as she came aboard her suitcase was put in his room. Then when the trial was ordered, he put it down in the hold."

I called the purser at once and had him bring the chief mate, the steward, and the chief butcher to my quarters. In the presence of all three I asked the butcher, "Did you bring the German girl aboard?"

"No."

"Do you know how she came aboard?"

"No."

"How did she pass the guard at the gangway?"

"I don't know."

"What about her suitcase?"

"She asked me to keep it for her."

"Then you must have known she was coming aboard." No answer.

"What did you do with the suitcase?"

"I put it down in the hold."

"Did you have it in your room?"

"Yes."

"Did you know that I was on trial before the United States Coast Guard for allegedly trying to smuggle that girl into the United States?"

"Yes, sir."

"Why, at that time, did you not speak up to help me?"

No reply.

It was obvious that the butcher, a German-born naturalized citizen, was withholding information.

"You have jeopardized my record and future," I told him. "You are withholding information vital to my complete exoneration from these charges."

I had no alternative but to log him $300 and make out a report to the Coast Guard in the hope that they would be able to get the full truth out of him. He signed the log book under protest in the presence of the steward, the mate, and the purser.

We arrived in New York December 8th and a few days later the crew was paid off. I turned the log book over to the shipping commissioner, and he interviewed both the butcher and myself, finally deciding that since the charges in Marseilles had been dismissed and since in any case the maximum amount the butcher could be fined was $50, he would let the logging stand at that amount. The whole matter was ultimately turned over to the Coast Guard and since I was never called again, I assume the charge was forgotten.

With the war over and most postwar duties discharged the time was approaching for a decision regarding the *Booker T.'s* future. Many Liberties were being disposed of to shipping-hungry allies and others were being retired in "mothball fleets" up the James River, the Hudson, San Francisco Bay, and other places. Happily, however, I learned that the *Booker T.* was one of those selected for peacetime service. We made one last voyage to Le Havre with general cargo, returning February 4, 1946. Then we were sent to the shipyards again, and stripped. Off came the gun tubs fore and aft, down came the emergency life rafts, out came the bunks and latrines built in the holds. For the first time we were decked out in the red and white bands of the Luckenbach Line, with the big white "L" painted on the black stack. The noble old *Booker T.* was not the same young girl when I saw her again . . . perhaps more like a middle-aged beauty who has just come from the salon, her basic structure still intact and a fresh coat of paint concealing the worn spots.

Most welcome of all was the information that we were bound for Tocopilla, Chile, on our first postwar voyage, breaking the monotony of the runs to the Mediterranean and Europe. We loaded cargo in New York, and cleared port late in August for the long run through the Canal and down the west coast of South America.

Although the war had ended a year earlier and we had traveled without convoy on our later trips, it was not until the *Booker T.* had been refurbished and we had set out for different oceans that I began to understand the pleasures of sailing in peacetime as master of a ship. There was no suspicion of submarines lurking off the stern, no bombers hovering on the horizon, there was not the simplest reminder of battles on the ship or on the tranquil sea. The crew was relaxed and cheerful, and Panama was brightly lit at night and free of MP's barring our way to restricted areas. Even the weather favored us.

Whatever the hardships of a life at sea, and there are many, there are benefits, too, and I never appreciated them more than on this first voyage of the *Booker T.'s* peacetime career. Life at sea is, first of all, beautifully and efficiently organized; the saloon is only a few dozen steps from your fo'c'sle, and not much farther from your job. Sixty seconds after I left the bridge I could be taking a cool shower or be stretched out on my bunk reading a good book. One pays for this convenience, of course, in not being able to drop in at a neighborhood movie, tavern, or park, but considering the inducements of most movies, taverns, and parks these days who would want to anyway? Indeed, a few days after returning from a long voyage, suddenly confronted by all the problems of shoreside life – noise, crowds, traffic, high prices, etc., many of us have wondered how people stand it!

The most interesting experience about these postwar

voyages, however, was the freedom to rediscover the sea, to recapture feelings I had not known, really, since the '20's or even since the old sailing ships. Throughout those decades from the end of the first world war to the end of the second it seemed that I had always been too busy or too concerned with pressing problems to *enjoy* the sea. Most of that time I had been concentrating on winning a promotion or fighting a union battle; too busy to pay attention to anything else. But now, at last, I was able to enjoy some of the leisure as well as the responsibility that comes with being a master.

Those who have never sailed the ocean, or have made only a trip or two, can never know the sea in all its magnificent aspects, or the fantastic forms of life it harbors. What shoreside entertainment, for example, can compete with an army of frisky porpoises playing at the bow, diving and falling, breaking away and returning, darting from port to starboard and finally, even though you may be plowing through the water at fifteen or twenty knots, flash ahead at double your speed and disappear! I have seen an army of them gather round the ship to convoy us through a starlit night, their serene, unbroken ranks undulating almost to the horizon. One of the most fascinating sights of all is to watch them hit a school of flying fish and skim just beneath the surface until the fish drop into their very mouths!

On the trip south, off Ecuador and Peru, we saw many whales, reminding me of the early days and Dad-Sonny's whalers operating off Frigit Rock, and of the old *Durbridge* and the *Sound of Jura*. I could recall the cry of the *Jura's* mate shouting, "Mulzac, overhaul those buntlines on the upper topsails!" Up I'd climb to the yardarms, 100 feet above the sea, and there, like as not, I'd spy a few whales breaching a mile or so away, and maybe a youngster trying to follow the lazy rolls of his mom and dad and managing only to look ludicrous and clumsy.

If our voyage down was thrilling even more so was our

reception at Tocopilla. Apparently many stories about the ship had appeared in the Chilean papers during the war and though Tocopilla is quite far North reporters from both *El Mercurio* and *Elmo Careo* of Antofogasta and Valparaiso were on hand when we docked. Our arrival was featured on the front pages of both papers. Local delegations from civic and union bodies had us for lunch and conducted us on local tours. We felt more like American envoys than merchant seamen.

Our return to the United States was equally interesting. We were ordered to Lake Charles, Louisiana, in the heartland of the segregationist South. The local population, both colored and white, had heard about the ship and wanted to visit us, and although the dockmaster had never permitted the townspeople to visit a vessel before the demand was so persistent that he finally capitulated. I opened up the ship for three days, the first for adults, the second for Protestant school children and the third for Catholic children. We provided refreshments for each group and held a little meeting. Later I was asked to speak in several of the schools and talked about democracy on the *Booker T*. The visitors and children could see that colored and white crew members shared the same fo'c'sles, showers and messroom.

Beginning in August of 1946 the *Booker T*. made eight speedy trips to such ports as Marseilles, Algiers, Cherbourg, and Rouen; and in March was chartered to run coal from Norfolk to Gothenberg and Malmo, Sweden, completing this assignment in October of 1947. During this whole period only two incidents took place, the last leading to a sharp disagreement between me and the Luckenbach company.

The first took place in Gothenberg. The Swedes, as everyone knows, have by and large remained uncontaminated by theories of racial inferiority. Colored and white members of ships in Swedish ports invariably go to restaurants, movies, and taverns together. Several of the

Booker T. crew members were in a dance hall one night, when an American sailor from a ship under contract to the AFL Seafarer's International Union suddenly accosted a *Booker T.* messman. "Hey there, buddy," he said, "you like dancing with white girls, don't you?" – and cracked him over the head with a beer bottle! A brawl followed.

The next morning a delegation of five Swedish students came to the ship to say that they had been present and explained what had happened. They begged me not to discipline the crew members; instead, they argued, "Send them back tonight. We'll be on hand to make sure nothing happens."

I learned from the police that the entire crew of the SIU ship had been restricted for the duration of its stay in port, and complied with the students' request. There were no more incidents.

The second occurrence however, was more serious and took place in Rouen.

As long as there have been ships at sea, or oxcarts on ancient trails for that matter, there has been smuggling. During and immediately after the war it was difficult for seamen to resist the temptation to buy a carton of cigarettes for sixty cents from the ship's slop chest, (no taxes or duties are imposed upon commodities sold outside the continental limits of the United States), and sell them in France for 600 francs a pack – roughly $10 a carton. On the *Booker T. Washington* we policed such practices very effectively by devoting educationals to the economics of the black market, showing how it bred inflation and how inflation hurt the poor most, and though we were on a sort of honor system I nevertheless inspected the ship thoroughly each time we entered port and was *extremely* stern in dealing with even minor violations.

Any official worth his salt, however, will admit that there are two kinds of smuggling: that conducted by professionals, who become seamen only to carry on the practice, and "amateur" smuggling conducted by seamen to get pin money to spend ashore. This is not to condone the latter, but the difference between minor and major offenses is recognized in all jurisprudence and the penalties are appropriate.

For example, during the war the National Maritime Union worked very closely with United States Customs agents in catching seamen suspected of large smuggling operations. On one big passenger ship carrying troops to Gourock, Scotland, and Liverpool, for example, thousands of pairs of nylon stockings were known to be sent ashore each trip in great laundry bags. The crew helped catch the culprits.

In Rouen the French customs agents discovered twelve cartons of cigarettes buried under the coal in the *Booker T.'s* galley, and levied a fine of $1,100 against the ship. I refused to pay the fine, first on the ground that it was excessive, and second that a thorough investigation could have established the man responsible. Therefore the fine should have been assessed against the guilty man and not against the vessel. The French were not interested in finding the culprit – they only wanted the fine. Finally, I was forced to draw the money from the Luckenbach agent and pay it.

When we returned to the United States, however, Luckenbach insisted that the $1,100 should be deducted from my salary, and I refused to agree. There was no precedent for such a step. In instances where the company has reason to believe that the master or ship's officers are accomplices to such undertakings, or that they have been lax in inspecting the vessel prior to arrival, the company has the option of discharging the officers, but penalties resulting from the operation of the vessel are the responsibility of management. Further, I proved that I had made three separate and thorough searches of the vessel and had, as a matter of fact, not overlooked the galley coal. The cigarettes must have been placed there *after* the third inspection. We did not come to any agreement on this point, however, and two years later the company used this charge against me in a public way.

17

The one certainty of life is change. Problems arise and are resolved, and in the resolution new ones arise which demand new solutions. Yet the dream of life *without* problems is unreal. It is only in confronting and trying to resolve them that we learn and grow, and through our individual frustrations discover that they are really resolved only at their root – in the social processes of which we are all parts and in which we must *consciously* participate.

When we tied up after Voyage No. 22 I had to ask for a leave of absence. I was suffering from a number of maladies and was run down from five straight years of sailing. There was no alternative but to place myself in the hands of the doctors at the Staten Island Marine Hospital. For eight weeks I relaxed there, slowly building up my strength to return to sea.

Some weeks after I had entered the hospital, however, I was notified that the War Shipping Administration and the Luckenbach Company had decided to end the *Booker T. Washington's* illustrious career. While I was indignant, it would be a mistake to say I was surprised. The *Booker T.* had served its purpose as a symbol during the people's war, but by 1948 it was obvious there was to be no people's peace. All hopes of postwar cooperation between the Western Allies and the socialist states had been blasted by the Truman Doctrine, the Marshall Plan, and Churchill's provocative speech at Fulton, Missouri, coining the phrase, the "Iron Curtain." America and her allies were busily converting friends into enemies and enemies into friends; the Russians were once more called "Communazis" and Francisco Franco, Salazar, Chiang Kai-shek,

Truijillo, and Syngman Rhee, butchers and hangmen all, were welcomed into the "democratic family." Every principle for which the war had been fought was flushed down the scuppers.

The *Booker T. Washington* had been one of the outstanding symbols of allied unity, but the cold war was a repudiation of that unity which our little Liberty ship could not survive. When she was sent to the "mothball fleet," however, I did not suspect I was to join her there. As a master with five years' experience with Luckenbach I had every expectation of being assigned to another vessel.

In the midst of all such speculation, however, an even greater tragedy struck — Marie, my bride of 1920, died abruptly. Just before completing the run to Valparaiso in 1946 I had received a wire from Una. Marie was in the hospital. Afraid of doctors she had put on a smiling face to conceal her pain, and by the time she was discovered to have diabetes it was too late. One of her legs had been amputated before I reached port. So while we knew she was in ill health none of us expected the end so quickly. By the end of the year, when I was finally released from the hospital, I had nothing but the memory of our twenty-seven years together — all too many of them spent away from her and the children — to look back upon.

A few weeks after I was discharged from the hospital I felt fit enough to make an appointment with Luckenbach's operations manager, Mr. H. M. Singleton. My reception was cordial. We exchanged pleasantries about the war years, my illness, and other matters, finally coming to the subject of the future. With some embarrassment Mr. Singleton explained that the number of vessels the company operated for the War Shipping Administration was steadily being reduced and that the postwar outlook was still uncertain. Even if the company doubled its prewar tonnage, he explained, it would still not be able to operate all the vessels it was presently operating — and thus he was unable to offer me a ship – though something might "turn up," of course.

The war was indeed over and the outlook indeed uncertain. Many who had sailed as master would now have to move a rung or two down the ladder, and until a master's assignment opened up, I then suggested, I would be willing to sail as mate. Mr. Singleton's face clouded; a number of Luckenbach masters were already sailing as mates, he pointed out, and unfortunately he could not give me any hope on this score either. Both of us knew that at that very moment dozens of young, white wartime recruits were working as officers on Luckenbach ships. We understood each other; there was to be no opening for Captain Mulzac or any other colored officer. There is no frustration greater than that of being completely powerless in the face of injustice. My five years of service for the company meant nothing; there was no union agreement to enforce my seniority privilege. As in 1918 I was no longer needed.

Thus, after twenty-two successful voyages during which we had carried 18,000 troops and countless thousands of tons of material, the *Booker T. Washington* and I were consigned to the boneyard. For a few short years that stout Liberty and the racially united, politically alert group of men who manned her, carried a message of peace, friendship, and hope for mankind to the ports of four continents. We had proved, as well as it can be proved to those who accept evidence, that colored and white can achieve together what they cannot even aspire to singly.

As for me, I had struggled all my life for that opportunity which came in 1942. As it had come, so it had to pass; there was only one thing to do – return to the struggle!

Yet it is one thing to struggle when you are twenty or forty, and another when you are sixty-two. My legs were not as strong as they once had been, and even I couldn't pretend that I was any longer in my prime. Setting out once again on my tour of the steamship company offices I discovered it was now no advantage to be reasonably well known. "Oh yes, *Captain Mulzac,*" some of the personnel people exclaimed – and not in a single instance did I ever hear from them again. Once again I began writing letters to every government agency having anything to do with waterfront hiring – and once again the replies were either non-committal or never came at all.

By June of 1948 I had discovered that I was not the only colored officer with an employment problem. During the war nearly 200 had served as deck or engine officers, but now not a single colored officer was left on the bridge of an American ship barely three years after hostilities ended. Only a handful – all in the engine department, as far as I could ascertain – still had berths. While making my rounds I ran into three others seeking jobs – Clifton Lastic, who had been chief officer on the *Booker T.* and later appointed to a vessel of his own; Philip Valdez, who was chief mate when the *Booker T.* was tied up, and John Godfrey, both of whom had had their own commands and were now unable to sail even as mates with their wartime employers.

One evening we all met and formed a committee to draft a letter to Major General Philip Fleming, then Chairman of the United States Maritime Commission, appealing for a formal hearing to present evidence of discriminatory practice in the shipping industry. We released the letter, and held a news conference. Though we received many expressions of sympathy, a little publicity and even a few contributions to help us carry on our fight nothing came of our efforts.

During this time it had become obvious that Luckenbach was hiring mates and skippers with far less seniority than I, not to mention years at sea, since there were few sailors in the entire American Merchant Marine who could show discharges going back to 1907. While there was no contractual obligation under the Masters, Mates & Pilots

agreement for companies to promote officers on a seniority basis, it was, nevertheless, a widely observed industry
practice. My only appeal, therefore, was under the New
York State Law Against Discrimination and on September 15, 1949, I filed a complaint against the Luckenbach Company.

More than a year later, in December of 1950, the trial
examiner ruled that I had been refused employment because of the cigarette incident in Rouen and *not* because I
was colored. It was the first time Luckenbach had offered
this defense. The company soberly asserted that it was
"entirely accidental" that not a single colored officer remained in its employ, though it was operating fifty-two
vessels at the time of the hearing – constituting, with
standby replacements, about 225 deck officers' jobs!

By October of 1949 I had been out of work for nearly
two years and was clearly back where I had started. The
American labor movement was not doing much better.
The wartime illusions of postwar labor-management cooperation had gone up in the smoke of the big 1946 auto
and steel strikes, and both sides had returned to the
struggle. Management exploited to the full the turn to the
cold war, with its invidious anti-Communism, and suc-
cumbing to these pressures the Murray leadership launched
a drive to clean the CIO skirts of any radical tinge,
expelling the progressive-led unions. Happily for employers this action took precedence over the drive for new
members or civil rights for colored members. A compliant
labor leadership, cooperating with the Truman administration, thus helped prepare the way for the McCarthy Era,
which did so much damage to labor and the nation.

During this period I happened to be sitting with a group
of friends one evening. We were thrashing over the problems of our race and our own bleak futures, wondering
where to turn, when someone began to enumerate the
areas where Negro progress had to be made. Jackie Robin-
son, I remember, had just won the most valuable player

award in the National League, firing our imaginations with visions of new fields to conquer, and my associate happened to mention discrimination at resorts. One of the things our people needed, he commented, was a travel agency, which over the years, through its influence with colored patrons, could fight the color bar on trains, planes, and in vacation areas.

The notion seized me the instant I heard it. Thousands of Afro-Americans, Puerto Ricans, Cubans, Haitians, and others living in Harlem and other Negro ghettos, visited the Caribbean every few years: didn't they need an agency to make arrangements for them? Thousands more were looking for places to vacation without humiliating racial intolerance and segregation – who was tipping them off where to go? Last but not least, who was better qualified to undertake such a responsibility than I? After all, in my forty-two years at sea I had visited almost every port in the world, had won a certain respect among my people, had a few dollars in the bank, and could probably do a very good and honest job.

Within a few weeks I had found an ideal location at 35 West 125th Street. The newspapers were warm to my project, as was my legion of friends. On December 16, 1949, I held a gala grand opening of the Mulzac Travel Agency, featuring *Sunbeam Tours* to resorts North and South. Sarah Vaughan, Billy Eckstine, Lionel Hampton, Errol Garner, and others showed up for the inaugural festivities and Hal Jackson, a popular local disc jockey, served as M.C. for a radio show. It was a great night, auguring well for the future.

Unhappily, customers did not batter down the doors in the following weeks. I consoled myself with the thought that it would take months to become established, but by spring I determined to analyze the situation.

There were two sets of problems, one comprised by the trade I had elected to get into, and the other by the particular public to which I was appealing.

In the first instance, to get my seven percent commission from the carriers I had to be approved by the International Air Transport Association. How did one get it? First, by showing evidence of a $10,000 cash balance. Travel agents are responsible to carriers – the airlines and shipping companies whose "space" they commission, and the carriers, naturally, demand proof of financial solvency for their own protection. While I had put away quite a bit of my $500 monthly salary during my years on the *Booker T.* I had not saved anything like $10,000 and moreover, I was reluctant to borrow it.

More than this, it turned out that to be approved by IATA you had to be endorsed by three carriers, and to win such endorsement you had to be in business for three years. How was the small businessman to stay in business three years without commissions, and how were you to earn commissions without staying in business three years?

The second set of problems was constituted by my Harlem "market." The citizens of Harlem, for entirely understandable reasons, turned out to be suspicious of *both* travel agents *and* airlines. Most of the citizenry believed the agency's profit was *in addition to* the fare and hotel fees, instead of a commission paid by the carrier and the resort. Most travelers therefore reasoned that they could save money by buying their own tickets and making their own reservations. Also, colored citizens had long since learned that the cheapest travel was the Greyhound bus – or the railroad. When they wanted to buy a ticket they simply took the subway to 42nd Street, bought a ticket as their fathers had, and *went!*

Now that time has safely intervened I can concede a third factor in my business failure – my lack of business acumen. The basic condition of free enterprise is competition, and competition means outsmarting not only your competitor but your client.

Travel agencies make their extra profits by charging visa fees, arranging "kickbacks" from resorts and hotels above normal commissions, and in many other ways. To prosper it is, if not absolutely imperative, at least *helpful* to be sharp in business dealings. I never was, and I suggest that such thinking is alien to the socially-conscious who are, after all, interested in getting *more* benefits for people, not fewer. In 1950 I discovered belatedly that I was not a businessman and after less than two years in business, reluctantly closed the doors.

When I closed the travel agency I was not only penniless, but, worse, had nothing to occupy my time, a most demoralizing problem for anyone, but particularly for one who has been active all his life. Two activities emerged from this frustration: participation in the political life in Queens, a borough of New York City, and painting.

With so much free time at my disposal I began to visit the offices of the American Labor Party, a "third" political party in New York which had been founded by Vito Marcantonio, Sidney Hillman, and others. In the beginning I helped out with meetings, mailings, and anything else that came up. My visits and work for the party produced unexpected results; at a meeting in the summer of 1950 I was nominated as the party's candidate for Borough President. There was no possibility of our winning – the Democrats and Republicans had established thorough political control throughout Queens as in the rest of New York, but we thought it was necessary to have a "second" candidate on the ballot since both my Republican and Democrat opponents stood substantially for the same things. We ran a hard campaign and lost, though 15,500 Queens citizens supported the ALP program. This was my first venture into politics.

The end of the campaign confronted me again with free evenings. I would return home tired and frustrated from my job hunting expeditions, and start casting around for something to do. One evening while puttering around I happened across a few old paint brushes and a ragged canvas I had buried in a closet when I left the *Booker T.*

I broke out a box of oil colors I had stashed away and began to fool around. But the next evening I could hardly wait to get home to work on a painting I had in mind.

Thereafter, except for "interruptions" that will be explained later, I became increasingly absorbed in my new-found pursuit. I even began to stay home mornings to work out preliminary drawings of harbors I'd sailed into, beach scenes abruptly called to mind, and scenes of the British West Indies familiar to my childhood and youth. Evenings I feverishly transformed these sketches into paintings.

At some point in this process a friend called my now quite substantial number of canvases to the attention of Carl Weiss, art director of the Long Island *Call*, a neighborhood newspaper in our Jamaica (Long Island, New York) community. Mr. Weiss came to visit one day, wrote a glowing review of my work for the paper, and got in touch with Allan Stoltman, head of the AFI gallery in New York. The result was a showing of my works.

Much to my surprise several were sold, one to the noted writer Walter Bernstein, for $450. *Art News* made several comments, including what I hope was a word of praise in describing them as "completely-unselfconscious." The resultant publicity led to further sales and made the year's effort not only aesthetically satisfying but modestly profitable.

While I have subsequently sold many paintings and continue to paint to this day, it would be dishonest to pretend that I have taken painting very seriously or have any pretentions to greatness. I have painted for pleasure, and the content of my paintings is the content of my life and of my people. My work is what critics call "primitive," and compared with the sophisticated abstractions that bring in thousands of dollars it certainly *is*.

Of course, painting could not provide me with an adequate income and by the summer of 1951 I was considering going back to the MM&P Hall to register. True, I was sixty-five and the work was not easy, but my feet itched to walk up a gangway again.

18

Working in my ill-fated travel agency, campaigning for political office, painting, and job-hunting, I had gradually lost touch with many of my old waterfront friends by 1951. In the summer of 1950 I had read that Congress had passed the Port Security Act, popularly known as the Magnussen Act; and later that President Truman had issued Executive Order 10173, granting the Coast Guard authority to screen off waterfront seamen and dockworkers whose loyalty to the United States was questioned. There was little public protest against the bill at the time, however, and since none of the men I knew had been screened I had no idea it would affect me.

One day in the summer of 1951, however, while I was walking down Front Street, I happened to run into an able seaman who had sailed with me on the *Booker T* We chatted awhile, and he remarked, "You know about the new regulations? The Coast Guard is issuing new papers – you have to prove you're not a security risk."

As I have explained. a seaman's papers are his passport, union book, and social security card rolled into one; I had carried mariner's documents since 1906 and wouldn't have felt like Hugh Mulzac without them. It therefore seemed like a normal precaution to be ready if I decided to go down to the union hall and register.

A few days later I presented myself at the Coast Guard offices and turned in my certificates for validation. The yeoman explained that it was not the practice to issue new papers on the spot – my old papers would be sent to Washington and I should return in about thirty days to pick up the new card.

Several weeks later I returned and the yeoman got out my file. "Your application has been rejected, Captain," he said carefully.

"What? *Rejected?* Why?"

"On the grounds that you're a security risk."

Blacklisting is like cancer – you know it happens to others, but you never imagine it can happen to you. Dumbfounded I heard myself exclaiming *"Security risk? But I'm Captain Hugh Mulzac of the Booker T. Washington!"*

"Can't help it, Captain . . . that's what it says here. I'm afraid you'll have to write to Washington. They're setting up a hearing board. You can appeal the ruling, you know."

It was only a few blocks from the Coast Guard headquarters to the office of William Standard, NMU attorney from 1936 until 1948 when the union's progressive leadership had been repudiated in a bitter election. Standard was not only an able lawyer but a warm personal friend, and there was no one in whose hands I would rather place my fate. We discussed the ruling thoroughly and decided to submit an immediate appeal. I was certain that the "mistake" would be rectified in a few weeks, for there were absolutely no grounds for the Commandant's finding.

A few days after I was notified of my exclusion from the waterfront, I received a letter from Meyer Stockman, Commander of the U.S. Coast Guard, in which he said:

Your presence on board merchant vessels of the United States would be inimical to the security of the United States. This finding is based on the belief that you are affiliated with or are sympathetic to an organization, association, group, or combination of persons subversive or disloyal to the government of the United States.

I was again dumbfounded. I had risked my life countless times during World War I and World War II in the service of my country. When I became a citizen in 1918 I pledged loyalty to this country. I had never knowingly been connected with any organization plotting its overthrow by force and violence.

I filed my appeal the very next day, July 6, 1951. The following January 31 my hearing was held by an appeals board consisting of one labor, one management, and one Coast Guard member.

One theme dominated this long day: my association with the Communist Party and its members; or "front" groups as designated by the Attorney General. The chairman of the board, Coast Guard representative Walter Lawlor, established the direction of the hearing in the opening moments when he declared, "We are delving into facts, circumstances and activities in the past of Captain Mulzac, which he has a right to bring forth here, to show that he has not been affiliated with the Communist Party or sympathetic to its policies or principles."

During my appeal Mr. Lawlor asked, "Did you associate with people whom you knew to be Communists?"

I answered, "No." It was a truthful answer. I never asked a person's politics because I had a simpler and more reliable way of knowing who and what people are. I judged them by their behavior when problems arose. In some forty-five years of working on the American waterfronts I have met many men who spoke the doctrine of Marx and Lenin, who distributed the *Daily Worker,* and who asked me for contributions to this or that cause. Virtually without exception they have been devoted trade unionists, firm friends of the colored and minority people, and I have helped them unstintingly – but I never asked to what party they belonged and I didn't care. Many of these men, like Ferdinand Smith, Al Lannon, Blackie Myers, and others who helped me during my lifetime have been deported, sent to jail or expelled from their unions on the grounds that they were Communists. I have no personal knowledge whether they were or not and of course could not so testify in a court of law or in my own appeal.

The examiners wanted to know if I ever read the *Daily*

Worker. Did the *People's World* ever print anything laudatory about me?

"Did you ever associate with Ferdinand Smith?" they asked me.

"Yes, I joined him on a nationwide speaking tour," I replied. The examiners pricked up their ears. I continued: "He and I campaigned on behalf of President Roosevelt in 1944." They lost interest.

I was interrogated regarding my attitude toward the National Council of American-Soviet Friendship and a scroll which the members of the *Booker T. Washington* had sent to the U.S.S.R. during the war. I reminded the Board that the Soviet Union had been our ally and that I had shared my responsibilities in the National Council of American-Soviet Friendship with such public figures as Eleanor Roosevelt, Secretary of State, Cordell Hull, and Secretary of Commerce, Jesse Jones.

The Board also questioned my membership in some of the organizations on the Attorney General's list, proscribed as Communist or alleged to be substantially Communist-dominated — for example, the National Negro Congress, the Negro Labor Victory Committee, the Council on African Affairs, and the Council for West Indian Federation. The National Negro Congress had been organized to fight for equal employment opportunities. The Council on African Affairs provided information on the various African independence movements and aided the native resistance movements. The Council for West Indian Federation was dedicated to the freedom of the British West Indian possessions from imperial rule. I was proud to be a founding member of it. (Little more than a decade later many African countries, as well as the British West Indies, had won their freedom, partly as a result of the activities of supporters abroad. And when Jamaica won her independence President Kennedy sent Vice President Johnson to Kingston, where he joined the Queen of the British Empire for the occasion.)

My interrogators presumed to be in possession of information which they refused to reveal to me. There were no witnesses against me. I was not told the source of the Coast Guard's derogatory information. It could have come from any sailor I had ever sailed with, possibly even from the butcher I had been compelled to log in France. It could have come from an official of any company I had ever worked for, and possibly from one whose ship I had helped strike. It could have come from a neighbor who disliked me. It could have been foolish gossip from a couple of gas hounds within the hearing of a paid agent of the FBI or one of the intelligence services. Indeed, it was in reference to such privileged information from secret sources that the Ninth Circuit Court of Appeals years later declared "The question is: Is this system of secret informers, whisperers and talebearers of such vital importance to the public welfare that it must be preserved at the cost of denying to the citizens even a modicum of the protection traditionally associated with due process?" The court concluded that it was not.

Throughout the day-long hearing, while I denied membership in the Communist Party or association with known Communists, I asserted unequivocally my dedication to the cause of Negro freedom and equality and to socialism. All my adult life I had fought discrimination to make the United States a better place for both colored and white citizens.

Within the framework of the President's order, the Coast Guard regulations and the Attorney General's proscriptions it was obvious from the beginning that the hearing was a mere formal and meaningless procedure. The finding had already been made against me. The board had no real power, it could only recommend to the Coast Guard. To the best of my knowledge the only appeals against the Commandant's finding which were ever won were those involving clear cases of mistaken identity, which I certainly could not prove. The board insisted repeatedly that it was not empowered to consider constitutional questions but was required to operate within the regulations established by the Coast Guard and the Magnussen Act. Therefore the mere fact that I admitted membership in some of the organizations on the Attorney General's list and conceded an acquaintance with Ben Davis, Ferdinand Smith, and others who had been deported or imprisoned under the McCarran or Smith Acts was enough to establish my complicity in a plot to overthrow the government by force and violence!

Accordingly, three months after the hearing Vice Admiral Merlin O'Neill wrote: "The review of your case before the local appeal board has been completed and you are advised that there appears to be no justifiable reason why the original decision in your case should be disturbed."

Before I could seek redress in the courts all appeals provided by the Act had to be exhausted. This provision of the Coast Guard regulations was calculated to delay court action and to so harass the victim with legal expenses and demoralize him with long and absurd hearings that he would give up his fight.

The next step was an appeal to the National Appeals Board. The Board provided me with a long list of questions, most seeking to determine whether I had been in Madison Square Garden on a particular night (at a political rally), whether I had ever called for peaceful negotiations to end the Korean War (a position President Eisenhower had already adopted). I answered all the questions truthfully. On September 22, 1952, Vice Admiral O'Neill wrote again: "The review of your case has been completed, and on the basis of the complete record I am satisfied that reasonable grounds exist for the retention of your classification as a poor security risk."

I was not the only seaman to be screened off the waterfront. According to some estimates about 2,000 seamen and waterfront workers were denied their credentials.

There are too many aspects of these so-called "loyalty" procedures to examine here, but a few, particularly with reference to seamen, should be pointed out. The first is that blacklisting is a convenient weapon for shipowners who want to rid themselves of militant trade unionists on their ships. Second, the screened seaman could not confront his accuser to refute his testimony. How reliable were those who asserted, with no fear of being forced to offer evidence, that an individual was a Communist, or even that Communists were subversive? A high proportion of such professional informers were aliens eager to escape deportation, congenital liars, publicity seekers, mental patients and even persons with criminal backgrounds. Some were rewarded with cushiony jobs in industry or other such for their cooperation. In all the security furor of the '50's it is often overlooked that not a single overt act was committed by any of the victims of the various witch-hunts, and this includes Communists prosecuted under the Smith Act or persons deported under the McCarran Act and all the merchant seamen, liberals, defense workers, ministers, and others who were and are still being hounded by the Senate Investigating Committee or the House Un-American Activities Committee. No military installations were spied on, no defense plants sabotaged, no railroad trains derailed, no military secrets given to a foreign power. Not a single overt act was ever committed for which the defendant could be hauled before a court of law and tried under criminal statutes.

Many gifted writers have written about the insanities of the Coast Guard screening procedures and other "security" measures initiated during the McCarthy era — many of which still prevail — but I suspect it will be decades before the stupidities of that period are finally assessed and understood. It is impossible to denounce too vigorously these blacklisting practices, these ruthless attempts on the part of the governing class to enforce conformity, this relentless hounding of dissenters, for they are violations of the Bill of Rights of the Constitution and an attack upon every basic principle for which America once stood and will one day stand again.

In short, these activities have to be seen for what they are: attempts to suppress independent political thinking, compel conformity, and to mobilize the people of America to support the adventures of a war-minded group of leaders who in their desperation can think of no way out of their dilemma but nuclear war to annihilate all mankind. Every dissenter from this national goal was to be labeled "Communist." As a result thousands of honest trade unionists have been hounded out of their jobs, hundreds of liberal college professors and teachers have been expelled from their posts and subjected to public obloquy, ministers have been driven from their pulpits by star chamber proceedings. Judges of the Supreme Court have been branded Communist. So has the NAACP. All these activities were as insane as the Salem witch-hunts.

These were bad years for me. The higher McCarthy soared the lower I sank. The Coast Guard ban deprived me of the only real resource I had, my more than forty years' experience as a mariner. The pittance I received from social security was not enough to sustain me, as any sexagenarian can testify, and jobs are not easily acquired by those in their sixties – especially colored men. For several months I worked as a delivery "boy" for a Manhattan jewelry firm, but the constant walking was too much for my tired legs. At other times I had jobs as an elevator operator, hotel clerk, or short order cook, but being on my feet nine or ten hours a day was more than I could bear. Mulzac's law, if I may formulate it, is that wages are in inverse proportion to the amount of time the employee is required to spend on his feet.

Late in 1953 the Queens Branch of the American Labor Party offered me a post as branch secretary, but by 1955 the ALP could no longer continue. Marcantonio resigned, and shortly thereafter was stricken with a heart attack and collapsed on the city streets. He was one of the few real friends the American people have ever had in Congress.

In 1954 a group of West Coast seamen, discouraged at the delay and expense of individual appeals and separate court tests, banded together to form the Committee against Waterfront Screening in San Francisco. In December of the following year a similar group, of which I was elected chairman, formed on the East Coast and we coordinated our efforts to push the court fight.

On October 28, 1955 the Ninth Circuit Court in California, in an historic decision known as the *Parker v. Lester* case, released a slashing indictment of the methods used by the Coast Guard to screen seamen from the ships. "Here plainly," the opinion read, "these plaintiffs have no adequate remedy in law. The damages of which they complain are irreparable. They have lost their opportunities for employment, some of them for months and some for years, and will continue to suffer such loss in the future if the defendants be not enjoined from the enforcement of the regulations complained thereof." The court ordered all screened seamen returned to their "original status."

A similar suit was quickly brought by the East Coast Committee before Judge Pine in Washington. D.C., since the Ninth Circuit's ruling was valid only within its own jurisdiction. Boudin and Rabinowitz, handling the majority of cases, and William L. Standard, made a joint representation, and a favorable ruling was handed down.

These decisions were the most heartening news any of us had had throughout the black years of the McCarthyist hysteria, and many of us began to pack our seabags.

Despite the emphatic and unequivocal rulings of the courts, however, for more than a year, in as fine an example of unmitigated arrogance as could be found, the Coast Guard refused to comply with the order. The Attorney General's office fought to delay and forestall the effect of the ruling with every device at its command. The government's intransigence finally led Judge Murphy to order our cancelled documents stamped "validated by order of the Ninth Circuit Court of Appeals."

This "California stamp" on the back of the certificates thereafter provided a convenient mark for union dispatchers, company personnel, U.S. Shipping Commissioners and Coast Guard representatives in differentiating screened seamen from those who had not been screened. The government, apparently fearful that an appeal to the Supreme Court might result in far-reaching precedents jeopardizing its loyalty program in other industries, eventually decided not to appeal and thus the "second phase" of our fight against screening was won in November of 1956.

But the government had still another trick up its sleeve: if the Coast Guard could not legally bar us perhaps the shipowners and unions could. The NMU, the powerful union we had built in 1936, now firmly in the hands of opportunists, agreed in amended contracts with the shipowners to do the Coast Guard's screening job for them. Seamen of "doubtful loyalty," which in practice meant all those with "California" papers, would not be registered or shipped.

Early in 1958, fourteen of us, later increased to twenty-one, filed a new suit against the NMU and the American Merchant Marine Institute, bargaining agent for American Export Lines, Grace Lines, United States Lines, Moore-McCormack, and most of the other powerful and heavily-subsidized shipping companies. It was another long drawn-out legal battle, but in April of 1960 Federal Judge Alexander Bicks issued an order which found the defendants guilty of illegal discrimination. He ordered us restored to all the privileges of union membership, and compelled the union and the shipowners to pay our $10,000 legal fee.

Thus in April of 1960, nearly ten years after it was begun, our long legal fight to recover our rights was won. Though our legal campaign ended in triumph it was a pyrrhic victory. Of the some 2,000 men barred from employment on the waterfront during the dark years only a handful ever returned. Many, like myself, were too old to return to sea and lost our pension rights. Others, harried through the years, found solace in little jobs in out of the way places, and surrendered the fight. Many, of course, have never even learned about Judge Bicks' ruling, which covered the twenty-one plaintiffs "and their class" (other screened seamen) who were, however, required to exercise their rights within sixty days. Those who never heard of the ruling, and they are scattered throughout America, or failed immediately to exercise their hard-won right to return to sea, would, if they wanted to now, have to fight the case through the courts all over again! Yet those of us who won *did* go back if even, as in my case, only in a limited way.

19

The present is a thin line dividing the past from the future. We live on that line throughout our lives, understanding only in rare flashes of insight how the past contains the present as the present determines the future. Ever since I was a boy romping the slopes of Tibree and Rafall, I have been mindful that the present was a sweet moment to be savoured and lived to the fullest, for it might never come again. Sinking my teeth into a succulent guava once I remember thinking, "Hugh, get every ounce of goodness from this guava, for tomorrow something may happen and you may never taste guavas again!"

My immediate "present" is seven decades later but the feeling is the same; what I fail to do today I may be unable to do tomorrow, and therefore every moment is vital. Yet time is running out. Throughout the years of the government-shipowner "security" ban I was getting older. On March 26, 1960, a few weeks before Judge Bicks' order to the NMU and the shipowners went into effect, I reached my seventy-fourth birthday, and while I marched into the Masters, Mates and Pilots Union Hall the following day with a considerable feeling of triumph, I was not the sailor I had been when I had marched down the gangway of the *Booker T. Washington* thirteen years earlier. If, through some lucky pierhead jump, I was called to serve as master and 100 miles at sea ran into a brisk North Atlantic gale, would I be able to stand out on the bridge for two or three days straight running as I had once? Of course not. Or if I came upon an A.B. struggling with a tricky sixstrand Liverpool wire eye splice, would I be able to take the work out of his hands with my old assurance and show him how to do it? No. Our senses falter, our memories fail, our limbs become less sure; seventy-four-year-old bodies, whatever the spirit that commands them, cannot take the punishment they once did.

Such presumed opportunities of course, were academic, for fifteen years after the war there were still more mates and masters than the nation's dwindling fleet could employ. By 1960 nearly ninety percent of America's foreign cargoes – a disastrous drop from the nearly 50-50 ratio at the time of my trial – were being shipped in foreign bottoms. (Nearly half of this ninety per cent was being carried in American-owned "flags of convenience," a delightful euphemism for the vessels which the big, heavily subsidized American owners place under Honduranian, Liberian, and Panamanian registry to escape United States taxes, wage scales, and safety regulations.)* As I have explained, the MM&P had never won the rotary shipping

* This was the issue initially at stake in the 1961 maritime strike, when the SIU and its associate unions, with contracts on the unsubsidized lines, and the NMU, representing the big subsidized companies, made the right to organize the foreign flag vessels a bargaining issue. The NMU broke the united front of the maritime unions by agreeing to accept a 23-cent-an-hour "package" in exchange for dropping the foreign flag issue.

system for masters and chief officers. These were privileged positions and those who enjoyed them were reluctant to surrender their posts for democratic shipping privileges. The old timers, especially, were against it. They looked forward to shoreside jobs when they retired, though here too there were many more retiring applicants than there were opportunities. They clung tightly to their seniority rights, even though these were guaranteed only by the company's good will. Many indeed, though they were required to maintain MM&P membership, had never been in the union hall in their lives, and even paid their dues by mail.

Nevertheless the shipping companies were required to call the union for night mates – replacements for the regular officers when the vessel was in port and the crew was on port watches, 8 a.m. to 5 p.m. Within two weeks from the time I registered I was assigned to my first vessel, the *Transborinquen,* a Trans-American SS Co. C-2 under contract to the NMU.

The only way to explain the feelings I had walking up the *Transborinquen's* gangway is to compare it with the first time I marched aboard a ship after the 1936 strike, or when I climbed the gangway of the *Booker T.* for the first time – I had the *right* to be there. She was not the best maintained ship I have ever seen, but I barely noticed her flaws, especially since vessels are traditionally ill-kept in port.

And whatever criticisms I had were forestalled by the generous welcome I received from several of the crew members when they turned to at 8 a.m.

The duties of a night mate are routine and simple, consisting principally in protecting the ship against sudden changes in the weather and the tides. One or two A.B.'s are always left on night watch to do the physical work – replacing burned out bulbs in the night lights, taking in or letting out the head and stern lines, etc.

My only task was to check unauthorized visitors, make

routine entries in the logbook, and supervise loading the nights we took on cargo.

Even though I wasn't going any place it was good to feel steel plates under my feet once again, to stand on the bridge of a ship overlooking New York instead of on a New York dock overlooking a bridge. When my four-day stint came to an end I returned to the hall, and was dispatched a few weeks later to the *Mormac Swan* ... and thus did I spend the balance of 1960.

My reassociation with the waterfront was helpful in more ways than one. In the first place at $28.60 a night it helped pay the rent. Second, it was sweet to savour the triumph over those wee men in the Coast Guard who, from the vantage point of cushiony shoreside jobs, are so capable of determining who is willing or capable of defending America.

Finally, it has rounded out my education to see what sailors and union ships are like today, twelve years after the NMU succeeded in ridding itself of the "Communist menace." To a man the sailors reported that conditions on the ships, despite the much higher wages, were not nearly as good as they were when the union enjoyed progressive leadership and when militant sailors fought for every point in the contract. With the disappearance of jobs the sailors have become apprehensive and conservative; many have begun to "marry" their vessels, staying aboard for years to earn the goodwill of officers, annual vacations, and to avoid the long months ashore awaiting to reship. They have abandoned any semblance of political action, or even an open expression of their sentiments, and union meetings aboard ship have become more and more infrequent.

This point bears emphasis. Back in 1949 millions of American workers were persuaded by their union leaders – backed by business, government, and the nation's press – that if only they would throw out the "left-wingers" all of their problems would be solved. It was the era of the cold war, and intense wage consciousness; the United Electrical Workers, the Mine-Mill and Smelter Workers, the International Longshoremen and Warehousemen's Union, and others were expelled from the CIO, and the remaining unions embarked on intense witch-hunting drives.

Now, fourteen years later, the facts can be assessed: unemployment for November of 1962 was higher than it had been in any postwar month, the grandiose organizing drive in the southern states has been completely stalled for years, colored workers are still segregated in jim-crow locals in many unions and the CIO-AFL is wracked with jurisdictional battles.

The National Maritime Union is a fine case in point. In 1946, when the union enjoyed progressive leadership, it led in forming the Committee for Maritime Unity, the alliance of seven unions representing about seventy-five percent of the water front workers of the country. Though confronted by the equally united employers the massive power of the CMU enabled it to effect a historic breakthrough in the conditions of waterfront workers, winning for the first time the forty-four-hour week at sea, the forty-hour week ashore, and many other advances.

Today, sixteen years after the CMU was destroyed by the charge of "Communist domination," the NMU faces its contractual negotiations virtually alone. Although it has won wage increases and improved fringe benefits – hospitalization benefits, pensions, an old sailors' home, unemployment payments, and increased vacation time, the job of organizing the unorganized has come to a virtual standstill, meaningful political action has ceased and union dues, initiation fees, and officers' salaries have trebled. The union has embarked on a real estate program as if its goal were to become a large, property-owning corporation rather than the organization of the workers to gain *real* security in increased employment opportunities, laws insuring a more stable economy and improved maritime regulations.

More important, throughout this period the shipowners have steadily transferred their vessels to foreign registry until now only ten percent of United States commerce is carried in national bottoms. Subsidies from the taxpayer have been increased, employment has dwindled, and the NMU members will inevitably face the day when having abandoned sailors on foreign flag ships and having failed to weld a united approach to the employers, they will be helpless to bring any real pressure upon the shipping interests.

There is an even more serious aspect of such "business" trade union leadership: the deterioration in morale of the union members. Many seem to be interested only in making a few fast dollars so they can retire to the proverbial tavern or chicken farm.

Today, gambling through the "numbers" racket is rampant on most of the big passenger ships, with seamen often betting a week's wages in a single pool. And especially on the big passenger ships, which have become floating casinos, when the supper dishes are cleared away out come the green baize tablecloths and the dice and poker games begin, with powerful groups of professional gamblers holding seamen's papers taking the house cut on every game.

Does it take much imagination to contrast this kind of program with that of the *Booker T.*? Or to understand why skippers like myself have been screened out of the industry while men who encourage, or at least permit the above offenses, are rewarded with commands and shoreside jobs when they retire? Does it take any great insight to figure out why Ferdinand Smith, longtime National Secretary of the NMU and persistent battler for Negro rights, was deported to Jamaica? Or why Hugh Bryson, president of the West Coast Marine Cooks & Stewards Union, one of the CMU allies of the NMU, was indicted under the Taft-Hartley Act and was sent to jail while his union, with the cooperation of the National Labor

Relations Board* was destroyed, its membership turned over to the Republican SIU leader, Harry Lundeberg? Or why Joe Ryan, International Longshoremen's Association leader, was allowed to prosper for thirty years while Harry Bridges, scrupulously honest and principled leader of the rival ILWU was four times brought to trial in fruitless efforts at deportation?

Yet, despite this bleak picture, there are solid rays of hope. One of the advantages in getting to be seventy-six years old is that one has lived enough history to begin to understand its processes, to know that this era too, will pass. Workers were just as unschooled in the '20's, union leaders just as venal, and yet the '30's witnessed the most militant demonstrations, the swiftest growth of union organization and class consciousness. History prepares not only the problems, as Karl Marx once remarked, but the conditions for their solution. The consciousness of men, after all, is determined by their *being,* not their being by their consciousness. Whatever their thoughts, however much they elect to compromise, men's actions are rooted inevitably in the real conditions of their time – a fact which skeptical and cynical liberals invariably overlook. And these real conditions are hurling the waterfront workers, as they are hurling workers in other industries, into new periods of depression, unemployment and very possibly war. The more the employers succeed in "perfecting" their economic machinery the more workers are put out of work, the more tenuous are the jobs of the still employed. Over the long run the rationalizations will become less effective, the dreams and pretensions will prove

* The Marine Cooks & Stewards, as was earlier explained, represented the steward's department on West Coast ships. In an election held in 1954 the NLRB permitted the deck and engine department members to vote in an election to determine the bargaining agent for the stewards, who, though they voted heavily for the MC&S, were outvoted by the other two departments and were incorporated into the SIU.

to be dreams and pretensions and a latent recognition will become operative. Workers will discover once again that individual "salvation" is a snare; that there are only *social* solutions to *social problems*. Once again, as during the '30's and in the war against fascism, they will take their working-class consciences out of the capitalist pawnshops, and *act*.

And so today, at seventy-six, night-mating when I can get a job, meeting with other members of the Seamen's Defense Committee (for even now there are bills in Congressional hoppers to bar us from the sea again), working as my strength allows in church and neighborhood groups, and participating in political campaigns, I do not despair. I have seen progress in my lifetime, and while it has not been as rapid as I would have liked, I realize that it could have not been, in those decades, any faster. I, and others like me, did what we could do, as the Freedom Riders, those who are fighting the House Un-American Activities Committee, and those who are fighting for peace and civil liberties are doing what they can today. If my son and daughters are not growing up in an America free of racial taint, or their sons and daughters, well, maybe *their* grandsons and granddaughters will.

The confidence and determination that have sustained me through the years have not deserted me in my seventy-sixth year – far from it! Indeed, looking around the world – at the *real* Freedom Fighters bravely storming the citadels of reaction in the South, at the people of Africa and Asia taking their rightful places at world conference tables, and at cosmonauts circling the earth – my confidence in man's future and in a world free from oppression and prejudice is stronger than ever. Today two broad currents of progress are discernible – the fight of the newly free and still struggling colonial countries, aided by the socialist nations, for economic and political freedom, with all the implications this has for diminishing imperialist power; and the gradual awakening of more and more

Americans, especially the youth, colored and white, to the real meaning of our country's heritage When I was young neither of these currents was discernible; England ruled the world, socialism was unborn, and America was brusquely entering upon the epoch of its greatest economic expansion, oblivious to the aspirations or rights of its colored minorities.

Today the truth is clear for all to see. Man's future, once a glittering dream, is close enough to seize. Who could be faint-hearted?

Best of all, in the process, I have myself been freed from the narrow ambition that drove me, and have understood that my success in achieving my limited goal was due only to the national struggle for full rights for minority peoples. Without the earlier battles launched by men like Dr. W. E. Burghardt Du Bois in the early days of the NAACP; without the fight of militant trade unionists such as the sailors of the NMU in the '30's, without, in short, the continuing effort of so many million decent citizens throughout the decades, I never could have been appointed master of a garbage scow, let alone of the *Booker T. Washington.*

And this, indeed, is my message to the youth of our nation, colored or white. When one is young, one is likely to look at the world confidently, thrilling to the surge of blood through youthful veins, and to feel that no problem is too great to be overcome by one's wit and ingenuity. We disdain cooperative action; we are raised in a competitive society, nursed on the philosophy of rugged individualism, and we rely exclusively upon our individual resources.

In later years one begins to measure one's performance against one's goals, and to understand there were problems and obstacles undreamed of. We begin to realize that others, too, had such ambitions, and to see ourselves as parts of society, *as part of the people.* The importance of private goals and selfish dreams diminishes as we understand that our dreams were not really our own, but illusions planted in our heads by a class-dominated educational system, by corrupt newspaper and magazine editors, and foolish prophets to lead us *away* from the *common* battle of *all* people for a life of freedom and plenty. And we discover that *only in common, cooperative action can all of our individual dreams come true.*

This freedom from our own narrow and selfish ambitions is the truest freedom that, as members of class society, we can win – and the most difficult. But winning it we can begin to see our lives and efforts as tiny tributaries feeding the river of human freedom. We can begin to understand clearly the function of those who would divert this mighty current into harmless streams, those who would dam it up, and those few Canutes who would command it to move backwards, and to *know* that their efforts must come to naught. Because *we know who and what we are,* and *what we represent,* because *we know who our allies are,* and because *we join them in the struggle,* we can never really know defeat or frustration.

Confidence and courage flow from our commitment, full and inextinguishable.

And if, therefore, there is any sense I can impart to the younger generation it would be this: *commit yourself!* Fight through the early private illusions as speedily as possible, admit, as quickly as you discover it, that separate, individual actions will get you nowhere, and join the common struggle. Fight for the liberation of oppressed people everywhere, fight for an honest, moral political system, fight for the fullest appreciation of every human need, for fighting for the good life for *all* people is the only way to live and win it for yourself. Thus does life become worth living.

I am only sorry I did not discover it long before I did.

Briefly,
ABOUT THE AUTHOR

Hugh Mulzac was born in 1886 on Union
Island. From his earliest days, he knew the
beauty and the bright warmth of the West
Indian Archipelago, and a love of the sea.
There was in him a searching spirit and a
longing for brave deeds (inherited perhaps
from his Scots grandfather) and a deeply-
rooted sense of responsibility which came
down to him from his mother's family – men
and women of pure African descent who were
the ordained clergymen and school teachers
of the Island. He was eighteen when he began to work with ships; twenty-one when he
first sailed. Eleven years later, in 1918,
he was the first Negro to win a Master's
license. For twenty-five years, he fought
bigotry and the chains of segregation for
his right to be a Captain. It was not until World War II that he finally was given
a ship. This book tells the story of those
years; the story of one man's success won
in struggle. Thus it becomes the story of
a courageous people facing a way of life.
Hugh Mulzac has related the happenings of
his life to two journalists, Louis Burnham
and Norval Welch. They bring his story to
you in his words, keeping to the chronolog-
ical order of events as he recounted them.
Captain Mulzac died on January 31, 1971
at the age of eighty-four.